Félix Guattari

Modern European Thinkers

Series Editors: Anne Beech and David Castle

Over the past few decades, Anglo-American social science and humanities have experienced an unprecedented interrogation, revision, and strengthening of their methodologies and theoretical underpinnings through the influence of highly innovative scholarship from continental Europe. In the fields of philosophy, post-structuralism, psychoanalysis, critical theory, and beyond, the works of a succession of pioneering writers have had revolutionary effects on Anglo-American academia. However, much of this work is extremely challenging, and some is hard or impossible to obtain in English translation. This series provides clear and concise introductions to the ideas and work of key European thinkers.

As well as being comprehensive, accessible introductory texts, the titles in the 'Modern European Thinkers' series retain Pluto's characteristic radical political slant, and critically evaluate leading theorists in terms of their contribution to genuinely radical and progressive intellectual endeavor. And while the series does explore the leading lights, it also looks beyond the big names that have dominated theoretical debates to highlight the contribution of extremely important but less well-known figures.

Also available

Alain Badiou
Jason Barker

André Gorz
Conrad Lodziak and Jeremy Tatman

Georges Bataille
Benjamin Noys

Jürgen Habermas
Luke Goode

Jean Baudrillard
Mike Gane

Guy Hocquenghem
Bill Marshall

Walter Benjamin
Esther Leslie

Julia Kristeva
Anne-Marie Smith

Pierre Bourdieu
Jeremy F. Lane

Slavoj Žižek
Ian Parker

Gilles Deleuze
John Marks

Félix Guattari

A Critical Introduction

GARY GENOSKO

PLUTO PRESS
www.plutobooks.com

First published 2009 by Pluto Press
345 Archway Road, London N6 5AA and
175 Fifth Avenue, New York, NY 10010

www.plutobooks.com

Distributed in the United States of America exclusively by
Palgrave Macmillan, a division of St. Martin's Press LLC,
175 Fifth Avenue, New York, NY 10010

British Library Cataloguing in Publication Data
A catalogue record for this book is available from the British Library

ISBN   978 0 7453 2821 8   Hardback
ISBN   978 0 7453 2820 1   Paperback

Library of Congress Cataloging in Publication Data applied for

This book is printed on paper suitable for recycling and made from
fully managed and sustained forest sources. Logging, pulping, and
manufacturing processes are expected to conform to the environmental
standards of the country of origin. The paper may contain up to
70 per cent post-consumer waste.

10   9   8   7   6   5   4   3   2   1

Designed and produced for Pluto Press by
Chase Publishing Services Ltd, Sidmouth, England
Typeset from disk by Stanford DTP Services, Northampton, England
Printed and bound in the European Union by
CPI Antony Rowe, Chippenham and Eastbourne

CONTENTS

ACKNOWLEDGMENTS

I began work on this book in earnest while I was in Sydney, Australia in 2006 as a visitor in the Department of Philosophy at the University of New South Wales and the Department of Art History and Theory at the University of Sydney. I am grateful for the personal and professional assistance graciously provided by Paul Patton and Alan Cholodenko. Andrew Murphie warmly welcomed me into his intellectual community, and Ross Harley was extremely generous with his time and energy. I was able to present some earlier versions of chapters at the Universities of Melbourne, Monash, and RMIT (Royal Melbourne Institute of Technology) thanks to the kind invitations of Felicity Colman, Anna Hickey-Moody, and Hélène Frichot. In the arts field, I was helped along my way by Maria Fernanda Cardoso and Elizabeth Day. The intellectual camaraderie of Melissa McMahon and Roger Dawkins was vital.

I am indebted to the research assistance of Adam Bryx, and to an ongoing dialogue about the expanding fields of transversality with Bryan Reynolds. Paul Hegarty was indispensable in helping me acquire European materials. I would also like to thank the four reviewers of this project for their good advice, and David Castle at Pluto Press for bringing the project to fruition.

Finally, I want to dedicate this book to the irrepressible Iloe.

INTRODUCTION

Overview

The late French activist–intellectual Félix Guattari (1930–92) is perhaps best known for his collaborations with philosopher Gilles Deleuze on a series of groundbreaking books in post-'68 French thought around the sprawling thematic of capitalism and schizophrenia. There was much more to Guattari than this collaboration, however, including numerous other joint and group projects with philosophers Antonio Negri and Eric Alliez, to name only two. Guattari's aberrant career path led him to take up psychoanalysis; he was trained by Jacques Lacan, with whom he had a stormy relationship, and worked with the Lacanian analyst Jean Oury at the Clinique de la Borde in Cour-Cheverny, originally a private clinic shrouded in myth and supercharged with as much intellectual cachet as terror, for most of his adult life. He also had his own private practice. Guattari died at La Borde in 1992 at the age of 62. He is buried in Père Lachaise cemetery in Paris. The evening of his death on August 28, as remembered by Labordian Marie Depussé, began with an ordinary meeting during which Félix fielded concerns from a number of patients and proffered solutions designed to elicit the participation of those either disinclined or incapable of such engagement:

> Félix died that night.
>
> He always thought that there could be a dialogue between groups of speaking patients and the most withdrawn and delirious. Not any groups, he said, but those which 'allow to surface the most accomplished image of human finitude, every undertaking of my own finds itself dispossessed in the name of an instance more implacable than my own death, that of its capture by the existence of others ...'

The next day in the lounge the inmates cried when O[ury] told them of Félix's death.

'Thank you for telling us like that,' they responded. In exchange, even if many wandered that night, unable to sleep, they did so politely, tenderly, without a sound. The night was calm.[1]

Guattari was a restless experimenter, an habitué of far-left groups from his earliest years; a militant suburban Trotskyite in the late 1940s who was labeled a 'dangerous "Titoist" propagandist'[2] (that is, anti-Soviet and imperialist) by angry and likely paranoid, thought Guattari, youth members of the French Communist Party; and a supporter of a myriad of good, lost, and forgotten causes, not to mention a vocal and visible agitator for progressive social and political change in Europe and elsewhere. His stomping grounds were not the universities, except when they were reeling from social upheavals or fraying at the edges as knowledge made its difficult passage into society and social change disrupted the prerogatives of the ivory tower, but the little journals (beginning with a Trotskyite bulletin in the 1950s, for which he wrote under a pseudonym), the transdisciplinary research groups, social experiments and public protests. As a committed intellectual he modeled himself on Jean-Paul Sartre, even during a time when Sartre had fallen out of favor and to speak of engagement was a provocation. Yet Guattari cites so many influences that it is impossible to categorize him simply as Sartrean. He lived in multiple worlds – young philosophy student at the Sorbonne and militant on the fringes of communism, visiting Yugoslavia and China, and strong adherent to Lacanian structural psychoanalysis by 1954 (spending hundreds of hours talking with Jean Oury at the psychiatric clinic in Saumery). He once referred to himself as a Leninist who was not very Leninist because he didn't believe in centralism, calling it an absurdity, and found the organized party as a detachment from the working class – ten wise men pulling proletarian strings – equally so; this was not unlike his Italian colleague Franco Berardi's self-description as 'more hippie [sometimes Buddhist] than Bolshevik.'[3] Guattari even considered his Trotskyism to be 'ambivalent.'[4] He was not at all ambivalent about the camaraderie he found among his 'young *ajiste* [hostellers] mates' from the youth hostelling movement, another important trying ground. In the early 1960s, for example, Guattari was also a Maoist of sorts, assisting in the founding of the 'Comité d'initiative pour une association populaire franco-chinoise,' whose newspaper *Bulletin d'information* was very short-lived, with his old friend Jean Baudrillard.[5]

By the mid 1960s Guattari had developed a formidable battery of concepts organized around the problem of delivering therapy in institutional settings. *Psychanalyse et transversalité* (1972) exposed the limits of the psychoanalytic unconscious by arguing that it was not a concern of specialists treating individuals but rather perfused the social field and history. For Guattari the subject was a group or collective assemblage of heterogeneous components whose formation, de-linked from monadic individuals and abstract, universal determinations like the Oedipus myth, allegedly rigorous uses of mathematical symbols, Lacan's so-called 'mathemes,'[6] and part-objects (not partial objects lacking wholes), could be seen through critical analyses of the actual vicissitudes of collective life in which patients found themselves. A Sartrean-inflected theory of groups emerged, distinguishing non-absolutely between subject (actively exploring self-defined projects) and subjugated groups (passively receiving directions), each affecting the relations of their members to social processes and shaping the potential for subject formation.

The heteroclite essays in *Psychanalyse et transversalité* cover the period from 1955 to 1970 and include many journalistic pieces, autobiographical reflections, and position papers. The core theoretical material dates from 1964 to 1969, that is, from two decisive interventions: first, the development of the concept of transversality in the institution; and second, the critique of linguistic structure by an ingenious 'discovery' of a disruptive machine already at work in structural thought that, once nurtured in the right way, disturbs the key structural principles and is in part the fruit of Guattari's reading of Deleuze's reflections on structuralism in *Logic of Sense*.[7]

The foundation of what Guattari called 'schizoanalysis' was laid in *L'inconscient machinique* (1979). As he matured intellectually Guattari no longer considered himself a psychoanalyst – his disagreements with mentor Lacan were as fierce as his criticisms of the technical elitism of the guardians of the Lacanian legacy; Guattari coined the term 'schizoanalysis' to give direction to his concern with problems of the psyche as breakthroughs taken in the context of the institutions that help shape them and the social currents to which they are attached. In other words, Guattari's concern was with an unconscious loosened from the individual psyche, an unconscious that was everybody's concern, an unconscious that wasn't confined by the interpretive matrices of psychoanalytic theories that shortchanged desire in the name of castration, Oedipus, psychogenetic stages, and myriad forms of repression; in short, for Guattari, the unconscious was neither confined or analyzed by pre-established coordinates. In other words, Guattari held a positive and productive conception of the unconscious that brought together desire and machines as desiring-machines, first hinted at by him in 1969 but explored more fully with Deleuze in their joint masterwork *Anti-Oedipus* of 1972. Famously, the disruptive, viral machine of Guattari's early writings, once conjoined with desire, ensured that desire never stops working, producing and reproducing its component parts, in the factory of the collective unconscious. Machines help liberate desire from the seductions of having specific objects, the deceptions of prohibitions, and the yoke of signification.

Schizoanalysis requires a practical, detailed semiotic critique of language-centric theories of meaning, which would lead one to reject outright the claim that the unconscious is structured like a language. It entails a politically progressive and provisional transformation of concrete situations and predicaments of living. The schizoanalyst's micropolitical task is to discern in a particular subjective assemblage of components the mutational potential of a given component and explore the effects of its passages in and between assemblages and milieus, producing and extracting singularities by undoing impasses, alienating and deadening redundancies: 'Rather than indefinitely tracing the same complexes or the same universal "mathemes," a schizoanalytic cartography will explore and experiment with an unconscious in actuality.'[8]

Micropolitical schizoanalysis will map, in a way specific to each passage, delinguistified, and thus mixed and plural, semiotic lines flush with matters of expression: all kinds of signs are in play, not merely linguistic signifiers. Rhizomes are released from constraining arborescent structures: tree thought is hierarchical and centered around a trunk and its roots, branches, stems, and leaves; by contrast rhizome thought does not have a center, since connections may be established at any time between disparate parts. The schizoanalyst pursues the smallest and most tangled, and hence molecular–rhizomatic, lines on the run from stultifying bureaucracies, looking out for ways to introduce new machinic connections and breaks, regardless of their level of formation, and reach across the social field.

The emphasis on molecularity entails a socio-political analysis that privileges creative, oppositional flight and eschews so-called professional neutrality – what Freud once modeled on the 'emotional coldness' of the surgeon[9] and Lacan on the exposed 'dummy' hand in bridge.[10] Guattari introduced the machine as a productive connectivity that forms assemblages of component parts, each running at the same time, but without forming a whole. Guattari advanced from a sociological conception of the group grounded in his experience as a young militant of leftist committees faced with impasses generated by rather onerous investments in their particularity ('my group, my tendency...'[11]) and false derivations of collective identity through the image of (and phantasms about) their leaders and the discipline they inspire – not to mention roles into which one projects oneself – to a strategy leading to the creation of new forms of revolutionary subjectivity (collective 'groupuscules'). These new forms would neither be modeled on party nor family; and surely not on the individual! For Guattari, revolutionary theory has completely neglected this dimension of struggle, and it becomes for him a question of the first order.

The essays in *Psychanalyse et transversalité* revealed Guattari's deep debts to Lacan, even though the largest of these debts involves the extent to which, for Guattari, it was Lacan who, perhaps despite himself, initiated the machinic unconscious. Guattari rebrands Lacan's *objet petit 'a'* (small 'a' object) as an *objet-machine 'a'* (object machine 'a') for two reasons. This object is already a machine in the way it works because, first, it effects a cut and, as the cause of desire (desire's dynamic), the subject's alienation; and, second, it is detached from oneself and is irrecuperable since it symbolizes loss (insofar as it is missing). It may be a hidden treasure that motivates a search – though one doesn't know what it is – hence a symbolization of lack like the McGuffin of Hitchcock films.[12] It is useful to think of the object machine 'a' as a bug in some computer code, with the proviso that it is a pretext, the cause of hacker desire, for rewriting and improving such code, or an alibi for geek grandstanding, regardless of whether or not it really is a glitch that needs fixing.

Guattari finds in the little 'a' the machinic force of disequilibrium that generates a decentering operation from which the subject cannot recover by regaining a secure and certain refuge; as Guattari put it, 'the object "a" erupts into the structural equilibrium of the individual like an infernal machine.'[13] Guattari characterizes the *object 'a'* as a machine that, because it is lost and outside of signification, returns in new fantasy guises, which can lead to quite dramatic misadventures, such as the Y2K preparations.

Guattari resists Lacan's definition of the little 'a' as a cause of desire and instead calls it a machinic representation of the subject's desire: 'the machine's essence is precisely this operation of detaching a signifier as a representative [représentant], as a "differentiator," a causal cut, heterogeneous to the structurally established order of things.'[14] It is this linkage of desiring subject-machine, ultimately worked out as a desiring-machine, that displaces the subject and situates it 'alongside the machine.'[15] Eventually, the representation of desire by the machine will also be superseded once Guattari conceives of collective subjects that 'liberate' their machines from the burden of representation – 'no need for these things to represent: technical machines do it better!'[16] It is significant that this early Lacanian Guattari did not write of the desiring-subject but instead clarified where desire 'is'

– not in the subject, since the subject was sidelined or beside the machine, but rather the machine invades desire in an unconscious that is a factory or laboratory.[17]

However, it would be churlish to claim that the machine is a mechanism by means of which Guattari altogether escaped the influence of Lacan; he continued to despise Lacan*ism*, and rejected the ethics of non-intervention in general, exemplified by Lacan's school, which was dominated by neutral silences and non-prescriptive measures precluding the pursuit of social-justice issues. Rather, the Lacanian legacy of graphs, schemas, knots, and algorithms is visually evident, even if structural–linguistic imperialism ('imperial discourse')[18] is rejected outright, in the myriad of diagrams that populate Guattari's *L'inconscient machinique* and later books. Indeed, the assessments of Lacan's thought in *Anti-Oedipus* are consistently laudatory and conform to the idea that his thought has been stripped of its deep complexity and self-critical deployments of linguistics and Oedipus by his disciples – 'the oedipalizing interpretations of Lacanism.'[19]

The two editions of *La Révolution moléculaire* (1977) contained advanced semiotic methods, modified from diverse linguistico-philosophical roots, adequate to the 'semiotic polycentrism' necessary for engaging in a genuinely radical analysis of the expanded fields of the unconscious, with a less woodenly dichotomous sense of superego on one side and socius on the other. Guattari's writings on social and political developments in Italy, especially the Autonomia movement, a loose alliance of left-wing cultural and political groups and tendencies of the late 1970s, underlined their potential for new molecular forms of collective action beyond the party form, in what he called 'generalized revolution'; eventually, in his collaborative writings with Alliez and then Negri, Guattari worked through the shifting characteristics of capitalism and the prospects for resistance to it through a renewed sense of communism as 'a continuous reaffirmation of singularity'[20] (freedom and autonomy) directly arising from the Italian experience with a blossoming of far-left political culture, the turn to armed resistance by one tendency, and its wholesale repression by the state.

The essays in the overlapping volumes on molecular revolution at the level of the formation of subjectivities introduce some important distinctions and new ideas: Guattari carefully outlines his relationship with the anti-psychiatry movement, offering criticisms of its major figures and veiled beliefs and placing himself in the alternatives-to-psychiatry movement that arose in Europe in the mid 1970s. He sketches a theory of cinema in relation to the accomplishments of alternatives to psychiatry; Guattari was interested in a cinema of madness, with the capacity to conjure up allies and get them thinking and feeling in new ways by means of exploring the singularities of madness. Further, Guattari developed an original theory of semiotics dedicated to his understanding of machinic capital – a type of part-sign that functions automatically and, as Maurizio Lazzarato has astutely observed,[21] perfuses everyday life in the many machine-mediated transactions into which subjectivity enters and to which it is subjected. Importantly, while this machinic enslavement of subjectivity to networks and technical components – allowing it to be coded, controlled, surveilled, and integrated as a kind of relay – works by means of a-signifying signs that set into motion processes (they function rather than mean) like the movements of information that open and close entry and exit points, the link between this semiotics and politics is what makes Guattari's insight original and valuable today. Some readers of Guattari suggest that machinic subjectivity is *subjectless*, inasmuch as it 'pulverize[s] the traditional notion of the subject as the ultimate essence of individuation ... [and] deploys itself as much "beyond" the individual as "before" it.'[22] In place of the subject there is only subjectification – processes neither anchored by the mental nor an effect of language, but guided by desire and the proliferation of singularities, tuned by connective refrains. Subjectivity becomes by means of an array of components provided by an increasingly machinic milieu whose potential for the creation of new assemblages is explored and enunciates without the benefit of a ground that pre-exists the enunciation itself. For Franco Berardi, this makes schizoanalysis a post-human pragmatics of subjectification, the aim of which is to make habitable, coherent, and sharable the singular maps each of us draws.[23]

Cartographies schizoanalytiques (1989) and *Chaosmose* (1992) elaborated non-representational maps of the self-engendering processes of subjectification, pragmatically attending to the specific ways in which singularities come together, through four ontological functions of the unconscious, their interfaces, and the character of their components. Although I will not go into detail in this book about Guattari's ontology, I want to indicate that these functions are presented in a square bisected equally by one vertical and one horizontal line. The ontological square consists of four equal parts. On the bottom left side one finds material–energetic *fluxes* and on the top left side, the machinic *phyla* and their diverse technological strands; on the bottom right side, there are the existential *territories* of subjectivities (human and non-human and inorganic) and on the top right side, incorporeal *universes* containing values, points of reference, relations with others, aesthetic experiences, utopias, imaginings, etc. On the left hand side of the square (flux and phylum) are technomaterialist functions expressed discursively, whereas on the right hand side (territories and universes) are ethico-aesthetic concerns and a myriad of qualitative issues organized non-discursively. One way to read Guattari's ontology is to think of the meeting of systemic forces (techno-science) and subjectivities (art). The way these two sides meet requires some further explanation.

Guattari borrowed the semiotic terms 'expression' and 'content' from Danish linguist Louis Hjelmslev to describe the left and right sides respectively. This designation means that the sides are mutually interdependent, as their relation is purely formal. There is no way to privilege expression over content, in the way that the signifier is privileged over the signified. However, whereas Hjelmslev went on to further divide his planes of expression and content into constants (forms of expression and content) and variables (substances of expression and content), Guattari characterized the bottom functions of flux and territory as real and the top functions of phylum and universe as possible. Thus, reading from left to right, bottom to top, the real–expression and real–content quadrants are fluxes and territories; the possible–expression and possible–content quadrants are phylum and universe. Simplifying, real–expression fluxes like monetary, libidinal, or semiotic flows are additionally designated *actual* because of their link with necessity and materiality. Real–content territories engage pathic (affective) dimensions of existence and have a stronger charge of *virtuality* (unrealized potentiality) that is still finite; this makes them more heterogenetic. The combination of the possible–expression in the machinic phylum in which technologies enter into a kind of evolutionary drama of selection, deletion, and residuality (not becoming extinct but subsisting in cultures of collecting), in a tangle of irreversible development, brings together the actually possible in a somewhat chaotic process; the most interesting arrangement is the content–possible of incorporeal universes where the possible entails a schizoanalytic midwifery of showing the way towards singularities which can truly unfold and constellate with one another. Universes are the most open, abstract, and rich in unactualized potential of the functions, about which not much is known. They are purely virtual yet have no meaning on their own as they need to be activated. Guattari has built a brand new kind of four-sided sign, a complex semiotic assemblage, with his square of fluxes, territories, phyla and universes, intersected by a number of qualifying characteristics and mediating measures. He used this conceptual vocabulary to punctuate his descriptions of schizoanalysis.

In a given situation a schizoanalyst tries to bridge (with bidirectional traffic) the right and left sides by discerning something of their incorporeal potentiality in attending to how things are actually working out relationally betwixt manifestation and possibility, processually and expressively as subjectivity ever emerges and the components composing it are massaged by flows and acculturate to large-scale changes. Using the functions and their articulations, Guattari diagrammed what he called 'meta-models', which would retain the particularity of 'self-referential enunciation'[24] – this describes the self-positing of subjectivity towards an emergent consistency or crystallization of components in a readable constellation, a more or less coherent universe. Guattari's question is deceptively simple: How does subjectivity engender itself as an existential territory? And how can this agglomeration of projects and perspectives, which is incarnated (but not merely) someplace, be mapped/diagrammed in a way that respectfully extracts some element (singularity) that shows some capacity to open up new vistas (universes) without disturbing material flows (fluxes) or ignoring adjacent connections (phylum)?

Guattari's fundamental problem was always how to traverse multiple fields in his own life and work. His own auto-modelization across fields of social struggles, institutional commitments, analytic treatments of psychotics in group settings and other patients in private practice, without forgetting writing philosophy and fiction, gave rise to a unique analytic method.[25] One of the hallmarks of this method is the proliferation of diagrams.

Readers of the *Cartographies schizoanalytiques* and *Chaosmosis* often wonder what a schizoanalyst does. Further, are there any schizoanalysts other than Guattari? The answer to the second question is probably no, for the time being at least. But the first question is a little more difficult since it involves consideration of what Guattari meant by meta-modeling. Both these theoretical texts concern meta-modeling operations. In Guattari's thought, diagrams are irreducible to icons because icons remain encysted in pre-established coordinates, beholden to a given meaning they can do without. Diagrams are non-representational and upload what they map as they map it – they give meaning. It is via diagrams that the passage from modeling to meta-modeling takes place; this passage is none other than that of expression plane to content plane. The diagram's productivity entails that meta-modeling is productive of new references; it functions; forces things together; doesn't need meaning, just the manufacture of it. Diagrams get models (existing coordinates of thought on the side of expression) moving, and in full flight they become meta-models, imbued with potentiality. Meta-models must be able to account in some way for their own vigor. They cannot simply be, of course, modeled (slowed down, solidified), but are themselves philosophically diagrammable (mappable yet a bit sketchy). Diagrammaticity is like a slice of chaos released by a meta-model and which opens up a new universe through which it coils itself along, like a virtual worm. Yet worms are circumscribed, they have territories. This is the meta-model's mechanism of constraint. The diagrammatic meta-model remains exploratory, fulfilling, and not at all static, because its constraints are productive, yet they filter pure potential in being embodied and someplace crossed by various flows. Meta-models are, in this respect, models of hybridity. Meta-modelizing maps do not interpret unique auto-references of individuals with reference to a pre-existing set of coordinates (referenced to childhood 'events' or 'traumas' of the human race), but attempt to respect self-positing trajectories in order to see if they are helpful in freeing up blockages in a given situation by taking risks with certain technological phyla (e.g. by taking up driving again). Schizoanalytic meta-modeling is forward looking, inventive, and actively experimental: 'within the diverse cartographies in action in a given situation, it tries to make nuclei of virtual autopoesis discernible, in order to actualize them, by transversalizing them, by conferring on them an operative diagrammatism.'[26] The schizoanalyst listens for or observes the emergence of something that can get a subject in a closed world moving again, rebooting desire and transporting one into unexpected places, regaining a footing in actual territories in drawing a singular diagram of a process of self-creation. Guattari specifies that this process is based primarily on ethico-aesthetic principles (rather than scientistic postulates and neutral posturings) that involve the analyst who, like a spectator drawn into the orbit of a work of art, connects with an artist's cartography, participates in a kind of interactive co-management of the worlds evoked – what for Guattari entailed a 'transference of subjectivation'[27] between subjects and lines of influence across disparate domains (e.g. between obsessional rituals and economics).

Schizoanalysis tries to understand

> how it is that you got where you are. What is your model to you? It does not work? – Then, I don't know, one tries to work together. One must see if one can make a graft to other models. It will be perhaps better, perhaps

worse. We will see ... And the criterion of truth in this comes precisely when the meta-modelization transforms itself into auto-modelization, or auto-gestation.[28]

A schizoanalytic cartography is the existential territory it engenders. This coincidence of subject and object, of map and territory, of problem and solution, means that the schizoanalyst lives in the 'field of the possible that is carried along by the assemblages of enunciation.'[29] In others words the map is its own cartography, its auto-model, that brings forth solutions – modifying behaviors, opening vistas, renewing fields of reference, building confidence: 'Respond to the event [e.g. a patient mentions in passing 'I feel like learning word processing'] as the potential bearer of new constellations of universes of reference.'[30] Schizoanalysts make risky, yet pragmatic interventions that give patients a chance to reorganize and rebuild infra-personal components by finding and forming new matters of expression, even if these don't communicate very well; it sounds a bit like social work, Guattari admitted, in reflecting on his role in getting a patient set up in his own apartment in order to assemble his own isolation, but the analytic truth is in the analyst's openness about his uncertainty and his refusal to imprint a pre-established diagnosis that would blind him to something really laden with potential.[31] New cartographies produce new subjectivities.

Why Read Guattari?

The question of reading Guattari today is embedded in a long-standing problem within the secondary literature of Deleuze studies. Ian Buchanan neatly summarizes the problem:

> [T]he fact that Guattari did have a career outside of his collaborations with Deleuze does seem to need emphasizing because so far the secondary criticism on the work of Deleuze and Guattari has tended to overlook his contributions altogether or consign them to a merely secondary role.[32]

Despite this entreaty, Guattari's criticisms of structuralism in all of its variations remain a sticking point for his widespread reception by those whose theoretical commitments, especially in psychoanalysis, remain attached to this master discourse. This is most evident in Slavoj Žižek's recent book on Deleuze, *Organs without Bodies*, in which he claims that Deleuze expresses a certain 'relief' in his collaborative writing with Guattari, even though it is 'fake.' Why? Because the fluidity that, according to Žižek, Deleuze finds in the co-written works 'signals that the burden of thinking was successfully avoided.'[33] Summarizing, Deleuze succumbs to the Guattari-introduced temptation to demonize structuralism against his better (that is, earlier) judgment, in which he endorsed this method in some measure. The idea that Guattari's critique of structure, initially launched by jump-starting a machine already located in structure, is not reducible to such facile scapegoating is never seriously addressed by Žižek, who doesn't *read* Guattari. There is more. Later, Žižek characterizes Guattari as an indulgent, delirious thinker who favored 'interpretive delirium'[34] and whose work doesn't need to be quoted accurately but simply presented in bracketed comments. This caricatural dismissal of Guattari by Žižek's rhetorical flourishes is only in defense of structuralism's rescue, which must resort to conservative character-bashing in order to get off the ground.

The context of critical reception provides a twofold reason why Guattari needs to be read today: to correct the tendency to elide his contributions to jointly written works and actually engage with his own texts instead of having recourse to marginalizing his contributions by erecting a straw man.

Once these impasses have been surmounted, Guattari's contributions to contemporary debates in social and political theory can be better appreciated. Although his two books about molecular revolution are unwieldy, in their pages Guattari outlines a critique of capitalism that begins with a historical appreciation of its heterogeneous forms and the implications of the definitive dominance of production (over the state and market) tied to a subjugating technico-scientific-informatic deterritorialization from the boundaries of nation states, witnessing the globalization of capitalism (Integrated World Capitalism) and the emergence of immaterial labor on a mass scale. In *Empire*, when Hardt and Negri discuss immaterial labor they begin with the involuted relationship in contemporary network society of informatization and affectivity, which describes Guattari's sense of the condition of machinic subjectivity.[35]

Guattari is an anti-capitalist thinker of the first order. For him, capitalism becomes a kind of total social fact by means of which all the dimensions of life – all of life's rhythms and textures – are knotted together in a subjugating and colonizing ensemble across a computerized planet: 'capitalism aims above all at controlling *the whole of society.*'[36] In this sense, Guattari also contributes to the critique of globalization that carries beyond the ideological, cultural, and institutional parameters of the phenomenon normally set out, that is, beyond capitalism's cyberneticization, liberalization of markets, privatization of public assets, permanent restructuring and endless crises, mobile factories, labor precarization, enforced flexibilization, and hyper-exploitation, etc. Guattari's insight is that capitalist production targets *subjectivity* and produces it in ways that resemble and serve capital's mobile and fluid aspects and interests. In Integrated World Capitalism everything is productive, and subjectivity – imagination, creativity, multiple energies, fascinations, facility with symbols – is a new kind of exploitable content. Cognition in the most general sense (encompassing memory, perception, imagination, emotions) is the raw material of contemporary capitalism. Immaterial labor produces immaterial (non-tangible) content wrapped in 'material' clothes: computer code for video games, for example. With subjectivity itself at risk, the political stakes are very high. The multitude, Hardt and Negri insist, can and must regain the social relationships and 'forms of life' produced for cognitive capitalism in the time of immaterial labor, but turn them to new forms of social and political self-organization.[37]

Behind the many pages concerning the resistance of the multitudinous militant in Negri and Hardt's *Empire*, one can hear Guattari's voice: empire produces and assembles subjectivities for different places and with a variety of matching forms; yet this subjugation is incomplete. Subjectivity as a collective (social) assemblage of components held together in a myriad of ways besides the category of 'person,' regains an active profile in pursuit of autonomous spheres of expression and the right to singularity, an incomparable inventiveness. Subjectivity meta-models itself differently by resisting, resignifying, and reappropriating the technologies that attempt to model it as a pliable citizen consumer; for example, mobile media – wireless technologies – are turned to politically progressive, non-exploitative ends in recomposing mobility as a cooperative project, either sporadically or in more enduring self-organizing formations. Guattari never abandoned the machinic dimension of production, for the same reasons that Hardt and Negri stay with the problem of communication: subjectivity is machinic as 'the means of production are increasingly integrated into the minds and bodies of the multitude.'[38] Wresting control for autonomous, alternative, and other purposes of the machinic dimension is vital. In short, there is no way out of the machinic through an easy humanism. For Guattari, in the age of planetary computerization machines and humans have mingled in so many ways along the path of self-reference and exploration of the potential for creative singularization that the demand for the right to singularity is immanent to the vast machinic phylum of globally networked systems that cover the planet, albeit unevenly.

Guattari is just the sort of militant for the present that Hardt and Negri evoke in the final pages of *Empire*: he expresses the multitude's skill at continuous agitation, cultivates joyful innovations of creative singularities in cooperation, while displaying facility with the molecules of revolution: forging tools for transversal organizing, engaging the new semiotics of info-capitalism, and displaying an acute grasp of the power of affect for both capitalism and its enemies.

Through his challenging ontology, Guattari directs activist–intellectuals to pose the problem of subjectivity, because it sits at the crux of large systems of change conveying multiple fluxes and collective struggles to build territories in which other universes can be imagined and inhabited by human beings whose forms of life are undergoing fundamental mutations.

As more and more of Guattari's own writings are translated into English and the secondary literature on his life and work slowly expands, the vexing issues that once concerned his readers will give way to considerations of his own insights into fundamental political challenges. From his final vantage point in the early 1990s, Guattari intuited that the struggles of the millennium were assuming startling shapes and sketched what would need to be done to successfully understand and meet them with the right weapons at the ready.

Chapter Outlines

This critical introduction explains Guattari's major socio-political ideas and practices through chapters organized around key dimensions of his life and thought, while delivering rich contextual material and explanations of concepts and how they are relevant for today. In the first chapter, 'The Formation of a Young Militant,' I put into historical and theoretical context Guattari's cryptic remark in *Chaosmosis* that his militant training as a youth involved participating in a host of extreme left groups including the youth hostel association. This portrait of Guattari as a young hosteller, a so-called *ajiste*, initiated into the movement by mentor Fernand Oury, helps to explain how he came to develop important concepts around the invention of institutional matter through the collective publication of journals. Guattari's early experiences in hostelling, under Oury's direction, as well as his focus on creating institutions, stretched in his lifework from the period of the youth hostels, through the groups for studying groups of the 1960s, the publication of the journal *Recherches* and, much later, with Deleuze, the co-editorship of the journal *Chimères* and organizational experiments at La Borde. I do not claim that he merely reanimated these earlier experiences. His own warning about 'ecosophy' in *The Three Ecologies* is heeded: 'Rather than being a discipline of refolding on interiority, or a simple renewal of earlier forms of "militancy," it [a new ecosophy] will be a multifaceted movement, deploying agencies and dispositives that will simultaneously analyse and produce subjectivity.'[39] If, as Guattari wrote, 'schizoanalysis only poses one question: how does one model oneself?'[40] it is prudent to begin by asking this of the schizoanalyst himself. How, then, did Guattari model himself?

In Chapter 2, 'Transversality and Politics,' I explain the significance of the diagrams of institutional collective life at La Borde, *la grille* and *la feuille de jour*, as transversal tools; I will use the term 'tool' even though Guattari was certain that machines are more ontologically basic than tools because they determine the 'collective dance' of specific tools and certain human bodies under the conditions of related social and technical ensembles.[41] I then turn to assess the political trajectory of the concept: how Foucault's sense of transversal struggles dovetails with Guattari's overriding concern with the production of new forms of subjectivity. Guattari praises Foucault for his 'radical questioning of the philosophical tradition of the "founding subject"' and 'discovery of a vast domain of forms of collective production and technical modalities of the construction of subjectivity, virtually unrecognized until then.'[42] Guattarian micropolitics and Foucault's microphysics of power relations both concern the political fields in which new subjectivities resistant to inherited individuations are created in a pragmatic orientation, a cartography of 'analytic singularity.'[43] But I will also consider the use of transversality in global political theory. Transversality becomes a new model of dissent, and this emphasis places Guattari at the heart of the theorization of anti-globalization struggles and technopolitics. At the same time, though, I express a number of critical misgivings about the use of transversality as a watchword for dissident vectors, to the extent that the Foucauldian view tends to edge out the Guattarian sense of the concept.

The third chapter, 'Subjectivity, Art, and Ecosophy,' takes up the key ideas presented in Guattari's bold tri-ecological vision in *The Three Ecologies* (1989), involving biospherical, social, and mental dimensions. In a detailed consideration of Guattari's thought, I explain that his real innovation was to develop the relationship between art and ecology through his core problematic of subjectivity. For Guattari, 'one creates new modalities of subjectivity in the same way that an artist creates new forms from the palette.'[44] Guattari believed that ecology, generalized as ecosophy, could help summon forth new, productive traits of subjectivity. His positive models were drawn from a range of arts, and in his view aesthetics had to be supported by an ethical responsibility that traversed micro- and macro-levels of concern. The prospects of transdisciplinarity as a non-transcendent ecology of knowledge are also explored through examples of ecosophic aesthetic and ethical practices drawn from his writings about specific artists and events that animated his tri-ecological vision. One issue that Guattari did not address was that his conception of ecosophy – the concept that articulates the three ecologies and is sometimes another way of expressing schizoanalytic method (meta-modelization) when it is itself articulated by the four ontological functions – was not linked to the extensive discussions of the concept during the 1980s in the work of Norwegian philosopher Arne Naess and his followers. Instead, Guattari used as a foil the Gaia hypothesis advanced by Lynn Margulis and J.E. Lovelock – their conception of the biota as the sum of living things on Earth, understood as a cybernetic control system that together actively maintains the environment from the inside and with respect to changing rather than fixed set points (homerrhetic vs. homeostatic) – and thought it was too mythically animistic and vitalist.[45] Guattari's reference point was not a system of living beings but its relation to an extrinsic coordinate – the machinic phylum, his idea of what drives history, the heterogeneous (non-linear) causality of a creatively mutating material substrate, the potentialities of which are actualized by drawing out and developing the most promising implicit traits. The interactions and crossings between the machinic phylum and living beings, humans with their non-human attributes, continuously re-create the world and give rise to genuinely singular machines. Guattari is proposing neither a post-human nor a post-natural ecosophy. A machine is at its simplest just a component – an object that enters into material and semiotic fluxes and assemblages – and 'is something that situates itself at the limit of a series of anterior machines and which throws out the evolutionary phylum for machines to come.'[46] The implications of this view shaped Guattari's sense of autopoesis: it is no longer a feature of living homeostatic systems but extended to other systems as a generalizable assumption of autonomy, nourished by its lineages, by social, semiotic, economic, and a range of incorporeal machinic assemblages.[47] Moreover, it is in the arena of green electoral politics that we glimpse a final public engagement by Guattari, despite his misgivings about professional politics. As another 'tool for transversality' (following Ivan Illich's 'Tools for Conviviality'), ecosophy served the 'aspiration for individual and collective reappropriation of the production of subjectivity.'[48]

Guattari's original contribution to semiotics is his theorization of a-signifying part-signs, which I take up in detail in Chapter 4, 'A-signifying Semiotics'. Although this type of part-sign or sign-particle is akin to a signal, in that it lacks a semantic dimension of content and meaning and is non-representational, Guattari adds that its molecular dimension, which is flush with material intensities, is marked politically. The example I develop is the magnetic stripe on bank cards, where the charged particles are aligned on rows thoroughly colonized by the aviation and banking industries, but which make machines enunciate (this is the domain of non-human enunciation and actions by machines on one another and data), integrating human users into the ensemble. Guattari has theorized, I believe, a new type of sign whose importance may be appreciated in the context of info-capitalist networks, which he accessed through the use of such cards. Although Guattari's contributions to a semiotic and political critique of the technoverse through a-signifying part-signs is remarkably temporary and written as it were before the letter of the Internet and explosion of wireless networks, my strategy is not to position him as a Netizen before the letter.[49] Although Guattari was an early cyber-enthusiast, especially when it came to the question of choice presented by new media – by means of keyboard and screen he could communicate with like-minded people about the dreams of Kafka[50] – he understood that the post-mediatic promise of singularity was easily corrupted by the intrusion of corporate mediocrity into the medium at every level, as he witnessed with the free-radio movement in France. Guattari was wary about the computer as 'pagan god', but meditated on the paradox of the relationship between singularity and mass media – the two canceling each other out as the mass desingularizes (decreasing the autonomy and creativity of its users). Post-[mass]media promised a number of key innovations: personal programming through media convergence brought about by the information revolution; a new kind of literacy in a post-linear communicational paradigm characterized by hypertext and the interactions of multiple users; redefinitions of producers and users as mutually dependent creators 'wedged like a crowbar between the private and public';[51] unanticipated or 'indirect' social practices arising from new information technologies and folding back upon the directions taken in research and development; and a call for a critical media education program arising from the distortions of news reporting.

In *A Thousand Plateaus*, the second volume of *Capitalism and Schizophrenia*, Deleuze and Guattari elaborate upon a number of models of smoothness and striation: a technological model contrasting the amorphous and supple felt and quilt with loom-woven fabrics; a musical model in which a smooth space draws a diagonal across the striated horizontal lines (melodic) and vertical planes (harmonic); a maritime model of a smooth sea of intensities subject to navigational striations (bearings and points); and a mathematical model contrasting two types of multiplicity: non-metric and metric. My question is what would an informatic model look like? In Chapter 5, 'Informatic Striation,' I revisit the smooth/striated distinction in order to show, through two detailed examples drawn from Canadian Inuit and Australian Aboriginal histories of capture by a colonizing British Crown, how information striation is a form of subjugation of previously smooth, non-bureaucratic space. I want to add a new dimension to the smooth/striated pair, that of information, in order to show how striation as social regulation disrupts many social practices. I also suggest that the resignification of out-of-date informatic striations, comically, artistically, and in other ways, relaunches these detested regimes in different registers and thus smoothness comes to perfuse the margins of the network society. In other words, I am proposing that informatic striation comes from without and imposes itself on indigenous peoples as a set of codings that reach deep into existing cultural practices. In turn, indigenous peoples resist informatic subjugation by colonizers and reprocess such codings in creative and innovative ways in the perpetual interaction of metamorphosis and identity inscription, of cutting loose and binding.[52] Informatics provides personal identifiers that master the variations of a people by division, linking number with space, arresting movement. Censuses, passports, and identity cards all attest to this counting as a form of occupation, as Deleuze and Guattari specify, while acknowledging that 'treating people like numbers is not necessarily worse than treating them like trees to prune.'[53] Through my two case studies of indigenous colonial capture I wish to show the deep mutual imbrication of the smooth and striated within the domain of an identity-ascribing informatics.

Guattari's somewhat scant writings on cinema primarily revolve around the investigation of alternative psychiatric strains in documentary works that offer insights into the institutions of madness. His interest in independent, activist cinematic works opens onto an international arena of the use of film as a medium of institutional critique, that is, a micropolitical cinema focused on the specific goal of 'shaking up opinion about the fate reserved in society for the mentally ill.'[54] The connection between anti-psychiatry – about which Guattari remained ambivalent – and cinema arose for Guattari in a concrete way at the first meeting in 1975, convened by family therapist Mony Elkaïm, of the International (originally European) Network for Alternatives to Psychiatry in Brussels. The urgency of anti-psychiatry's political goals across the globe may be indexed to the Kennedy Act of 1963, which closed psychiatric hospitals across the United States in a misapplication of anti-psychiatry's strategy of deinstitutionalization which the administration of the time conflated with dehospitalization, precipitating massive homelessness and swelling the prisons with ex-patients in the name of ill-conceived community health centers/half-way houses (read private rooming houses). The screening of the remarkable film *Fous à délier* (Silvano Agnosti, Marco Bellocchio, Sandro

Petraglia, Stefano Rulli, 1975) was a revelation for Guattari, even if his praise was muted in view of the film's idealism and the outdated solution of inserting psychiatric patients into the industrial proletariat. It was a few choice cinematic examples from the early to mid 1970s that enabled Guattari to shift away from the demagoguery and guruism that infected the anti-psychiatry movement. In Chapter 6, I work through the implications of Guattari's turn to this minor cinema, akin to minor literature, as an attempt to summon a people with whom to connect in expanding and deepening alternative psychiatric struggles. It will be useful to introduce Deleuze's conception of the minor in *Cinema 2* (primarily through Third Cinema examples) in reading Guattari's theory of minor cinema in *La révolution moléculaire*. However, Guattari's minor cinema cannot be cleanly grafted onto Third Cinema categories, and his brief discussion of films in no way corresponds to the divisions of filmic material in film studies, as he weaves a path between documentary cinema, big Hollywood fiction, and European auteurs without deference to genre and with great dexterity.

Today, anti-psychiatry is almost forgotten and seems to rear its head in the rants of Scientologists and the market liberalism of mental health consumerism. But during the late 1960s and early 1970s, anti-psychiatry as a coherent social movement displayed a range of political positions – militant to utopian – in the critique of medical power, objections to the loss of patient's rights, the valorization of countercultural lifestyles, and the exposé of psychiatry as an unsubtle form of social control. While the exploration of madness and critique of social normopathy – capitalism's schizophrenia – was a widespread cultural phenomenon during this period – think of psychedelic rockers Pink Floyd's magnum opus *Dark Side of the Moon*[55] – anti-psychiatry promoted widespread change in state institutional organigrams of power around the world, with each national struggle adopting different tactics and finding specific opportunities to explore its territories within and beyond the walls of hospitals and clinics, and national health systems. Despite the waning of anti-psychiatry, my goal here is to engage directly with one of the key socio-

political milieus that animated Guattari's thought and look at the
decisions he made at the time to critically valorize certain media
of aesthetic expression, without abandoning his own clinical
work that furthered anti-psychiatry's fundamental commitment
around the diffusion of roles (decentering the doctor's traditional
authority),[56] despite his thorough critique of psychoanalysis as a
reformist retreat from the social into myth-based interpretation
in a sterile analytic encounter of patient and doctor.

Chapter 7, 'Affect and Epilepsy,' provides a further contextu-
alization and application of Guattari's analyses of minor cinema
as a privileged medium for the exploration of minoritarian
becomings. Within the context of alternatives to psychiatry, one
film stands out because of its exploration of epilepsy within the
disabling environments of the family and in terms of its constraints
on public performances. The key film for Guattari was Marco
Bellocchio's *Fists in the Pocket* (1965); Bellocchio counts as one
of Guattari's favorite directors and he was part of the collective
that made *Fous à délier*. How does epilepsy function cinematically
through depressing and distressing atmospheric viscosities that
confirm affect's autonomy, affect's capacity to resist discursive
and representational capture? Affect comes from elsewhere, in a
flash, to 'exist in you,' like a seizure, and with a brutal specificity
that sweeps the subject away.[57] To this end I will also consider a
contemporary 'biopic' concerning Ian Curtis (actor Sam Riley),
former lead singer of the post-punk band Joy Division, director
Anton Corbijn's *Control* (2007). My aim is to show Guattari's
original contribution to the theory of affect, a concept of such
widespread contemporary philosophical importance; I am not
suggesting that Guattari liked Joy Division (he didn't like punk,
anyway). It is in the unity of affect and epilepsy that Guattari
innovates. I am questioning after Guattari's founding of affect on a
certain conception of epilepsy that is autonomous and atmospheric
(viscous and immobilizing) but in a manner that opens questions
about what philosophers of affect have detected as the 'positive
connotations' of affect's unassimilable, uncapturable, vital, and
open characteristics.[58] What is positive about affect's epileptic
foundation? The rhythmic transductions of epileptic seizure in

Fists in the Pocket and *Control* reveal only the misery of affect's void, and thus this chapter issues a corrective of sorts, rebalancing affect's much vaunted transformative potential for critique, with a sobering thought about how readily it can turn towards death. To this end I present a detailed study of how epilepsy shaped Guattari's theorization of existential affects, showing how he derived the concept from phenomenological psychiatric sources, including Eugène Minkowski's important book *Lived Time*, and explaining how this illness informed his delineation of different kinds of affect and their effects on subject formation. For epileptic seizures are intensities to which subjects are susceptible, and yet they appear to bring few opportunities for creative engagements with the real, and little room for positive metamorphosis (more sadness than joy, death rather than flight). In deploying two filmic examples, however, I am aware that they present restricted viewpoints and thus I will also suggest what a Guattarian epileptic subject might do with or develop the differentiating, intense affects of epilepsy.

My concluding remarks emphasize the trajectory of Guattari's original theorization of machines and the implications of his conception of the vast machinic phylum that constitutes a technological world history for evolving productions of subjectivity (machinic subjects for machinic ecologies). For Guattari, micropolitics is about pragmatically intervening at the smallest levels in order to ensure that the dominant kinds of subjectivity produced by Integrated World Capitalism do not win out: 'It is no longer a question merely of reappropriating the means of production or the means of political expression, but also of leaving the field of political economy and entering the field of subjective economy.'[59] In the subjective economy the domain of struggle is defined by developments on the machinic phylum.

1

THE FORMATION OF A
YOUNG MILITANT

While many of us were excitingly entering the workforce for the first time as part-time laborers in the tertiary sector, Guattari was already at 16 years of age politically precocious. He was a child of the Liberation, and all of its 'extraordinary wild imaginings,' above all those of the youth hostel movement.[1] Radical pedagogue Fernand Oury (1920–98) was instrumental in getting Guattari involved during the summer caravans from one hostel to the next that he organized in the Paris suburb of La Garenne-Colombes for youth like Guattari, who grew up in the same department, and already knew Oury as his science teacher.[2] Indeed, in his journal Guattari recalls a dream sequence in which there were 'two different paths for going out of my house at La Garenne. One was towards Fernand Oury's house.'[3] This chapter follows the path upon which the elder Oury (there would be another younger brother) set Guattari.

Fernand Oury's influence was decisive for Guattari in both practice and theory. Guattari once remarked that

> my presumed competence in this domain [setting up intra-hospital patient clubs and workshops at Clinique de Borde in the mid 1950s] was due to the fact that since the age of sixteen I had always been a 'militant' in organizations like the Youth Hostels and a whole range of activities for the extreme left.[4]

The Guattari that we have received is best known for his collaborations: with Deleuze, Negri, Alliez, etc. Guattari's career path led him to take up psychoanalysis after abandoning the study of pharmacy he began in the late 1940s, what he dubbed the 'family business.'[5] He was trained by Lacan, having entered the orbit of the master's seminar in the early 1950s and with whom he had a stormy relationship, and spent his career at La Borde. In return for freedom to experiment with the institution's organization, Guattari offered, in a confessional mode, 'constant fidelity to the local superegoism.'[6] He also maintained his own practice. Jean Oury – another Lacanian superego – helped Guattari escape from an internship in pharmacy, a path he abandoned;[7] Fernand initiated Guattari into a militant's life that prepared him for what his brother had in store.

The picture of Guattari I want to draw in this first chapter owes more to a little-known schoolteacher in suburban Paris than to the big names of post-'68 French thought. Fernand Oury was best known as a key figure in the movement that updated the ideas of Célestin Freinet (1896–1966) for a new era of barracks schools under the name of 'institutional pedagogy.'[8] The new large urban (primary and secondary) schools of the 1960s were far removed from the one- or two-room rural schoolhouses with small numbers of mixed ages in the primary grades that defined the Freinet movement. Fernand's name is closely linked with the birth of the institutional pedagogy movement (IP) in the early 1960s. This was a sub-movement – a 'recognizable strand'[9] – of Freinet teaching, located in Paris, although Freinet himself was not comfortable with IP's heavily theoretical discourse grounded in psychoanalysis, the 'case study' method of writing about children, and the creeping professionalization and desire for a pathway of accreditation (ideas alien to Freinet) of the teachers involved. In fact, the IP introduced an entirely new element into Freinet culture: academic research in education studies now had a role to play in Freinet activity.[10] Freinet's failed attempt to influence activities in the Paris group's journal (*L'Éducateur de l'Ille-de-France*) from his location outside of Cannes in the south of France led to the IP's expulsion from the Parisian Freinet group, the Institut Parisien de l'École Moderne.

Oury was not the only educator who influenced Guattari and assisted in his political education. Fernand Deligny (1913–96) worked with psycho-socially marginal children, offering them an alternative to hospitalization. He also created, circa 1948, a 'therapeutic caravan' known as La Grande Cordée, 'a network of lodgings for delinquents, pre-delinquents, and emotionally challenged children with the assistance of the Youth Hostel network. Children impermeable to psychiatric treatment were welcomed by "normal" adults.'[11] By means of sponsorships, funds from support groups, donations, and numerous moves in and out of Paris to encampments and communes, Deligny managed to sustain his peripatetic cure against the demands of professional teachers and those specialists who voted for the institutionalization of the children with whom he lived and worked, creating a 'suitable place to live.'[12] Eventually, in 1965, he landed on the doorstep of La Borde. Jean Oury and Guattari assisted Deligny's team by providing accommodation at La Borde, where part of Deligny's film *Le Moindre Geste* (1962–71) was shot by Josée Manenti and Jean-Pierre Daniel in 1965–66. Later in the decade Deligny would work on his film and short-lived journal *Cahiers de l'Aire* (1968–73) at Guattari's property in Gourgas, close to the commune where he lived in Monoblet. Despite Deligny and Manenti's differences with Guattari,[13] both were briefly involved in the production of publications for the Fédération des groupes d'études et de recherches institutionnelles (FGERI – founded in 1965). Indeed, Deligny is credited by some with the artisanal production of the *Cahiers de la FGERI*, including the early issues of the journal *Recherches*, directed (perhaps even dominated) by Guattari.[14]

Before Guattari coined the term 'schizoanalysis' to describe his brand of psychotherapy, he worked under the rubric of what was known as 'institutional psychotherapy,' that is, analysis undertaken by foregrounding the institutional context itself as a mediating object in collective life. This approach actively deconstructed the dyad of analyst–analysand and the familialism that perfused even the most avant-garde practices of psychoanalysis; indeed, access to the unconscious could not be made exclusively via language and the symbolic order by means of the transference, the psychoanalytic cornerstone. Guattari focused on how an institution contributed to the creation of certain kinds of subjectivity; likewise, for educators working within the Freinet-inspired IP, the focus was on how the school itself created certain kinds of learning disabilities in its pupils. The organization, artifacts, fields of reference, and group life of an institution emerging through its collective self-invention was not empirical sociology or organization studies, because the model was the psychoanalytic part-object that was irreducible to its objective description. The 'institutional object' (based neither on lack nor on a whole from which a part is cut, but understood in positive and productive terms irreducible to any totality, especially the kinds of identities that institutions bestow) could be known only through an analysis of a group's desire as it participated in and negotiated its creation with reference to proliferating reference points. This gave to groups the ability to occupy the creative spaces of an institution and contribute to its ongoing elaboration in a kind of sculptural process. This would have been extremely difficult in a 'barracks' school with large numbers of children managed only through quasi-military routine. Institutional pedagogy and psychotherapy were grappling with very similar problems around how institutional objects were received, that is, introjected, by their denizens.

Guattari was learning the ropes of institutional experimentation in the course of his training as a young militant, first visiting Jean Oury at the small psychiatric clinic at Saumery in the early 1950s. It was not until he joined La Borde a few years later and developed the 'grid' – literally the tabular representation upon which the evolving schedule of work rotation in which everyone participated was inscribed – that he developed a portfolio of practices for gaining access to the ways in which complex institutional inter-relations affected the psychical economies of actual groups and their members. Guattari set about experimenting with ways to heighten and maximize an institution's 'therapeutic coefficient' by unfixing rigid roles, thawing frozen hierarchies, opening hitherto closed blinkers, and modifying the introjection of the local superegoisms and objects. This role redefinition and displacement of fixed, hierarchical power relations and identities was scrambled micropolitically in ways that interrupted fantasies that would have otherwise bewitched the institution's denizens by trapping them in inflexible strata of authority and routines without any justification but their own continuation. As I shall explain in Chapter 2, the grid wasn't perfect and was a little centralist in bureaucratic inspiration at first.

Jean and Fernand had been active in the IP and had therefore a working knowledge of the battery of Freinet techniques. Fernand had been a member of the Freinet movement since the late 1940s. Jean borrowed Freinet techniques and adapted them to new forms of group work at Saumery and then La Borde.[15] In a sense, then, Guattari was absorbing from the Oury brothers lessons in modified Freinet practices.

The notion that youth hostels could be lumped together with other far left experiments is hard to reconcile with the broad inter-nationalist strokes of the hostelling movement. France was one of the original signatories to the establishment of the International Youth Hostel Association (IYHA) in 1932. Hostelling is a German creation, dating from the early twentieth century and catering to the country wanderer burdened only by a rucksack, with a foundation in educational experimentation – the elementary school hostel set up in Altena by Richard Schirrmann, widely considered as the founder of the youth hostel movement, in 1909. While the politics of the IYHA may be appreciated through its actions over a number of decades – its successful resistance to National Socialist attempts to dominate the organization in the 1930s and, later, its steadfast refusal to permit South Africa membership and its outright rejection of South Africa's proposed 'white' and 'black' hostel networks – the movement is centrist in its internationalism and valorization of youth travel, preferably in the country and on foot, and exposure to folk cultures in general. All the values of self-reliance and the benefits of fresh air and physical activity are found there, together with any number of restrictions (age limits for hostel use, division of the sexes in the dormitories, house parents, etc.). Organizationally, youth hostels are by-and-large voluntary bodies in the non-profit, NGO sector, organized around national councils with main executive bodies that conform to the basic standards set by the IYHA. Many national youth hostel organizations have direct connections with ministries of education and serve, in the manner of Schirrmann, as accommodation for traveling school classes, a kind of 'roaming school' or 'school country house.'[16] This is what Guattari suggests by the 'caravans' organized by Oury out of La Garenne, which used both schools and hostels as accommodation for roaming groups of schoolchildren during vacation periods; likewise, it is the same network that assisted Deligny in conceptualizing passages, circuits, and trajectories followed by children within much more strictly circumscribed areas, which he would map both on paper and on film (not so much as lines of flight, but lines of repetition and wandering) towards grasping the inscriptions of unique existential territories. But what is the relationship between hostelling, far left militancy, and popular pedagogy? What is the link between the youth hostels and Oury's institutional pedagogy and how did they contribute to Guattari's training as a young militant and influence his subsequent experiments with transdisciplinary groups?

The French Anomaly in Youth Hostelling

In the history of the youth hostel movement, France is an anomaly. Although it was not uncommon for national associations to be divided and subdivided along regional–territorial lines, in France competing associations emerged that were fractured along political and religious lines. This was a unique challenge for the IYHA. The original signatory for France was the Catholic wing of the movement, the Ligue Française pour les Auberges de la Jeunesse, long associated with the name of Marc Sangnier (1873–1950) and known for its pacifist politics, not to mention its conservative attitudes toward sexuality.[17] The first French youth hostel was established in Sangnier's country home in Bierville, south of Paris, and opened its doors in 1930.

In 1934 another French hostelling organization appeared, the Centre Laïque des Auberges de la Jeunesse (CLAJ). According to one historian:

[I]t drew on the latent anti-clericalism in French educational circles and gave political allegiance to the Popular Front Government; it emphasized the need for the young hostel-users to take a part in constructing and controlling their youth hostels, and large numbers of hostels sprang up all over the country like mushrooms ... Every group of hostel-users established its own journal which discussed in serious terms the mystique of youth-hostelling – the liberation of youth from the 'stuffy' tradition of the older generation. The movement could boast its own poet (the Provençal writer, Jean Giono) and its own collection of songs (Marie-Rose Clouzot's *La clé des chants*).[18]

There are several important points here that allow us to situate Guattari and Oury in this lay hostelling tradition. The first is the emphasis placed on the socialist politics of Léon Blum's Popular Front (Front Populaire), which had come into power in 1936 behind a left unified in the face of the threat of fascism. The Front's emphasis on cultural enrichment through leisure, and the secu-larization of education, gave impetus to the formation of many new organizations, but most importantly provided funding for many existing organizations, including the Centre Laïque and the Ligue. Leo Lagrange was the minister in charge of the Ministry of Leisure at the time and he later assumed the presidency of the CLAJ.[19] The lay hostels multiplied faster than those of the Ligue largely because of government policies that saw in them places where workers, who for the first time enjoyed paid holidays, could vacation. A mythic status has accrued to the 'communist' summer camps for children, the *colonies de vacances*, and the body that was charged with training its leaders (Centres d'Éntrainement aux Méthodes d'Éducation Active). Followers of Freinet were members of this body and Freinet's own school, which had room for boarders, participated in this scheme. At the time the government supported a wide range of programs geared toward youth organizations. Under the Popular Front, hostels, schools, and other facilities became points of intersection for popular education, new opportunities for leisure and the valorization of youth travel, and consensual political ideology machines within civil society. This enthusiasm was rekindled in the postwar years.

Just as significant was the character of self-organization attributed to the hostels within the Centre Laïque, which underlined self-reliance through workers' control. This extended to the actual construction of the facilities, thus regaining the original mandate of cooperative labor that animated the hostelling spirit and which accelerated in the postwar years in the face of the considerable task of rebuilding and repair. It may be added that some of the remote hostels in unoccupied France during the Second World War had been 'centers of resistance,'[20] just as psychiatric hospitals like St. Alban had provided refuge for progressive doctors, artists, and resistance fighters.

However, it is the central role given to a self-produced collective publication that cements the relationship between Guattari, Oury, the youth hostels, and institutional analysis. A key feature of Oury's Freinet-inspired pedagogy was the self-produced school journal and the collective responsibility assumed for its editing and distribution. While many national youth hostel associations had their own periodicals, including in France the Ligue's *Information et documentation*, these were not constitutive of the institution and stood apart from the project of its permanent reinvention. While many of these journals had 'romantic names such as *Au devant de la vie*, *Route joyeuse*, *Viens avec nous* and *l'Aube se lève*,'[21] publishing was not an activity separable from a hostel group's self-management. It constituted a key piece of institutional matter.

The IYHA would have preferred that the French organizations voluntarily merge into a single national body – a matter decided artificially during war under the occupation government in France. The international body encouraged this end by denying a splinter group from the Centre Laïque separate membership rights in the postwar years (1947–48), after a third group, the Union Française, had joined the Ligue in 1947 as the Fondation Française des Auberges de la Jeunesse (FFAJ). The 'lay' movement had suffered its own split as the Movement Laïque (MLAJ) set its own course.[22] It was not until 1955 that unity was achieved in France in the form of a Fédération Unie des Auberges de la Jeunesse.

Institutions in Question

Fernand's institutional pedagogy paralleled Jean's and Guattari's efforts at La Borde in the milieu of institutional psychotherapy. What both approaches appreciated was that the institutional context itself had to be analyzed. To this end, around 1960, a diverse group of therapists and educators gathered around the Ourys to discuss the problems of institutions, their production, their modification through creative organizational solutions, etc., under the name of the Work Group on Institutional Psychology and Sociology (Groupe de travail de psychologie et de sociologie institutionnelles, GTPSI). Groups of this sort proliferated: as noted above, in 1965 FGERI was founded and, later in the 1960s, FGERI would develop sub-groups such as CERFI, the Center for Study and Research into Institutional Functioning (Centre d'études de recherches sur le fonctionnement des institutions). I will focus explicitly on CERFI in my concluding remarks to this book because of its enormous significance for Guattari as a social-group machine.

The followers of Freinet aligned with Fernand organized the Nantes-based Group for Therapeutic Education (Groupe d'éducation thérapeutiques, GET), which participated in FGERI, and found themselves in the company of psychiatrists, anti-psychiatrists, philosophers, architects, urbanists, activists, and so on. Jean Oury brought to GET psychoanalytic models, like the idea of writing case studies about specific students in the context of their class.[23] The Federation of Study Groups was nothing less than a transdisciplinary experimental research assemblage that Guattari described as a '*detour* through other disciplines that allowed false problems to be overcome (relative to functions of space: volumes, levels, communications, and the institutional and micro-political options of instigators and participants).'[24] The confluence of militancy and transdisciplinary experimentation had the goal of creating scenes of subjectification – and this was how Guattari characterized F. Oury's efforts – that overcame the 'encasernée scolaire' (school-as-barracks) subjectivity, for the sake of an appreciation of student–teacher relations sensitive to heterogeneous components as well as local conditions that would be otherwise steamrolled if one arrived with 'prefabricated interpretive grids.'[25]

I want to emphasize the critique of the institution in the pedagogical context taken up by F. Oury and his colleagues in the Freinet movement. This perspective will help to explain some of the basic principles and influence of institutional psychotherapy and acknowledge Guattari's ongoing interest in the Group for Therapeutic Education, especially the role played by the importance given to singularization, a self-organizing process involving the constitution of an assemblage of components (intrinsic references), relations with other assemblages, and the analysis of their effects on subjectivity. For Guattari, this was 'constitutive of finitude and authenticity.'[26]

The principles and program outlined in Oury's classic co-authored statement on institutional pedagogy *Towards an Institutional Pedgagogy* (*Vers une pédagogie institutionnelle*, with Aïda Vasquez), picks up on themes vital to Guattari's concept of the group. Oury and Vasquez emphasized the act of writing as an individual and collective project that not only allowed for the expression of meaning and character by individuals, but realized success in communication, that is, being read or heard by one or more others (classmates, parents, correspondents beyond the school itself), like a subject group that speaks and is heard.

For Guattari the subject was a group or collective assemblage of heterogeneous components whose formation, de-linked from monadic individuality and seemingly bottomless interiority, not to mention abstract, universal determinations by complexes such as Oedipus and castration in the Freudian universe, could be seen through critical analyses of the actual vicissitudes of collective life in which persons found themselves. Guattari favored a Sartrean-inflected theory of groups, distinguishing non-absolutely between subject (actively exploring self-defined projects) and subjugated groups (passively receiving directions), each affecting the relations of their members to social processes and shaping their potential for subjectification. The problem of subjectification will be taken up in greater detail in later chapters. In the meantime, Guattari's interest was in how subjects were fabricated (in and against a capitalism in which machines like television and the Internet and sports equipment come to be more and more influential in the 'modelization' of subjects) from unsorted (neither hierarchically organized nor classified) components drawn from any field (human, non-human, organic, non-organic) and assembled together in an unstable, creative process of singularizing autoproduction. Subjectivity emerges from this de-differentiated agglomeration of components which 'autopoetical[ly] snowball' into a sense of self.[27]

Pedagogical scenarios of subjectification were organized that guaranteed the certainty of writing in order to be read through the circulation of published, reproduced texts. The pillars of this process were the individual and collective school journal, interschool communication and exchange of school journals, and the school printery. Correspondence was established between individuals, and between individuals and groups (entailing reading before the class, but only from those sections of one's personal 'free text,' in the language of Freinet, that would interest the group, and upon which they would pass a certain kind of judgment, making corrections, suggestions, editing, toward its inclusion in a collective publication), and geographically diverse school groups exchanged collectively written manuscripts (refocusing attention on otherwise overlooked everyday situations that would appear unique to other readers). For Oury, the 'school journal [composed of free texts] is a privileged technique'[28] in the constitution of a *third* object (that is never just a thing but always more than merely an object) that opens the students to multiple networks, breaking down the rigid teacher–student dyad in which the former superior *teaches* the latter inferior. Oury echoes a great chain of psychoanalytic objects – part[ial], transitional, institutional, *objet 'a'* – that would become less and less typical (representational and/or non-significantizable) and progressively singular, that is incomparable, with this third object of the published text and other mediators. These third, transitional objects are held in common by a given group and focus the attention of its members; they orient themselves by means of such objects, transit through them, and transform meaning by means of them. This Gutenbergian realization of the collective around the school printery and the collectively 'perfected' (not corrected) text in the real work of cooperative production may sound today, in the age of networked virtual communities and real time blogging, somewhat narrow, but the machinic dimension of the mediating third term remains intact since it opens the class to the world as relations between class and community serve pedagogically as a focal point for lessons about grammar, reading, and writing. This theorization of basic operating principles along psychoanalytic lines is beyond the concrete, classroom-focused thought of Freinet himself. Suffice to say that Freinet found the heavily psychoanalytic language of some of his Parisian followers to be alienating. Yet Freinet introduced at the material level mediating objects like the school journal, printery, and cooperative counsel that proved influential and indispensable for the Ourys. As F. Oury relates:

> The introduction of a *mediation* between therapist and patient is, at least in the first instance, the necessary condition of the cure. It is the characteristic, if one can schematize it in the extreme, of institutional therapy. Evidently mediations may be objects (tools or goals) or persons, or institutions, but these always prove to be more than objects or persons. At the Congress of 1957 Freinet said that a statue should be erected to the little printing press and not to him.[29]

The printing press is not a techno-fetish; its introduction into a school situation is not even original with Freinet. What is original is its role as a mediation, a transversalizing–transporting space in which hierarchy is restructured, responsibilities are assigned and assumed, functions and transformations of those functions are managed, and existing institutional structures at all levels, from the classroom through the school to the board, are called into question. Moreover, the printery is but one of many mediations, adequate to the specificities of the situation, by Freinet and his followers. Let's now look more closely at the school printery.

The School Printery

Freinet was a great believer in trial-and-error learning, and the École Freinet (the first of which opened in 1935 in Vence, France) was a school without lessons in which language (writing and reading) was acquired naturally but non-passively through technological mediations. The use of technologies of reproduction was at the heart of what Freinet called *L'imprimerie à l'école* – the school printery – also the name of the journal he began publishing in 1926. A few years later he added subtitles to this journal: cinema, radio, phonograph, etc. The Freinet School had one room devoted to a print shop housing then current technologies of engraving (linoleum and wood), movable type, and/or stencil and hand-turned Gestetner drum. Freinet had, in fact, designed a small press for school usage and marketed it to fellow travelers. Technology was put in the service of the school's communitarian life and was the means by which students made the school their own. Freinet and later Guattari thought that technology could be flush with micro-political activity, that real struggles were being staged by the deployment of a printing press towards the production of a newspaper as a source for lessons as opposed to the importation of a state-sanctioned reader. In other words, a connection is made between technical and political choices.

As Oury notes above, collective autocritique was embedded in the process of creating school journals for inter-school correspondence within and beyond France, as these were assembled from otherwise free texts created by individuals as they passed from drawing into language. The only school books were those created in the printery. For all of his focus on mechanical reproduction, Freinet refused to see the printing press as a panacea. It constituted a 'technique of free and creative work' and not a method.[30] Freinet's originality was not in selecting the use of printing, or even in emphasizing the production of a 'free text,' but in embedding these in an egalitarian and democratic atmosphere that began very simply with the removal of the teacher's raised platform and the refusal of a standard school reader.

A good deal rested upon this technique, however, for it was in mechanical reproduction that reading and writing found for Freinet both their justification and their motivation (not the creation of interest as such but the deepening of interest). For schoolchildren there was something magical about seeing their work in print, and Freinet wrote of the 'eternal enchantment, a permanent magic, which fires all the possibilities of expression, doubling the reach of new communications which totally integrates the scholarly effort into the complex process of contemporary life.'[31] Beginning with the fixing of expression in drawings and the wonderment of their perfect reproduction as stencils in black and white (with the option for hand-coloring) or in color,[32] Freinet observed the excitement and empowerment of young author–artists as they created their own books by adding new drawings daily as well as integrating works by their fellows. Some copies were sent to parents, while others made their way into the school journal, which was sent by post to other schools in exchange for their collectively produced journals. These kinds of activities were for Freinet 'efficacious stimulants of the child's desire to create, possess and communicate a work which is their own.'[33] These books are form and content: at first, letters to corresponding schools were 'written by the teacher as dictated by the children, recopied by them, and all this will lead the students toward the well-founded practice of writing independently of drawing.'[34] Copying gives way to independent writing: 'the miracle occurs: the cycle is resolved: the manuscript text that the child perfectly understands in its role of expression, is composed and then printed. It is now, black on white, a majestic page that has been illustrated and added to the book of life.'[35]

The Cooperative Council

Oury picked up Freinet's emphasis on democratic organization in the classroom through the weekly event called the *conseil de cooperative*, the cooperative council directed by the students themselves. It is adapted from Freinet's plan for a weekly meeting of the *cooperative scolaire*, the highlight of which was the reading and discussion of the mural journal containing under three columns – Criticisms, Congratulations, Requests – the week's record of non-anonymous student feedback.[36] This is far from the anodyne feedback or solicited comments popular in many schools under the cover of anonymity (the 'suggestion box') and discretionary bureaucratic responses. Each issue is discussed; positions are explained, defenses are mounted, students are reassigned to different tasks, when necessary: 'Nothing is as moral and as profitable as this common examination at once critical and constructive, of the life of the class.'[37]

In Oury's work with Vasquez, an institution is defined by

the places, moments, status of each according to his/her level of performance, that is to say according to his/her potentialities, the functions (services, posts, responsibilities), roles (president, secretary), diverse meetings (team captains, different levels of classes, etc.), and the rituals that maintain their efficacity.[38]

An institution, then, is composed of these activities; these are its matters, not all of which leave behind well-formed, archivable substances. In the meeting the teacher is one among many participants and, although s/he may at times veto motions, the class remains active as a self-directed group, as in Guattari's sense of a subject group that formulates its own projects, speaks and is heard, and puts itself at risk in pursuing its own ends and taking responsibility for them; indeed, the council is sometimes silent, faced with tumult, until it finds language. No one knows precisely how or where it will find it – at La Borde the emergence of local jargon derived from the laundry, and Jean Oury dubbed it 'lingistique' (lingerie/linguistique; linen/language).[39] In cases where either young students or psychiatric patients are concerned, there is always a risk that they will disappear, or simply be ignored, upon their insertion into the broad socio-politico-economic fields of normal child/adulthood. The *conseil* was for Oury the eyes of the group (witness of each persons' transgressions, successes, ...), its brain, as well, and heart – a refining machine: it was the 'keystone of the system since this meeting has the power to create new institutions, and institutionalize the milieu of communal life.'[40] In short, it helped to produce the institutional matter which could either be formed into semiotically well-defined substances or sidestep substance altogether by an a-signifying connection (more on this in Chapter 4) between form and matter that did not have a meaning effect (signified) or could not be totalized in a structural system of meaning production. The artifacts of this process of giving form to institutional matter are quite few since this articulation bypasses substance, if by this is meant concrete remainders. Much of the effort to bring form flush with matter remained on the cutting-room floor or unrecorded in the minutes of the school council, as it were, because it did not accede to semiologically well-formed substance.

The *conseil* is the pedagogical equivalent, on the organization level, of the collective bodies of *grilleurs* and *grilleuses* that arose as monitors of the work rotation schedules at La Borde; a vehicle, then, of autocritique following from auto-invention or self-management, with all of its shocks, especially in our era of privacy, in which it would be unthinkable for patients' dossiers to be open for discussion as they were at La Borde.[41] The system put into place had to safeguard against favoritism (e.g. parachuting people into certain positions), remain sensitive and adaptable to emerging resistances, implosions, and exploitations (e.g. the fears of staff hired to work in the kitchen about taking on healing tasks), allow for the segmentation of tasks, always complexifying itself along the way. The seductions of authoritarianism were always present, for both doctor and teacher.

Psychoanalysis in/of Context

The mediating third object is a fundamental principle of the institutional situation, following upon a critique of the dual therapeutic situation of psychoanalysis and the alleged neutrality of analysts. The red psychiatrist François Tosquelles, who had trained Jean Oury in the late 1940s, looked beyond the dual analysis at the openings provided by

multiple impersonal networks of the symbolic order ... [toward] a form of group therapeutics that is often established, with the doctor's knowledge, in psychiatric hospitals as a result of the material organization and the psycho-social interactions between patients and between patients and doctors.[42]

For Oury,

> the introduction between the therapist and the patient of a *mediation* is the necessary condition for the cure at least at the outset, and is also the characteristic, if one can schematize it in the extreme, of institutional therapy. The mediation may be apparently an object (tool or aim) or a person or an institution that always proves to be more than an object or person.[43]

Such mediations may take diverse forms and, in the pedagogical milieu, the school journal, published by the class, a collective assemblage of enunciation, together with the *conseil*, is an organizational institution created, reinvented, and maintained by the group over time. A mediating third object exists outside of one-on-one contact, and upon which work is done cooperatively, and for which responsibility is collectively assumed, through a series of obligatory exchanges (one speaks of the journal, apropos of a resolution, within a meeting defined by rules of order, etc.).

Less psychoanalytically, institutional experimentation in the tradition of Freinet is based on the principle of 'education by work.' Freinet's conception of work is arrived at through his deconstruction before the letter of the work/play distinction. He writes work–play together to indicate his idea that it is not manual work at issue, but a material and intelligent activity imbued with the spirit of integration. It is not imitative, like playing at working. He did not deny that 'education by work' had 'potential for an ulterior social production,' but he put the emphasis on the excitement it generated for the children without producing in the end 'a product directly useful to society.'[44] Guattari often had to defend himself against the claim that he was offering at La Borde a series of fixed tasks, a form of social adaptation though labor.[45] Likewise for Freinet work–play was neither a species of technical *apprentissage* nor a corrective of some kind. These interpretations would give 'prematurely a goal too directly utilitarian to childlike activity.'[46] By the same token, work–play mixed joy with fatigue, timidity with surprise, in a collective mode that organized the child's school world and did not permit a catastrophic distillation of play from work. Freinet refused to accept the separation, a 'social duality' typical of his time, between intellectual and active manual work within the school's physical layout, the latter functioning as an annex.[47] Here, again, is a mediating third figure, the work–play of the school printery loosening the hard and fast dualism of its definition as either training in a profession (work) or art technique (play). It is a question, then, of giving a greater amplitude to the interactions of teachers and students. The dual-protagonist model no longer sufficed and was for all those involved in the institutional movement extremely limited.

Students within the Freinet tradition are encouraged to become subject groups actively exploring self-defined projects, as opposed to subjugated groups passively receiving directions and living a kind of empty seriality; each kind of group affects the relations of their members to social processes, shaping their potential for subject formation, the amount of risk they can tolerate, and how they can use such groups. The modification of alienating fantasies of inferiority and failure, of stripping away the armor that many wore against encounters with otherness, would encourage creativity with imperfection. This was not an exercise in remodeling subjectivities but, rather, in producing new forms of subjectivity through restless, almost baroque micro-sociological variations. A key medium for this dynamic refashioning is, as we have seen from the example of the youth hostels forward, the collectively produced journal embedded in 'the institutional matter engendered throughout the tangle of workshops and meetings, as well as in daily life in the dining rooms and bedrooms, in sports, games and cultural life';[48] to which may be added, in the common rooms of hostels; and in the undertakings of the cooperative council. Guattari did not believe that the grid at La Borde was generalizable – 'no single model being materially transposable in this way.'[49] Still, the youth hostels and institutional pedagogy of Fernand Oury as well as the institutional psychotherapy undertaken at La Borde involved

complementary forms of transversal experimentation. Chapter 2
considers transversality in greater detail.

Transversality

> tends to be realized when communication is maximized between different
> levels and above all in different directions. It is the object toward which a
> subject group moves. Our hypothesis is this: it is possible to modify the
> different coefficients of unconscious transversality at different levels of
> an institution.[50]

In order for groups of students to realize their potential for transversality, they need to escape from the ghetto of passively receiving
the experience and meaning of school; they are separated and
largely segregated from this by layers of static administration
and preformed semiotics (books, uniforms, gestures, etc.). As a
group, school children normally have little real power. Their transversality would remain latent to the extent that its institutional
effects would be extremely limited by the lack of opportunities for
manifesting it. In order to modify this situation, popular pedagogy
reorganized the educational institution and redefined it through
permanent reinvention by means of collective creation (in which
the source of a group's unity has been internalized and shared
as a common property) from the material to the cognitive level,
bringing together roles and responsibilities hitherto held apart. A
privileged institutional matter for the students' creation of their
school experience was the school journal. This kind of collective
publishing has been a constant in Guattari's life from the hostels
through the journal *Recherches* by FGERI and then CERFI. It
is important to observe the influence on Guattari of the Freinet
journal scolaire – the school magazine consisting of perfected free
texts – and also to acknowledge how it differs from the school
newspaper or yearbook, or even the militant broadsheet under
the yoke of one or more editors (or meddling teachers or dues-
collecting professional bodies). The collectively produced journal
is a transversal tool used in subjectivity production by a radicalized
institution. Such a journal contributes to the collective creation of
institutional matter and is not merely a product engendered by
an institution (and into which it inserts participants); rather, the

institution is in part a product of a journal's collective elaboration and refinement over time, including everything that befalls a project of this kind, even the plight of serial repetition as the production of the next issue or version handcuffs an editorial group with a penchant to rest on its laurels and nurture its transversality with opportunities for entropy – since it might really enjoy what it cannot get done! Freinet underlined the success of the school magazine/journal/periodical strategy by pointing to numerous international examples – in Europe and Mexico and South America.[51]

These reflections on collective auto-production and the formation of institutional matter which give to artifacts of semiological substance such as journals a central role move in the direction of an interpretive strategy that sees in journal runs and editorial assemblages resources for the investigation of the processes of institutionalization. The journal–artifact is the key feature of the institutional matter engendered through editorial and other activities; indeed, not all the wide-ranging desiring productions, fantasies, positionings vis-à-vis a field into which a collective wants either to insert itself, or whose main markers it wants to elude through creative transversal crossings, find such substantial formedness. However, perhaps simply because they survive as concrete resources, such publications are indispensable. One way of grasping Guattari's intellectual formation is to situate him in the world of journal publishing, not on a stage-by-stage basis, but as a way of mapping a territory on the basis of whose projects he built himself territories and created new universes of reference – political, aesthetic, cognitive, etc.

The Role of the Timetable

Historians of the Freinet movement place much emphasis on its concern with classroom organization and scheduling, especially the daily timetable. Briefly, the day begins with the composition of a 'free text' by each student, at the level of one's ability; this text is read aloud, and one is selected by vote, written on the board, and edited ('perfected'); after a short break, class reconvenes for lessons required by the ministry, but which are delivered using the 'free text' in conjunction with the information cards held in the school's 'library' (*fichier documentaire*) consisting essentially of clippings and pedagogical materials produced by Freinet covering lessons on a variety of subjects; a vegetarian lunch (although students from the local area would go home for lunch) was followed by the printing process, each of several groups cycling in and out of the print shop from other activities such as listening to records or making handicrafts; a formal lesson was presented by means of either readings drawn from the card collection or from a text received from another school; after the short afternoon break the day ended with the so-called 'stop-gap' – whatever else needed to be covered. The daily schedule was embedded in individual plans of work–play using the cards, the weekly cooperative meeting, and a variety of collective activities (gardening, crafts) as well as the need to cover certain subjects.[52] Here we see how democratic goals, scheduling of work–play, and the rotation of activities dovetail in the grid adopted at La Borde; further, it is also evident how regular collective events provide a mechanism for feedback and the means for rebalancing the schedule. Guattari learned his Freinet scheduling from both Fernand and Jean Oury. Guattari described the grid as a double-entry table[53] for the management of time and task in daily, weekly, monthly, and even longer parameters, as well as on a rotating basis. The grid is first and foremost an instrument (evolving and increasingly sophisticated) for the management of personnel. The meaning of 'militancy' in this context is far from the romance of revolution, and even agitation must take a back seat to management skills. But this is no compromise: it is the very texture of the lessons about organization that Guattari learned in extracurricular youth activities in the hostels movement and from institutional pedagogy. Followers of Freinet were, after all, known as *militants Freinet*. And many self-styled militants were expelled from the Freinet movement because they sought to professionalize themselves and adopt the current trends of eduspeak! In the following chapter I will consider in more detail the problem posed by the schedule within a theory of transversality: as Foucault put it, 'the timetable is an old inheritance'[54] that seeps into the body in the form of controlled gestures and rhythms in the production of docility.

There is a remarkable coherence in the transversalization of institutional life that runs from Freinet, the great organizer, through the Oury brothers to Guattari, as well as the constancy of machines like journal publishing from the school printery to *Recherches* (but also including 'free radio' stations like Radio Vert that Guattari helped set up in the offices of the newspaper *Matin Paris* in 1977).[55] The key touchpoint is popular pedagogy and the collective auto-production by various groups of institutional matter through publishing projects. This is not a traditional philosophical universe of reference. Just as Freinet democratized the classroom by rewriting the teacher–student relationship, Guattari desegregated the medical–non-medical personnel relation and rewrote existing doctor–patient scenarios. Institutional militants from Freinet to Guattari have forged transversal social tools for the communication and articulation of individual and collective affects through the creation of institutional matters and the exploration of their potential for social creativity. Such tools and their supporting techniques are the privileged means of recomposing the components of subjectivity so that new kinds of responsibility can be taken, ways of seeing and living may be favorably achieved. These tools ensure that constructive, anguish-free institutional matters are engendered.

2

TRANSVERSALITY AND POLITICS

What is transversality?

Transversality is a core critical concept introduced by Guattari in a paper entitled 'Transversality' in 1964, in the context of a conference on theatre and therapy. The concept's development took place on the ground as a therapeutic and political tool in Guattari's analytical critique of and experimentation with intra-institutional formations of subjectivity at Clinique de La Borde. However, in 1964 Guattari was still beholden to Freudian theorizations of the unconscious (an intra-psychic depth model structured by universal complexes and lodged in individuals, the purpose of which is to modulate drives) which had not yet acquired, as it would over the course of the next five years, a machinic character. Guattari in his own words was a 'borrower and shuffler' of ideas,[1] and eventually a machinic dimension would be shuffled into the psychoanalytic unconscious, entailing the following statements: representational contents are not centered by language; the syntax of universal complexes are not adequate to grasping the singularities arising in specific circumstances; intersubjectivity bypasses universal structuration and is engaged by non-subjective arrangements, extra-human and non-organic components not necessarily available for interpretation; there is no use exclusively falling back on inheritances of the race and the big instincts because the here and now must also enter into consideration; the unconscious is contingent upon time and place and evolves in each instance; the analysis of such an unconscious is not the purview of specialists.[2]

Although Guattari admits to being a shuffler and even a thief of ideas, this admission may be taken the wrong way as a license to uncritically attribute the invention of some of his strongest conceptual work to others. For example, the portrait of Guattari that emerges in François Dosse's monumental intellectual biography of Deleuze and Guattari is that of an ideas thief; yet the claims of others are presented without any interrogation: psychologist Ginette Michaud claims she suggested to Guattari the concept of transversality;[3] and Dosse considers that the 'grid' was developed by Claude Jeangirard and exported from the Clinique de la Chesnaie to La Borde by Guattari.[4] Concepts like transversality do not spring up fully formed and remain static entities, a matter Dosse fails to appreciate.

Guattari reintroduced social demands, problems, and material realities into the analytic encounter. Originally guided by Freud's remarks on the fundamentally social being of individuals in the survival of sources of anxiety beyond the stages of psychogenesis, Guattari considered the object of institutional analysis to be outside both family, linguistic structure, and Oedipal myth. The problem of social reproductions of superegos (political leaders, for example, despite their actual influence) as constant sources of anxiety in advanced industrial societies (capitalist and socialist) led Guattari provisionally, and a little stiffly, to 'arrive at a modification of the superego's "accommodation" of data by transmuting this data in a kind of new "initiatic" reception, clearing from its path the blind social demand of a certain castrative procedure to the exclusion of all else'.[5] The goal is to bring about the acceptance of new data, rather than interminable castration anxiety precipitated by every superego figurehead (the great chain of the same Daddy in psycho-analytic terms), primarily by establishing new demands and setting up innovative points of reference within existing attachments (both real and imaginary) to institutions. This reworking of the superego was Guattari's earliest explanation of his activities at La Borde, where all sorts of experimentation and testing of hypotheses were played out. Guattari's therapeutic focus shifted away from the dual analysis of psychotherapy and onto patients in the places where they actually find themselves in clinical settings. This directly challenged innumerable inherited analytic methods.

But perhaps the greatest shift beyond both Freud and Lacan was that at La Borde psychotics were treated.

Guattari foregrounds institutional attachments by analyzing groups – everyone in a group has an analytic role to play. The desire of a de-individuated subject, considered as a group or collective assemblage of heterogeneous components freed from abstract determinations such as the archaic inheritances of Freudian analysis, or the official objects that support the symbolic order (defined by Lacan, Winnicott, or Klein), is understood through critical analyses of the organizational textures of actual groups. The machinic unconscious produces it own objects. Guattari insisted that the machinic unconscious was not exclusively available through talking and involved all sorts of expressive matters and contents.

Transversality overrode the psychoanalytic concept of transference (movement of positive and negative affect back and forth between patient and doctor). In another essay, 'The Transference,' originally published in 1964, Guattari clarifies that

> in the transference there is virtually never any actual dual relation ... At the moment we envisage this relation [of mother and child] in a real situation we recognize that it is, at the very least, triangular in character. In other words, there is always in a real situation a mediating object that acts as an ambiguous support or medium.[6]

The object detached from the intersubjective encounter is reinserted into the problem of groups in clinical settings – it is neither universal nor mythical–archaic. Transferential phenomena constitute spaces of potentiality and creativity grounded in stituational and contingent encounters.

If transference is the artificial relation in which the unconscious becomes conscious, transversality is the measure of an institution's influence on all its denizens. It is the group's unconscious, which entails that a descriptive analytics of overt power relations and objective laws inscribed in either vertical (pyramid) or horizontal (field of distribution) terms is insufficient. This is an unconscious that perfuses the social field and history – it is not eternal but transitory.

As Deleuze explains, one of Guattari's most significant contributions is the political idea of '(non-hierarchical) transversal relationships.'[7] Thinking in terms of life inside psychiatric facilities, but also of political groups, Guattari specified that transversality was neither found in vertical relations, as in a managerial pyramidal structure based on hierarchy and the division of labor based around specialisms, nor in pure horizontality, as one finds among groups of senile patients or even among the most troubled, manic patients in their section of a ward.[8]

Neither/nor, but what, then? Guattari continues:

Transversality is a dimension that strives to overcome two impasses: that of pure verticality, and a simple horizontality. Transversality tends to be realized when maximum communication is brought about between different levels and above all in terms of different directions.[9]

Transversality avoids getting stuck in hierarchy, and thus in a fixed point of order giving and taking, up or down the chain of command, and also resists sliding into mere accommodation – what can be done under the circumstances.

Transversality, Guattari posited, is an unconscious dimension of an institution (the residual Freudianism of the early Guattari is on display here in the manifest–latent dyad that determines his sense of levels), which can be accessed through the analysis of how its coefficients are manifested in and through group relations. Using a non-human example, Guattari considered the predicament of blinkered horses in a field: the opening of their blinkers would reduce the traumatic encounters produced when they were closed. The coefficient of transversality in a field of blinkered horses is low. The idea of the opening of the field of vision or in general, reference, through the adjustment of the horses' blinkers enhances transversality's coefficient by actually increasing the quantity of communication available that would otherwise be tied up in vertical and horizontal impasses; whereas a further closing of the blinkers would decrease the potential for transversality. 'In the hospital, the coefficient of transversality,' Guattari wrote, 'is the degree of blindness of each member of the staff.'[10] Here blindness is artificially induced by 'blinkers' like vertical traps and horizontal accommodations, pecking orders and gendered divisions of labor, and no end of professional peccadillos. Guattari is careful, however, not to prevent a kind of severe blindness, and the resulting trauma, from providing input about the analysis of an institution's transversality. This may be seen in the other important contribution, as Deleuze noted, that he introduced in support of the idea of transversality: subject groups.

For Guattari, a subject group has the goal of maximizing transversality. This group articulates its interests and pursues them in relation to an outside, for instance through dialogue with other groups. This openness is, however, precarious, because outside interactions and interventions threaten to overwhelm the resources the group has available to manage its relation to the outside. Nevertheless, subject groups attempt to balance this openness that brings with it threats to their own security, by developing internal or borderline forms of madness. It is in response to a double-edged alienation – open yet fragile, desirous of expansion yet inclined to contract – that subject groups grapple with their finitude.

On the one hand, the modification of alienating fantasies would permit creativity, remove inhibitions, and encourage self-management, whereas a subject group could decay into a subjugated group through an auto-mutilation (bureaucratically, in the case of a fixation on the fantasies of a leader and his/her mythic power that shuts down transversality; or with recourse to a despair that perfuses the group because it is not the revolutionary 'subject of history' to which it aspires, and can only occupy this position with the knowledge that its speech is co-optable by another group when circumstances present themselves).[11]

On the other hand, the members of a subjugated group may be encouraged to withdraw and vegetate in the group's rules and rites, in its 'structures of misrecognition.' Guattari noted that subject groups state something in a dialogue and subjugated groups have their causes heard – but without knowing where or by whom.[12] The subjugated group is subjugated by what it receives from the outside and by its inability to pursue its own ends. This group puts into play mechanisms that permit its members to spin their wheels, and refuse to face up to threats and the meaninglessness of their projects. But the important part is that even the most shut-in subjugated group that has rejected all hope of enrichment through negotiating otherness may harbor a key to an intractable situation. This is the non-mutually-exclusive character of the subject–subjugated distinction, which Guattari described as two angles or sides of the same institutional object. However, in subject groups there is a greater risk for individuals in facing up to external threats because of the possibility of compromising their group standing, but simultaneously the potential is there to lift the scaffolding of symptoms that individuals erect around themselves.

Guattari focused his attention on subject groups negotiating with the outside within a transitory group project:

> from the moment the group becomes a subject of its own destiny and assumes its own finitude and death, it is then that the data received by the superego is modified and, consequently, the threshold of the castration complex, specific to a given social order, can be locally modified.[13]

This is the positive result of the risk assumed by a member of a subject group in exposing him/herself to an outside. This is the very structure of transversality in the group. Guattari returned to this point again and again in his explanations of transversality.[14] It was for him a jumping-off point, circa 1964, embedded in the Freudian nomenclature of the superego (with its need for castrating punishment) and its ability to lord over representations of real external threats and to manufacture such threats internally.[15] It is evident in the Freudian schema, transmuted into Guattari's thinking about groups, that establishing a relation with an outside is a sine qua non of dealing with the psychoses, but through the modification of objects introjected by the superego, and that both kinds of group can potentially receive input in a new productive way. The introjects need to be stripped of their familialism and cleared of Oedipal residues, including the blind demand of castration anxiety, not to mention other reactionary psychoanalytic formulations, so that the superego can admit new unburdened objects (disconnecting guilt and desire) in a context in which other ideals and social demands would be made available by tools for transversality in a progressive institutional setting. In Freudian psychoanalysis, the superego sets up shop in between the internal and external worlds and turns the latter into the former, which Freud likened to turning the present (outside) into the cultural past (phylogenetic inheritances). The ego, on this account, curries favor with the superego by denying itself pleasures.[16]

Tools for Transversality

Transversality poses, then, a 'how to' problem in the process of thawing frozen institutional organigrams of power/knowledge, and in putting transportation back into the analytic transference relations as a means for transformation (in promising therapeutic outcomes). How, then, is the superego to be given access to something that doesn't trigger repression? Guattari's task was to create the means to increase transversality in the group. In this respect transversality requires a workable solution embedded in the everyday life, the local politics, of an institution that would modify its coefficient so that it would not trigger the superego (Guattari first envisioned the erasure of certain symptoms and inhibitions and then the entire erasure of the topography, because for him desire was not territorializable and assignable to specific coordinates). For Guattari, the superego was the key term: the Freudian topography (ego, id, superego) set up the superego as a gatekeeper and (third) party crasher: 'It all boils down to these alternatives,' Guattari stated; 'either desire comes to desire repression and actively supports its aims, thus preserving itself as desire, or desire revolts against repression and loses itself as desire. Quite a clever mechanism!'[17] On many occasions Guattari railed against the idea of a 'general father' in the same old familial triangle triggering a tired complex.[18]

The aforementioned François Dosse has perhaps set back Guattari's critique of psychoanalysis by some 40 years by constructing a primal scene, an *Urszene*, in which a young Guattari at nine years of age, living with his grandparents, experiences the death of his grandfather in a rather inopportune situation: Guattari's grandfather expired while sitting on the toilet listening to his favorite radio broadcast, while young Félix played with his paper dolls at his feet. Dosse isolates this anecdote provided by Guattari during his fifties and uses it to explain his subject's life-long anxiety about death – a fear of mortiferous repetition – and restless comportment, including an insatiable desire for change and novelty. Dosse does not provide a theoretical justification for his unreconstructed Freudianism.[19]

Transversality needs tools. But not any tools. Those tools sitting on the shelves in your local hardware store are not the ones at issue. Rather, tools for transversality need to be forged, that is, invented for the work of institutional change. Readers of Ivan Illich will note the connection between tools for transversality and those for conviviality, to the extent that Illich wrote of fundamental institutional change – removing the managerial class – through the use of tools that fostered autonomy, creativity, and sharability of meanings, against the dull thuds of 'large tools for lifeless people'[20] imposed by and shackled to the industrial model of production. Both Illich and Guattari were quick to distance themselves from the single and simple recipe for happiness that an increase in transversality or conviviality may be thought to bring to group relations. Likewise, neither thought that the same tools were applicable to different institutions at different points in their development.

Guattari put into place at La Borde a work rotation schedule known as the 'grid' (a double-entry table consisting of rotating times and tasks) that engaged everyone in the clinic, not merely on a single-day basis, as one sees in corporate trading-places experiments in which CEOs take a position in the warehouse and, vice versa, material handlers get bumped upstairs, but on a rolling basis. Non-medical personnel, medical staff, and patients were integrated into the rotation, and both times and tasks became more subtly differentiated and responsive to successes and failures as the schedule developed in a non-linear fashion, building in layers of supervision and review as it unfolded. The grid was put into play in order to maximize the transversality of the institution by demystifying the physician–patient relationship, and it was supported by a range of collective activities with internal and external orientations – clubs, committees, assemblies, commissions, performances, and workshops. The structural redefinition of everyone's roles in an institution like La Borde differs fundamentally from the imposition of change from above or pressure from below. *La grille*, or the grid, was, then, a transversal tool through which 'individual assumptions of responsibility [were] instituted, the only remedy to bureaucratic routine and passivity generated by traditional hierarchical systems.'[21]

In a typical training hospital at a large university, groups like interns suffer under conditions of labor that limit their potential for institutional transversality, because they are encysted in the hospital's entropy and their transversality is unavailable for effecting change; they are in residence – undergoing training, working long hours, following physicians around – and are less experienced than nurses, but identify strongly with a position above them in the medical hierarchy. Yet, if inserted into the work rotation calendar, their institutional position suddenly becomes mobile and moves them into new territories and new relations of responsibility (they may even find themselves working side by side with their former superiors, as equals, on a non-medical task, or with non-medical staff, with whom they can attempt to dialogue in a new way). By the same token, their transversality within their own group may be highly charged in affective terms, yet caught up in rituals of incapacitation into which they retreat every weekend (binge drinking and the stuff of television hospital dramas). Nevertheless, mutually enriching encounters were set up so that individuals did not fall back into old roles and the repressive fantasies attached to them, or succumb to retrogressive habits of how to respond to authority, and fixed ways of communicating which were residues of family life (and, of course, to escape once and for all the requisite acceptance of mythical psychoanalytic complexes as a form of social regulation and religious mystification).

The Problem of the Timetable

When Foucauldians respond to the grid, they invariably point to the passages in *Discipline and Punish* about the timetable and 'disciplinary time', with the goal of calling into question this tool of transversality. Foucault's observations on the control of activity through the imposition of occupations and their repetitive regulation, in addition to the obligatory rhythms embodied in collective and individuals actions, all show how 'time penetrates the body and with it all the meticulous controls of power.'[22] Foucault's emphasis is on finer and finer, as well as purer and purer, divisions of time, and restraints on bodily movement in the production of docility and economies without waste.

Deleuze emphasized that, understood abstractly, panopticism in Foucault is a diagram, an abstract machine, a spatio-temporal map of relations between forces immanent to the fields of their application.[23] Any timetable is a diagram's concrete assemblage of time and task in a given institutional matrix. And at first glance the grid fits into this schema. Indeed, Guattari thought of it as an abstract machine:

> Let's consider what we call at La Borde *la grille*: regardless of its different actualizations, its various stages, one can say that it involves the emergence of an abstract machine. The problem that faced us was how to conjoin temporal fluxes, work fluxes, duties, and monetary fluxes, etc., in a way different than what is generally found in similar institutions and may be perhaps characterized by the existence of a relatively static functional organigramme. *La grille* employs time – inscribed on paper; a machine for 'rotating' duties – inscribed in a gestural semiology; the modification of hierarchical categories – inscribed in a juridical and social semiology. These are particular manifestations of the same abstract machine expressing a certain mutation – certainly localized and without widespread repercussions – of relations of production.[24]

It is important not to freeze the grid in a synchronic slice, stripping it of all dynamism and diachrony in order to fit it into the timetables described by Foucault that contract into smaller and smaller units, and thus greater and greater control over bodies stripped of the ability to innovate, indeed, even to move freely. Moreover, an abstract machine may be appreciated, at its simplest, as contact between form–matter unmediated by representation; that is, it is not anchored by an anterior referent, and is irreducible to a finished substance. The grid assembles heterogeneous semiologies and semiotics (and a wide variety of matters out of which it creates the institution itself), and arrays a large number of bodies in a local context. Of course, the manifestations of abstract machinic conjunctions may harden into routines and degenerate into rigid models of enforced behavior (summoning everyone to a meeting at 6 p.m. each day). An abstract machine has the capacity to produce a new kind of 'rolling' and inventive reality and in this respect it is dynamic and not bound by one or another of its instantiations (which are not generalizable). The easiest way to understand an abstract machine is to consider it as a diagram. The grid is a diagram of an institution that does not yet exist, which is to say that it doesn't represent La Borde at this or that moment, but guides its ongoing creation, yet not towards a pre-given end. The grid is not, then, a formal program, but an unfinished work, open to modifications and perfused with informalities and unpredictable elements. Stephen Zepke writes about art as an abstract machine and reminds us that the diagram's destructiveness is the condition of creation's emergence:[25] it has to do some damage and clear away the detritus before it finds the means to generate something new (it is not easy to get professors to pick up brooms, and the lack of cooperation in some areas was part of the process). This was the negative task of transversality in relation to existing organizational models of the division of labor and chains of command in psychiatric institutions and in terms of the practices and dogmas established and disseminated through the psychoanalytic schools.

The dynamism of the grid lies in the paramount importance placed at La Borde on *les roulements* – rotations. The rotation of tasks wards against, but cannot wholly eliminate, sterility, rigidity, and the fantasies that come to be attached to remote specialists (head doctors and nurses). In principle, but not in practice, it was possible for everyone to familiarize themselves with all the facets of the clinic. In writing about La Borde, Guattari almost always underlines that the grid was one of many diagrams through which he set out to explore new ways of being together. Another feature was that this novel way of organizing collective labor could not be found in a manual, but had to be cobbled together out of bits and pieces of his youthful experiments in collective self-determination.[26] All of the breakdowns, friction, refusals, and errors that he met or made along the way were components, once the diagram of the grid was set in motion, of the assemblages that emerged and formed part of the analysis of the life, the very ontological texture, of the institution. Guattari understood recalcitrance, emotional cul-de-sacs, and diversions of every kind to be necessary to the ongoing elaboration of the constraints (all of the codes introduced by the ministry, by different personnel, silence of the catatonic, refusal of non-medical personnel to give needles, demands to be treated by 'real' doctors, etc.) that filtered the diagram; constraints that helped to make it productively imaginative, working matter transversally into new forms, by bringing together disparate components, persons, times, places, and tasks. It is not such a simple matter, Guattari taught, in the manner of Illich, to 'take the syringe out of the hand of the doctor' for the sake of lay access to otherwise specialist tools.[27] Deleuze elegantly and simply characterized as mobile and diagonal the transversal line along which Guattari moved between heterogeneous poles, without totalizing or centralizing them, guided by the abstract diagram written on a large piece of paper containing names, tasks, hours, places.[28] The piece of paper is abstract in the sense that it is not fully formed. And it is a diagram since it needs to be worked out through a very long process that began in the late 1950s. But this is not the whole story, for the truly incorporeal abstract machine never fully passes into the material, especially in a way station like a piece of paper. The virtuality of the abstract machine is not emptied by its incarnations or actualizations. Such potential (virtuality) is not a standing reserve, a preformed form, a surplus. It is too vague, too sketchy, for this sort of economic treatment. To be sure, the virtuality of the abstract machine of the grid appears on paper, but this actualization is quickly virtualized by the refusal to fetishize the document and acknowledge how the diagram rolls forward in the original languages and social relations resulting from the encounters it maps; indeed, the resistances that arise in and from different quarters must be acknowledged. The key register here is becoming: although one may be struck by the seemingly inflexible coordinates of a timetable, which specify that you will be there at a certain time, tasks themselves had a tendency at La Borde to fuse, to spin off, and even to become fissile. Along the way, new languages developed in order to communicate about this – acronyms, sub-codes, insider jokes – all sorts of constraints on the diagram's unfolding. There is even a *petit glossaire labordien*.[29]

Sometimes a diagram throws out a line, like a new eye on a potato. *La feuille de jour* is a good example. This collectively produced events listing is published each day and posted at some 30 locations around the clinic. Everybody reads it. It contains information about what is happening in the clinic and is described as a 'melting pot of information.' It even has an aesthetics based around the uniformity of its design, its introduction of supporting appendages, or its adoption of a parodic mode. It is a tissue that touches transversally all the sectors of the clinic, as well as orienting new admissions and posing the philosophical question of coordinating space-time and movement into the near future.[30]

Any history of the grid may include *la feuille de jour* as an outcrop dating from 1984. The grid does have a history that runs at least since 1957, although a pre-grid period of natural amicability between doctors, patients and non-medical staff is posited from the clinic's inception in 1953. As far as the historical strata of an analytic diagram are concerned, things really start to heat up around 1958. The temporalization of the diagram in its historical dimension involves a certain amount of periodizing, at least according to the members of CERFI (the Center for Study and Research into Institutional Functioning).[31] Briefly, three periods are presented:

1. 1958–66: highly structured and centralized;
2. 1967–70: strongly decentralized;
3. 1970–73: strongly centralized but with decentralized elements.

Eschewing an elegant Hegelian synthesis, this history marks the waxing and waning of the diagram's systematicity in relation to the periodicity of work rotations and their enforcement in blocks of day/week/month, and the analytic function of a *grilleur/grilleuse* monitoring the movement of bodies and bearing witness to the 'implacable rhythms' of the automatic changes in the rota system. When the automatic changes in the work rotation and the monthly ordinate were discontinued in the second period of the grid, there was a sigh of relief, because this interruption, that seemed to intervene just as things were getting interesting, was deprogrammed. But then a new recentralizing tendency emerged; yet the group structure shifted as well, entailing a more atomized configuration of 5 or 6 mixed groups of 25 persons per unit, organized spatially in terms of a variety of responsibilities, each with their own micro-grid and monitor, whose role is to negotiate directly with other monitors trade-offs and rotations between their groups. The textures of transversality in the clinic changed along with the diagram's shifting manifestations. Since the time at stake is not disciplinary (not exhaustive and lacking precision in movement and gesture) but therapeutic, and not ergotherapeutic (a kind of therapeutic training involving the simulation of common tasks towards the reacquisition of skills), the emphasis was not on the diversification of work skills, nor on the circulation of bodies, nor even on the fixing of schedules, but, rather, on 'transferential potentialities' in the sharability of affects, the passages of phantasms, and the analytic opportunities presented by certain locations, sometimes in quite unpredictable ways, with sudden valorizations or ghettoizations of the laundry or kitchen (awakened in many patients by old identifications). In other words, Guattari used the grid as a tool to transversalize the set coordinates of analysis itself toward the apprehension of the singular scenes composed and modified by each participant in relation to the relevant collective constraints and institutional matters that emerged in the process. This is not an ideological experiment in radical democracy and anti-hierarchical auto-formation, Guattari insisted, since it retains the therapeutic axis of patients and caregivers, and the goal of finding ways to apprehend all the dimensions of their singular maps.[32]

Still, even when one appreciates the complexity of the cycles and interactions involved and the details on the maps of as many as 150 persons in rotation over long periods of time, Guattari thought of these as too connective, that is, insufficiently unbound by 'unconnective connections.'[33] In order to hold back from the drift toward reductionistic unity, transversality must behave transversally and remain ontically unbeholden to a whole, the very sort of whole into which Foucault pushes his analysis of docile bodies: composition of an efficient machine that integrates parts into 'whole ensembles' and coordinates chronological series in a 'composite time.'[34] While similar mechanisms of articulation are present in disciplinary timetables and the rota system of the grid (distributed and articulated with other bodies), the latter are deployed in the service of the production of new forms of subjectivity that emerge only processually in relation to all the dimensions of the institution to which participants are exposed. It would be reductionistic to claim that Guattari understood time in the grid as an objective factor to be calculated in relation to place and task; on the contrary, time is in how it is beaten, that is, in the existential refrains that are extracted from all of the significations at work in any encounter in order to assist in subjectivity's production; such motifs provide consistency and persist as markers for a variety of functions. But they are not fixed, because they undergo qualitative changes, complexifications, and singular valorizations that do not correspond to objectively classifiable coordinates, whether these are calculated in terms of skills, objects, or tasks completed. For Guattari, 'of primary importance ... is the mutant, rhythmic trajectory of a temporalization that is capable of holding together the heterogeneous components of a new existential structure.'[35]

The Globalization of Transversality

The problem of a unidimensionalizing unity that would capture the singular productions of subjectivity aimed at in a clinical context, through the creative deployment of tools for transversality such as the grid, poses further questions about the concept's application to a larger socio-political field. In order to appreciate this problem, it is instructive to consider several examples from recent political theory.

In Richard K. Ashley's characterization of global politics, transversal struggles are without boundaries; are unfinished; obey non-Cartesian spatial coordinates; are non-essentialist, without absolute purpose, etc.[36]

David Campbell figures transversality as the 'an-archical condition of postmodern life' that arises after the failure of political representations based on transcendent principles ('first principles').[37]

Following Ashley and Campbell, Roland Bleiker thinks dissent is a transnational boundary-defying phenomenon: transversal struggles break the state-centrism of international political theory and cannot be spatially represented by the divisions typical of global politics (attributions of agency, state behavior, national sovereignty, transnational relationality). Transversality inspires Bleiker's 'disruptive reading and writing' of global political life. His primary example is the fall of the Berlin Wall: 'an inherently transversal phenomenon – one in which various discursive dynamics and various forms of agency were operating in a multitude of interconnected spheres, including terrains of dissent that ranged from street protest to the publication of underground literary magazines.'[38] The interpretation of this event must be adequate to the event's character, hence the need for multi-modal, mobile, multi-leveled analyses that disrupt standard categories and call into question existing models.

Michael Hardt and Antonio Negri describe, in *Multitude*, how the organization of guerrilla movements were transformed in a coordinated fashion in relation to changes in economic and social production, that is, after Fordism, the network society and the rise of affective labor. This entailed that the distributed-network structure became the model for a truly democratic organization;[39] the multitude as a kind of subjectivity emerges from an open network of singularities (differentiated and plural) ceaselessly maximizing creative connectivity (through communication) toward common goals (singularity and commonality are non-contradictory) shared and produced along the way (the multitude ultimately learning how to organize and rule itself). In general, by going beyond its institutional definition, in Hardt and Negri transversality passes into a larger field, because the common life that the multitude produces together requires a coordinated subjectivity with institutional resources (tools) that make it possible to link and organize diffuse singularities. As Ned Rossiter underlines, the issue here is translating between common capacities and singularities within an organized network.[40]

In these ways transversality jumps the rails of the psychiatric clinic and becomes relevant for political struggles against global capital. Of course, transversality in La Borde was never meant to be exportable wholesale from the institution to the bio-political production of social life itself (the tools for transversality will be different, not merely of a different brand!); yet the problem for political theory is how to define its contribution in positive rather than negative terms within the expanded range of the concept's applicability. Although, to be sure, the theoretical interventions cited above are short on concrete proposals, the first three additionally display negative deployments of transversality based upon Foucault's – and not Guattari's – sense of the concept's relation to power. Negative deployments betray the elegance of Foucault's meditation, however brief, on transversal struggles at the nodes of minute webs of microphysical power relations. Foucault may begin with negative criteria, but he quickly moves forward.

In 'The Subject and Power,' Foucault reflected on transversal struggles beyond a negative definition:

1. they are not confined to nations, specific types of economy, or governments;
2. they concern power effects (e.g. of the medical profession over the body);
3. they are 'immediate' in two senses: proximity to the power they criticize, and their choice of target (an immediate enemy); and

belonging to the present and not to the future of a revolution yet to arrive;
4. importantly, such struggles resist individualization and its normopathic subjugations;
5. they are concerned with the effects of power linked to knowledge, as they expose 'mystifying representations';
6. and they regain singularities obscured and occluded by individualizing definitions and categorizations that make certain kinds of subjects to the exclusion of others.[41]

What I am suggesting is that Foucault and Guattari moved the consideration of transversality into the realm of struggles aimed at transforming the production of subjectivity away from inherited models, and that this movement turned from negative to positive criteria in the transition. The Guattarian and Foucauldian senses of transversality share in the valorization of horizontality (over the 'verticality of thought,' as Guattari noted while remaining wary of valorizing just one orientation)[42] and the goal of transforming subjectivity without collapsing the subject onto a delimited monadic individual. These are resistant struggles, not simply anti-authoritarian, Foucault specifies, but clearly exemplified in feminism, anti-psychiatry, and children's rights, among many other social movements. Transversality is what they have in common: a transformation focused on the production of new forms of subjectivity. Guattari turns point 1 into a positive attribute, since transversal struggles 'are to be understood as emerging from the particular context of the country in question.'[43] This is Bleiker's approach to the fall of the Berlin Wall and his emphasis on the transversal flows of exiting populations, linked to the effects of political reform in the Soviet Union, Hungary's decision to open its borders to Austria, defiant mass protests in the cities of East Germany, etc. This is not how Guattari saw things at the time. For him the transversal potential unleashed in the fall of the Berlin Wall called into question previously solid axes of thought (left and right; East and West), but in the context of the uncertain consequences of the East's liberation – 'the immense subjective revolution there will be difficult to channel'[44] for a capitalism burdened by its own chronic crises – given the simultaneous rise of religious extremism, racism and the birth of the network society. When a society loses its axes of valuation and reference through a process of depolarization, Guattari maintained, it risks amorphousness and loses internal consistency at every level and in all its institutions, yet remains open to a repolarization of the proliferating 'microscopic' initiatives across the socius.[45] In the early 1990s, in the wake of the fall of the Berlin Wall, Guattari made a key political decision to repolarize around a 'new progressive axis' of the worker's movement (following a critique of unionism shrunken in its outlook by its size and frozen in an outdated hierarchical party model), women's rights, and ecosophical practices, each 'putting into play procedures leading to mutual recognition, exchange, consultation, and research which works towards a general enrichment.'[46] The new axis Guattari theorized was most often multi-componential and fluid, but boiled down, at least in his most public statement, to a renewal of relations between the worker and ecology movements, with the reinvention of subjectivity at the crossroads of this ongoing dialogue. What Guattari diagnosed was a vast deterritorialization of a European population that would have to confront the illusions they held about the West in encounters with everyday totalitarianisms and archaic retrenchments the likes of which they thought they were fleeing.

If we consider the implications of Foucault's point 3, it is evident that he parts company with Guattari on the issue of immediacy against potentiality, to the extent that both reject Revolution (with a capital R – the 'old schema' of Revolution stuck between 'impotent anarchy' and embryonic party organization)[47] yet Guattari finds in tools of transversality the envelopment of a potential that militants can release, affecting and being affected in the process. The immediacy hypothesis drains potential into the present and does not adequately respect the transversal militants' task of transmitting impulses of potentiality across singularities towards the invocation of a people to come (the multitude is ontologically 'always-already' but politically 'not-yet')[48] in 'a future that is already living.'[49] I will return to this issue in relation to minor cinema in Chapter 6.

The irreducible plurality and polyphony of the Guattarian process of subjectification, its self-positing and auto-producing singularity in a collective process before and beyond the 'person,' calls forth a transversality equal to the task of subjectification in the age of a vast machinic phylum that sees organic and inorganic interlacings emerging across all fields. Foucault's points 4 and 6 directly concern subjectification: in constraints on the cultivation of difference and repairing linkages broken by the straitjacket of identity; and in the bureaucratic inscriptions of identity that are the power effects of corporate and governmental categories and profiles, data generated through administrative surveillance, and subjugating informatic striations of all kinds. In Chapter 5 I shall develop the concept of informatic striation as a kind of 'dividuation.' In Foucault's estimation, transversal struggles have the goal of releasing individuals from subjection (what ties one to oneself) and from submissive forms of subjectivities (hegemonic capitalist–consumerist subjectivity). Guattari agreed wholeheartedly and stakes the same claim in *The Three Ecologies*, even if this is only one (mental) of three ecologies in which a nascent subjectivity needs to install itself, having thrown off the 'neuroleptic cloaks' of 'stagnant individualization' that protect it from encountering incomparable otherness and achieving a measure of creative autonomy.[50] The relationship between subjectivity and ecology and art will be taken up in the next chapter.

Guattari and Foucault's shared interest in the production of subjectivity points directly to the key role that tools for transversality can play in turning potential for change toward emancipatory ends grounded in an ecosophical ethos. Transversal tools such as the grid and *la feuille de jour* are the existential supports for subjectivity's enrichment in an institutional context defined by treatment and inspired by heterogenesis – the diversity and irreducible differences out of which subjectivity takes shape in a collective setting. This is another of three ecologies – a social, institutional assemblage. The three ecologies become, much later in Guattari's career, further tools for transversality, but predicated on the same development of the potential for subjectivity to reinvent itself through eco-praxes that cross the domains of the individual, collectivity, and environment (which in Guattari's mind is machinic, since it concerns an artificial mechanosphere encompassing all of science, technology, and information). The transversal tools for large-scale change are more difficult to isolate, because the field in which their effects are felt is less circumscribed. But never has the phrase 'the right tools for the job' been more appropriate! The tools required for influencing the course of propitious existential ruptures in an emerging web of events must be the 'right' ones – at the right scale, at the right moment, forged for the job – in respect of local conditions because such tools do not merely manipulate pre-existing conditions, but participate in their creation and nurturance. Try to imagine the protests against the World Trade Organization in Seattle in 1999 without the Internet. Tools for transversality not only adjust to the changing conditions they help initiate, they may be modified in and through and by the processes in which they participate.

3
SUBJECTIVITY, ART, AND ECOSOPHY

Why did Guattari settle on a fixed number of ecologies in his book *The Three Ecologies*?[1] How many ecologies are there, anyway? Well, if we believe Guattari, there are at least three. I do not know precisely how he arrived at this number. In lieu of what might count as solid autobiographic, explanatory evidence, then, or even other kinds of justifications based on precise theoretical or practical considerations, let's consider this number as a way of critically appreciating the tasks to which Guattari set these ecologies. But the questions pile up: How do these ecologies cohere? What are their constraints and combinational possibilities? How are strong charges of transversality carried across them?

The number of ecologies answers to Guattari's delineation of the ethical, aesthetic, and political foundations of transdisciplinary knowledge. In fact, he brings together ecology and disciplinarity in order to pose the problem of what the passage from inter- to transdisciplinary knowledge looks like.[2] Guattari's overriding political concern was with the production of subjectivity, and his green politics were no different. In fact, the problem of the subject's fabrication posed in the context of ecological struggles raises the question of the vast mechanosphere of the globe in the age of advanced informatics which must come to be under human mastery, Guattari claims, if the most pressing problems facing the Earth are to be solved. His position on mastery of nature does not rehearse the domination thesis popularized in the 1970s, but calls for the necessity of a mastery that can keep pace with the environment's reinvention in a time of rapid and widespread technico-scientific progress and crisis. The effects of the machinic phylum on subjectivity becomes Guattari's major ecosophical preoccupation.

Ecology is, in its plural, heterogeneous forms, not a conjuration (supernatural) but a conjugation (as in an interchange of closely related elements) with important qualifications and implications. Ecology in the plural does not offer a magical solution to the question of how disparate knowledges and practices cohere. It is not some sort of general model or pedagogy, a training course for which one might sign up. Guattari clearly rejected such a notion in order to exclude any pretenders to such specialized educational expertise.[3] Indeed, to invoke in the same introduction transdisciplinarity and ecology is not to solve anything. It may even appear tautological if by 'transdisciplinary' one means more than a juxtaposition of many (multi-) and greater than a coordinated interconnection (inter-); thus, a somewhat rebellious and always critical kind of ecology of knowledge. When transdisciplinarity is used as a buzzword, an abracadabra word that merely anoints a project in the eyes of potential funders, as Guattari once put it, it changes nothing, because nothing really changes at the level of process.[4] Ecology served Guattari as an example of how to pose the question of transdisciplinarity on a large and stratified scale. The prospects of transdisciplinarity are thought through in terms of three intersecting ecologies, the articulations of which demonstrate the difficulties, potentialities, and stakes of knowledge and action in the face of global challenges. Although transdisciplinary ecology goes beyond the multi- and inter-disciplinary pretenders, it is not a higher-level synthesis or a transcendent solution.

The Winding Road to Non-transcendent Ecology

In terms of intellectual biography, Guattari shifted his exploration of transdisciplinary projects from groups and institutions to that of ecology later in his life, which is say, during his fifties. He spent most of his career experimenting with combinations of knowledge; indeed, from the time of his youth forward he lived a life of transdisciplinary implementation. Guattari created numerous experimental groups and publications, and participated in many other projects and institutions whose purpose was the exploration of organization through flexible participatory organigrams, such as the evolving schedule of job rotation at La Borde, which I discussed in detail in the previous chapter. This system was an analytic instrument (transversal tool) by means of which individual and collective affects could be articulated with institutional demands (material, social, bureaucratic, therapeutic tasks) towards the goals of enriching social relations, promoting the assumption of responsibility, participating in collective inventions (local jargon development, forging of new tools, rediscovery of means of expression), not only for patients, but for doctors and support staff as well. In short, he envisaged the transformation of those involved in the extraordinarily complex negotiations and interactions (progressive and regressive) entailed within the clinic on daily, weekly, and monthly bases, and in longer cycles. Like the institution thus reconceived, ecology is a similar kind of hyper-complex operator, a catalyst of change, a caretaker of concern, with great and grave stakes. But the most important stake is the development of a new kind of subjectivity.

Guattari came to ecology in the mid 1980s as an antidote to what he dubbed the 'winter years' of the first half of that decade, which saw the rise of many conservatisms and neo-liberal economic policies, and the ascendency of 'vague vogues' like postmodernism, which he despised.[5] Despite his personal access to French government through his working relationship with Minister of Culture Jack Lang, the political field of French socialism, perfused by the exponential expansion of what Guattari called the unidimensionalizing forces of Integrated World Capitalism, on the back of rapid technological change yoked to reactionary social archaisms (the rise of Front National in European elections, the French–Spanish agreement on extraditing Basque separatists),[6] almost led to his permanent relocation from France to Brazil. In accordance with Franco Berardi's description of how the personal is pathological and the pathological is political, Guattari during this period did not pay sufficient attention to depression.[7] In this respect, Guattari's encounter in 1982 with Lula da Silva, presently Brazil's president, but then radical leader of the recently legalized

Workers' Party, allowed him to find some much-needed energy in a revised, open unionism consonant with that of Solidarity in Poland.[8] After the mid 1980s Guattari sought distance from the disappointments of French socialism and the dirty tricks of the French secret service, specifically the sinking of Greenpeace's ship *Rainbow Warrior* in Auckland harbor on July 10, 1985, in the newly formed political party 'les Verts.' The left–right split in the French Greens, Guattari's experiment with joining both factions, much to the chagrin of the party, and his attempts to manufacture a 'rainbow coalition' of the left, forced him to take his distance from traditional party politics under the cover of green. As he put it in no uncertain terms in his final book *Chaosmosis*:

> If you ask ecologists what they intend to do to help the homeless in their suburb, they generally reply that it's not their responsibility. If you ask them how they intend to free themselves from a certain dogmatism and the practices of small groups, many of them will recognize that the question is well-founded, but are quite unable to suggest any solutions![9]

During the lead-up to the Paris regional elections in the spring of 1992, Guattari wrote of his 'hope' that disenchanted voters would gravitate towards 'another vision of the future'[10] contained in ecology's inventive political articulations of the everyday and planetary. Downplaying the split in the French Greens between two factions, Guattari urged voters not to be transfixed by such sectarian machinations – 'the ecological "movement" has nothing to do with the leadership struggles' – and called for 'respect for plurality and the diversity of components' in a hoped-for 'recomposition' of the party. A brief glance at the list of candidates put forward for the Paris elections includes under the Green banner a remarkable range of persons, and Guattari, too.[11] The electoral success of the Greens in the spring of 1992 – in the low teens in terms of the percentage of the vote – did not include a victory by Guattari. Still, for the next few months he continued to turn towards the theme of overcoming sterile axes of political reference through a more complex and critical approach to the question of ecology.

The year 1989, original publication date for *Les trois écologies,* was not propitious for the environment: recall the massive oil spill in Prince William Sound off the Alaskan coast, caused when the *Exxon Valdez* tanker ran aground, creating long-standing ecosystemic damage. But by the same token, 1989 was a good year for thinking about the potential for collective social reinvention, as Communism came crashing down with the Berlin Wall, inaugurating a whole new set of relationships with an emergent eastern Europe.

What sort of ecologies do we get when a practicing analyst and political radical schooled in far-left social movements and transdisciplinary experimentation gets hold of them? What we get are ecologies that can be represented by *écosophes* such as Franz Kafka and Samuel Beckett.[12] You won't find Kafka or Beckett in your *Dictionary of the Environment.* Suffice to say that Guattari's vision of ecology's psychological dimension owed less to such standard-bearers as Freud, Lacan, and Klein than to 'ecologists of the phantasm' like Marquis de Sade, or masters of the refrain, like Marcel Proust, to both of whom Guattari regularly turned when he wanted to tackle the most intractable problems of the psyche.

There are, then, arts and logics of the eco; but also praxes of large-scale change linking micro and macro; varieties of ecology that encompass the environment at the macro-level in terms of the extent of ecocatastrophes (Chernobyl, global warming); social relations at the intermediary level; and mental ecology at the micro- or molecular level.[13] The threesome is multi-leveled, but the hierarchy is misleading if it leads one to think that the macro-level holds the greatest value. For Guattari, precisely the opposite is the case: it is the 'machinic soup' – from which molecular disturbances bubble up, often in spite of large-scale determinations – that holds the greatest value.[14] It is perhaps not very surprising for a psychoanalyst to gravitate towards subjectification; nor for a seasoned thinker of collectivities to situate the social in-between. Yet even this is oversimplifying, since all the levels are intimately connected and solutions at one level entail changes at the others: earthly spheres, social issues, and worlds of ideas are not compartmentalized, and molecular social revolutions travel around the globe by means of planetary networks of communication: 'The difference between these kinds of molecular revolutions and earlier forms of revolution is that before everything was centered on ideology or the Program, whereas today the mutational models ... are immediately transmitted to the entire planet.'[15]

In an unpublished manuscript, the 'Great Ecological Fear,' Guattari wrote of an iceberg: the tip, above water and visible, represented environmental disasters and menaces; down below the waterline was the bulk of the worry, that is, the degeneration of social relations, like the rise of organized crime in the detritus of Stalinism, the hatching of parasites of hyper-capitalist growth, and mental pollution caused by media infantilization and passivity-inducing post-political cynicism, to which may be added the traumas of globalization and (anti-)terrorism. The iceberg represented a continuum of material encompassing the fabric of everyday life, large-scale crises, and habits of thought.[16]

My task is to interrogate Guattari's three ecologies in terms of their prospects for a transformative thought and action that has been, and will continue to be, transmissible by artists and through the arts in general as connectors of micro- and macro-dimensions. This is meant to imply neither that artists should subordinate themselves to ecological imperatives – say, the amelioration of aesthetic degradation – nor that artistic practices can be adequately judged with reference to a transcendent concept like ecosystemic balance. Ecology is not art's prop; neither is art ecology's secret weapon. These restraints are helpful, if only to underline that the interrogation of the three involves transits across, transformative powers, and nothing less portentous than, as Guattari claimed, 'the production of human existence itself in new historical contexts.'[17]

Three Ecologies

For Guattari, there are three fundamental types of ecology: environmental, social, and mental. These types – biospherical, social relations, human subjectivity – are also figured as registers and 'multipolar issues'[18] whose ethico-political articulation, as opposed to technocratic solution, is the proper concern of ecosophy. What makes this articulation superior to technocratic solution-mongering – for instance, the American model of emissions trading, which displaces industrial pollution instead of reducing it – is that it will effect a revolution of the subject formations and social groupings charged with tackling ecological issues. In the absence of such profound change at the level of mentalities, that is, of real existential mutations, even the proffering of technocratic solutions lacks the resolve for their authentic deployment. The will, in short, is just not there. This is not a wholesale rejection of technology and international environmental bureaucracies, environmental science, and eco-business, for that matter, which are often subsumed by and reduced to oft-repeated and poorly understood slogans – the Rio Declaration on sustainable development and the Kyoto Protocol on climate change, to cite two examples from the 1990s. To the extent that Guattari tried to get beyond tired left–right, east–west, socialist–capitalist, science–anti-science distinctions, international initiatives hold some promise in terms of the contribution they can make to the complexification of the contexts in which ecological issues are understood. During his lifetime Guattari was signatory to hundreds of good causes. Still, he sought to regain human values against an 'unbelievable scientistic myopia' that sometimes infects international conferences. Guattari had in mind the Heidelberg Appeal first presented at the Rio Earth Summit in 1992, and subsequently signed by thousands of scientists. This appeal constituted a discrediting in the name of techno-scientific elites of all naysayers as 'irrational' romantics.[19] What fails in such positioning is that the connection between the material and immaterial is not made, that is, the circle that includes the mutual need for change in material, social, and environmental conditions and in mentalities. This is what Guattari foregrounds in his conception of a generalized ecology, an ecosophy.[20] There is no easy trade-off in Guattari's work between a rejection of science and its replacement by art. On the contrary, he would reject any 'unequivocal ideology' because it leads to profound impasses and implosions. Guattari wrote with a kind of desperation about the need for biomedical success in the fight against Aids, for example. But such success would need to be channeled by ethical motivations 'in less absurd, less dead-ended directions' than those dictated by interests based solely on profit, property, scarcity, and restricted distribution.[21]

By the same token, Guattari's ecosophic perspective cannot be unified by the simple sloganeering of eco-revivalists; the three ecologies are 'complementary headings' and 'points of view' that are, in effect, like 'interchangeable lenses.'[22] Levels, types, views, visions, lenses, registers – Guattari shifts his descriptors throughout his book. His goal is to elucidate the 'common principle' of the three ecologies through his conception of subjectivity and how it is produced. This is his most original contribution to the theorization of ecology. Guattari's concern with the quality of subjectivity is what holds together art and ecology.

The Guattarian subject is not an individual, an individuated person, thinking and thus being. No climax of philosophical striptease in originary intuition; no ego shipwrecked from real territories of existence, as he underlined.[23] Rather, the Guattarian subject is an entangled assemblage of many components, a collective (heterogeneous, multiple) articulation of such components before and beyond the individual; the individual is like a transit station for changes, crossings, and switches. In the development of Guattari's conceptual language, assemblage came to replace group. This is not to deny the existence of core elements; on the contrary, there are nuclei or especially dense crossing points where interiority is found and from which energy can be extracted for further differentiation, complexification, and enrichment. Such nuclei replaced for Guattari the prevailing psychoanalytic languages of complex, system, and structure, making subjectivity irreducible to a universal syntax, mathemes, imagos, mythemes, etc. This subject is also polyphonic – of many relatively independent parts – because it assembles components in order to posit itself in terms of some points of reference (body, social clusters, etc.), in an existential territory, a field in which it is incarnated, but out of which it also ventures. For this productive self-positing is relational, subsuming both autonomous affects of the pre-personal and pre-verbal world, and multitudinous social constructions. Emergent and processual, producing and produced by mutual self-engenderings, the subject emerges as it finds a certain existential footing and coherence, without getting tied down to an identity once and for all, in the crossing points of components, in their intra- and inter-assemblage relations, sometimes deflating into involutions, blockages, and encystments; at other times taking off through transformations (potential consistencies). Open and full of potential, this subject is truly a work in progress/process, outflanking both essentialist and constructionist postulates. Radically creative and at times aggravating in its abstractness, 'subjectivity still gets a bad press,' Guattari admitted.[24] The stakes are high and this abstruseness is a cost of escaping from takeovers and annexations by fixed and single and exterior coordinates – psychoanalytic, structural, or postmodern plinths upon which the subject may be mounted like a botched taxidermic specimen.[25]

For Guattari, the three ecologies point the way toward emancipatory praxes whose 'major objective [is] to target the modes of production of subjectivity, that is, knowledge, culture, sensibility and sociability.'[26] Ecosophy's business is to attend to the regimes by means of which subjectivity is produced and to intervene in them; it is readied for this task by Guattari insofar as he shifts into the delineation of the dynamics of eco-logic – how the three ecologies communicate (the terms are affective intensities rather than delimited sets like stages, complexes, linear phasal developments, or universal structural coordinates). Although Guattari abandoned typical psychoanalytic psychogenetic stages for the sake of a hetero-genetic becoming (giving to singular-ization a constancy), he still needed to retain some sense of a self's prospective unfolding without slavishly adhering to a developmental model punctuated by decisive events and sticking points. Only an emergent self would suffice; and the phases of such an emergent organization, while at work over time from childhood through adulthood, would also be available in parallel at different degrees and in a variety of combinations over a lifetime.

One of the ways in which Guattari translated this insight into practical criticism may be seen in his observations on the American artificial realist painter George Condo. Guattari observed that critics of Condo's work experienced an acute disorientation before his paintings of figures (many with comic, contorted heads) in landscapes. The cataloguing of countless modern masters as seminal influences and the proliferation of reference points which a single Condo painting seems to visit, often subsuming several periods of a given painter's works, led Guattari to suggest the following to Condo about the polyphonic character of his work: 'all your periods coexisted – blue, clown, linear, volumical, monochrome, etc. It is like a symphony articulating all the levels of your "self", simultaneously exploring and inventing it through your painting.'[27] The details of this example are perhaps less pertinent than the translation of the coexistence of stratifications of subjectivity (with varying degrees of formedness, capacity to be shared, what one might call degrees of fixity) onto periods of painting each with a distinctive thematic, style, and color. This example of what might be called transversal criticism – a tool for the enactment of an adventurous connectivity that skirts around the abyss of a list of influences and precursors that only point towards the past and freezes Condo's work in a crowded representational space – brings the paintings flush with the engendering of a subjective territory.

Eco-logic concerns new incarnations of subjectivity in partially formed existential territories not yet yoked to normalized extrinsic pillars, whether these are certain family members, respectable academic grammars, religious fixations, aesthetic styles, or even lifestyles. This lack of fixity is a fecund amodality (an abstract, intense feeling of vitality not object-oriented or attached to causes) that is ripe for the eco-logic. This is where the logic turns to praxis. The eco-praxes 'scout out,'[28] somewhat opportunistically, 'catalysts of existential change' that lack solid support in the assemblage yet are full of passive potential for swerving from normality, running counterclockwise, as it were, but not running completely amok, either. Of course, this is also where things can go horribly wrong. Instead of summoning forth and assisting new traits of subjective particularity, incomparable singularities breed banal imitations, or we get another aneconomic myth of a return to Nature or some such similarly counterproductive manifestation (Sir Paul McCartney lending his face to the global media slaughter of Newfoundland sealers or another dream of Walden Pond). Eco-praxes are on the watch for dissident vectors, ruptures, and mutations of subjectification in all walks of life and thus in all the ecologies and in any existential territory. But these have to be delicately 'turned' toward productive and active ends and provided with scaffoldings and guy ropes so they do not just twist in the wind.

Eco-logic is by definition activist, but not in a narrow sense – vigorous, yes; dedicated, certainly; but not motivated by single-issue eco-politics, or animated by the generation of a paper trail of non-binding agreements. It is colored – perhaps a better term would be marbled – by a therapeutic ethos. Guattari doesn't simply exclude the political goals of single-issue ecological movements or attractive stereotypes like the 'eco-Indian,' but instead occupies different ground: 'Ecology,' he wrote, 'must stop being associated with the image of a small nature-loving minority or with qualified specialists'[29] in the rebranded environmental sciences.

Breakaway components of subjectification must be handled with care and sobriety; even so, the gentle loosening and tutelage of such catalytic components (or segments thereof) inevitably leads for Guattari to certain kinds of redundancies (what he calls existential refrains) in a given assemblage upon which subjectivity becomes focused or which fixes subjectivity in a way that interrupts the diversity of the components at play. Despite everything else going on, one can be glued to the television set, whose screen then becomes a circumscribed existential territory; subjectivity is produced flush with the screen and it is in this respect modeled by machinic systems.[30] Examples of complex refrain motifs are found by Guattari across the arts – in fiction, theatre, visual art – with a preponderance of musical examples, even in literature (the model being *la petite phrase* that captivated Swann in the salon of Madame Verdurin).[31] Refrains (recurrent beatings of time understood in relation to a milieu and its components) are established when motifs are detached from the flux of components, when an established texture is interrupted and a motif curls up without spinning around hopelessly, acquiring the ability to generate a positive process of self-reference. This is not such a rarified phenomenon, for after all it happens with those few notes from pop songs that occasionally come back to one as motifs detached from personal turning points or lingering, somewhat autonomous, affective qualities; but, instead of inviting us into rich universes of personal reference and reverie, reactivated in the present for the future, they find themselves hijacked and affixed to automobile tires or boxes of breakfast cereal. Subjectivity shifts, but merely onto the diversions of consumption (capitalistic refrains of advertising like annoying jingles), thus restricting the potential for enhancing and enriching itself through the exploration of its own universes of value.

Eco-praxes try to nurture the ruptures and flights of catalysts of change and their productive evolutions, keeping them from turning in circles, getting shut inside the Nintendo universe or trapped in the compounds of reality TV programs, or in the doped voids of classic-rock revivals; or merely taking the latest popular pill. Enthusiastically, but vaguely, some performance art, Guattari thought, 'shoves our noses up against the genesis of beings and forms, before they get a foothold in the dominant redundancies – of styles, schools, and traditions of modernity.'[32] Guattari draws on numerous examples from the arts, because for him these are positive paradigms, though at times vertigo-inducing, of how the full implications of subjectivity's mutational forward flight from consumerism and other 'steamrollers' and 'contractions' can be explored, both by creators themselves and by observers, critics, and non-experts, too. He even reserves art's traditional role of providing refuge for dissident vectors of expression.[33] Still, 'this is not about making artists the new heroes of the revolution,' Guattari insisted.[34] It is about the aesthetic dimension of eco-praxis. Ecosophic activism resembles the work of artists in extracting details that serve as path-breakers for subjective development and as guidance in responsibly negotiating refrains.[35]

Circa 1989, Guattari was moved by the work of New Yorker David Wojnarowicz, especially in terms of the queer activist aesthetics that this painter and writer knit into his provocative critiques of healthcare (especially redesigned money) in the United States that 'trigger an existential movement, if not of revolt, at least of existential creativity.'[36] This entails that ecosophic artists are engaged in a form of anti-empire critique, since work on the multitude of dissident, singularizing vectors of subject formation goes hand in hand with this, with the Guattarian proviso that there is no falling-back on old state socialism or the welfare state, nor any pre-fabricated dialectical solutions. Thus, Guattari tended to privilege so-called political art (for example, Wojnarowicz's production of an accelerated reaction of viewers with regard to the politics of the management of Aids as a global phenomenon), but not absolutely, since there are no guarantees that catalytic components will be engaged and ethico-aesthetic commitments will be generated. There are many possible strategies in this area. For example, Canadian photographer Ian Wallace treats the assembly of anti-logging protesters at Clayoquot Sound, British Columbia in 1993 through a style of disrupted documentation that attempts to provide some partial existential support for collective action by underplaying the highlights of protest and arrest and refusing to indulge in star-focused rally reportage (in one instance seated protesters are looking in every direction but towards a speaker with a microphone atop a van).[37]

The artistic examples that Guattari mentioned over the course of his lifework are too numerous and diverse to constitute a definitive aesthetic, except that this alone tells us of the importance of heterogeneity, yet his emphasis was on forging new value systems (not simply renewing existing traditions of militancy), short of offering a fully elaborated alternative. On this point Guattari was quite candid.[38] Yet the ethico-aesthetic contact point between art and its audiences involved for Guattari inducements precipitating the assumption of responsibility in an existential transference of singularities leading to the assembling of new constellations of components with their own intrinsic and extrinsic relations. The ability of buildings such as Shin Takamatsu's signature works of the 1980s and early 1990s in Kyoto and Osaka (ARK, Pharaoh, Kirin Plaza, Syntax, and Imanishi, for example) to effect a profound transformation of many of the facets of their urban environments was for Guattari a key example of existential transferences brought about by contextual mutations that trigger in each person gripped by the vision of the architectural project their own taking of initiative within the newly emerged territories and worlds of reference opening up before them.[39] For Guattari, stellar architectural projects provided evidence of changes in habits, routines, spatio-temporal coordinates, opening cracks in interpretive grids, and rearranging situatedness for those who occupy and work in them, pass through, or simply observe. Guattari was thinking less about influence than inspiration, a kind of affective contact with works that gets collective subjects moving towards the acquisition of the means for their own singular auto-productions and explorations of how to become different from themselves.

Refrains can be quite precarious. They may implode psychically in deathly repetition. But Guattari's myriad artistic examples possess a positive, open precarity, the capacity to sustain 'praxic openings-out' from an existential territory that do not remain trapped by exploitative coordinates or wrapped up in post-political alienation. Not only are these openings enunciated, but they find a consistency that makes them habitable by politically, ethically, and aesthetically engaged projects; this is certainly not the psychoanalysis that Žižek describes as miserably giving one the freedom to enjoy as much as one wants of what one does not want![40] Being carried beyond familiar territories into alterities of all sorts permits the emergence of new valorizations, new social practices, new subjectivities. Artists can provide the means for these creative forward flights, these breakaways. For Guattari, art begins with the expressive features of a territory that become for its inhabitants flight paths beyond its borders. Art begins not with a home but with a house, not with inner-directness, but with outer-directedness; when in 1993 Rachel Whiteread set up her casting operation on Grove Road in Bow, east London, she turned what was once a home inside out into a house, by filling in all the frames and planes and sections so that the work could not shelter anything, but simply point outward, the functional having become expressive and mobile.[41]

Tri-ecological Vision

The paths of this vision may be 'tangled,' but Guattari's call for the 'permanent re-creation of the world' begins by attending to a melody of nature and art that suggested 'renam[ing] environmental ecology *machinic ecology*.'[42] The unity of biosphere and mechanosphere means that biological life, including human being, is involved in the vast techno-informatic infrastructures in the era of planetary computerization and the IT revolution. Subjectivity is thus dependent on machinic phyla (telecommunications; synthetics; new temporalities brought about by increasing processing capacities; and biogenetic engineering of life forms) and engenders itself with machinic components from iPods to iris scans.[43] This does not displace the biospherical challenge of large-scale problems like ozone depletion, for instance; on the contrary, the machinic dimension of the depletion of stratospheric ozone by catalytic chain reactions initiated by imbalances introduced by CFCs and halons is well recognized. It also meant for Guattari that eco-praxes at the environmental level on 'natural equilibria' would involve more and more sophisticated interventions and transversal criticisms – like the quaintly named 'hamburger connection', which linked rainforest habitat destruction for pasture with fast food, but which is now more ominous as beef has become a vector for global food insecurity; or, the algae bloom in the Venice lagoon, which Guattari linked to the proliferation of exploitative New York real-estate redevelopers (Donald Trump algae) who generate unknown levels of homelessness and despair in poisoned social urban ecologies. The reconstruction of group belonging and institutional life, driven by processes of subjectification that find in realms both intimate, even phantasmatic and more distant, perhaps objective ways of reevaluating the censoring and concealing shrouds engulfing them, begins at the most 'miniscule level,'[44] but opens outward and swarms in all directions. The omnidirectional openness of subjectivity needs, Guattari also warned, to find real existential anchors and connective refrains that allow it simultaneously to install itself in all three ecologies, lest it fly away from lack of consistency and perspective.

Transdisciplinary Ecology

Asking after the number of ecologies is not really a quantitative question at all. Readers of *The Three Ecologies* are in much the same position as Deleuze before the triptychs of Francis Bacon. Deleuze discovered the non-linear distribution of forces whose laws of rhythm make visible invisible musical temporalities across the three panels, and this led him to boldly conclude, against the grain of the painterly record, that there are only triptychs in Bacon.[45] Guattari's three ecologies are themselves evidence of his refusal of transcendent judgment,[46] synthesized or subsumed; the three ecologies maintain the paradigm of creativity, soberly serving crossings and connections across disparate domains, running from the intimate, everyday to the planetary in scale. In theorizing this complex three, Guattari showed how to grasp the generality of ecological vision; perhaps this is firmly situated in the French tradition of transdisciplinary studies grounded in the human science of communications, but subject to occasional revisions as a 'science of the event' (sociology of the present) and then various rapprochements between the life and social sciences.[47] The three ecologies are an assemblage that shows how disparate domains constantly engage one another. There is a transference here between art's and ecology's hope in the creation of new universes of value. Putting on the lenses of the three ecologies one sees – better, one senses – a potentiality, not yet real, but unfolding itself toward actualization, and for which one is always responsible, as existential grounds are sought for the corporeal and incorporeal universes about to be brought into being.

Transdisciplinary ecology is inspired by the interdependent hyper-complexity of its object or problem – that of subjectivity. Unlike so many contemporary definitions of the term, this trans-disciplinarity does not seek a transcendent, extrinsic ground or plane for the subject from which its parameters and obligations issue forth.[48] The subject does not pre-exist the assemblage that gives it consistency and the potential to enunciate and project its own universes. Transdisciplinary knowledge is engaged, ethico-aesthetic, and political, for it seeks nothing less than creating conditions conducive to subjectivity's self-transformations. Guattarian transdisciplinarity does not seek to transcend, it seeks to transform. It doesn't recoil from chaos. It doesn't solve the problem of chaos by positing a fixed, univocal ground, thereby vouchsafing the differentiated 'subject.' It is not forever on the path back from chaos.[49] It doesn't retrieve a unity from the 'massive and immediate ensemble of contextual diversity,'[50] thus turning around the alleged degradations of flux, but in the very act of assisting in finding a position for subjectivity, a 'node' around which a territory can be built and universes of meaning find affirmation, chaos in all its discomfort is respected, its textures analyzed, and its tributaries explored. 'Emergence' in this sense is not toward a higher level of abstract integration, but is something that must be continuously confronted and permanently reappraised. Art can provide a model for subjectivity's heterogeneous and ecosophical explorations, without betraying its singular textures and crushing its desires. Of course, artists have to grapple with their own social ecologies of the schools, gallery system, art market, fickle arts councils, and fashions of criticism in which they place themselves.

More and more Guattari tended to refer simply to 'aesthetic perception' while eschewing stylistic categorizations. Through this perception one may be oriented towards ecosophic activism of the highest order by exploring refrains and extracting innovative segments of components in collective processes of subjectification, the existential impacts of which are never decided in advance. Near the end of his final book, *Chaosmosis*, Guattari stated: 'Perhaps artists today constitute the final lines along which primordial existential questions are folded?'[51] This sober 'perhaps' simply tells us that while artists do contribute important components to the tri-ecological vision, there are no guarantees: it is no easy task to throw off certain self-satisfactions of creativity, deal with anti-intellectualism and economic marginality, expand one's world so as to take responsibility for matters that were once conveniently outside one's traditional purview, and adapt one's means of working in accordance with the demand to subtract that is required in contributing to collective processes of subjectification – an inspiration and object that is, frankly, as much a matter of the self-transformation of artists themselves, through the artistry of living and ageing, as of the renewals and deviations initiated by works of art. In the end, Guattari claimed much the same about political ecology – it 'should concern itself, as a matter of priority, with its own social and mental ecology.'[52]

'Ecosophy' is a term often associated with the Norwegian sage Arne Naess. Guattari makes no reference to Naess's writings and the influence of his ideas during the 1980s. Readers of *The Three Ecologies* may be puzzled by this oversight, since it appears that Guattari considered the term to be, if not his own, then a constitutively defined neologism. While Guattari investigated ecology's potential through its contributions to subjectification in relation to aesthetic examples, at the core of Naess's conception is a similar attempt to broaden the restrictive sense of ecology as a sub-science of the field of biology and develop an ontology expressing an action-oriented and principled philosophical wisdom of the 'earth household.'[53] However, in Naess's hands ecosophy is a normative philosophical system in which norms and hypotheses from which they are derived achieve a progressive 'precization' by delineating concepts and interpreting statements guiding them. The so-called 'top norm' in Naess's ecosophy is self-realization, conceived processually as expansive of the 'unity of certain social, psychological, and ontological hypotheses: the most comprehensive and deep maturity of the human personality guarantees *beautiful action.*'[54] Ecosophy changes mentalities and builds solidarities between persons for a non-narrow Self that expands by means of identifying with other selves and non-human animals. Decreasing egocentricity, widening identifications, appreciating diversity and complexity, and engendering care are all tasks of such an eco-Self. Often this movement from the personal self to the large Self is figured in a transpersonal psychology involving a movement of expansion from part to whole controlled by a unified agent capable of cultivating commitments to others through empathy and acting in accordance with altruistic motivations.[55] The appeal to the mutuality of self-realization in Naess's cosmically expanding system of contacts is limited by its psychology, that is, the subject at stake, and the limits on self-realization for and by living beings, which doubly excludes the Guattarian problematic of a non-unified, non-pre-existing machinic subject (pre-personal and partial) interacting with a technological phylum, and the notion that incorporeal, non-biologic 'existential species' can participate in autopoetic potentialization. Guattari's concern is not self-realization through widening of a pre-given self, but processes of singularization that resist the frames of reference imposed by an identity (a process-collapsing circumscription) yet bear upon everything concerning the way one lives, feels, thinks, and acts.

Guattari's ecosophy is an ethico-aesthetics of eco-praxis, but its ethical sense is derived not from expanding subjectivity's field, rather, in turning machines to progressive ends and initiating real change, but without being able to predict outcomes (hence tolerance for uncertainty and courage to experiment), especially when trying to effect influential changes in ways of living through molecular eco-praxes; small isn't beautiful, it's bifurcating, mutating, with discontinuous effects, and doesn't back away or oppose more traditional ideas of social change through struggle at the scale of the party or the working class, but doesn't uncritically rehearse them. Molecular mutation bubbles beneath macro-social conditions: 'A mutation like that introduced by microprocessors changes the actual substratum of human existence and, in reality, opens up fabulous possibilities for liberation.'[56]

Media-induced passivity and the solitude of gadgetry may be rampant, but Guattari believed that the machinic phylum evolved in a way that introduces new opportunities for individual and collective creators to rework subjectivities in close contact with and overlapping machines. At the macro-level there is a kind of 'machinic efflorescence' that surrounds the planet and, at the micro-level, encounters with information technologies which had already effected, for Guattari writing in the early 1990s, 'a mutation of subjectivity that perhaps surpasses the invention of writing, or the printing press, in importance.'[57] At the heart of Guattari's project is an ethics arising from the interface between humans and non-human machines, in the midst of which ecosophic cartographies, no matter how sketchy and particularistic, are drawn. Guattari borrows from Hans Jonas an ethics that concerned the dealings of humankind with machines and which arises in view of the phylum's irreversible advance, magnitude, cumulative effects, and unprecedented accomplishments. Machinic evolution is the context and ethical horizon of responsibility for humankind's essential collective actions in and on the phylum. For both Jonas and Guattari 'technology ... assumes ethical significance by the central place it now occupies in human purpose.'[58]

4

A-SIGNIFYING SEMIOTICS

Signals are the poor semiotician's stock-in-trade. They are not considered signs proper since, as Umberto Eco explains, they 'can be computed quantitatively irrespective of their possible meaning.'[1] Signals thus on this view occupy 'the lower threshold of semiotics.'[2] Signaletic stimuli do not appear to require higher-level semiotic functions engaging cultural contents or the kind of effects that typically emerge in and from the movement between signifiers.

My task in this chapter is to rethink and regain the lowly status of signals through the explication and deployment of the category of a-signifying semiotics developed by Guattari. To this end two initial reorientations are required. First, the prejudicial hierarchization of signals as low-ranking phenomena, under the semantic horizon of cultural conventions of interpretation, will be suspended. Second, the quantitative or machinic qualities of signals will form a positive part of their reassessment, rather than serving to confirm their lowly status against a higher-order domain in relation to which, by definition, they can never measure up. Signals, in short, have a good deal to teach about a-signifying semiotics; indeed, the category of the latter considerably deepens and revivifies the former sort of 'lowly' sign type by unleashing, as a heuristic virtue, the characteristics of this status. Additionally and thirdly, Guattari insisted on linking informatics with the production of mutant forms of subjectivity that in quite radical ways progressively removed subjectivity, through the process of a generalized distancing and decentering, from traditional territories and coordinates (those of scriptural semiotics, for instance, in the era of hypertext and interactivity); yet this does not vouchsafe specific kinds of results.

In short, the techno-materialist analysis of a-signifying semiotics I will present advances the original suggestive analysis bequeathed to us by Guattari concerning the consequences for subjectivity of an existential dimension of the automated trigger-part sign, of an empty signaletics, in which something like a cold and remote computer voice – 'The door is ajar. Thank you,' or simply using a bank card in an automated teller machine – can deterritorialize components of subjectivity and open new and unfamiliar universes. Subjectivity is a 'raw material' worked by informatic capital within the expanding fields of its system of valorization, colonizing life by 1s and 0s and PINs and access codes, subjugating not by knots but by nets; in the process modeling subjectivity through 24-hour online banking, the protective 'pet' of automated tellers, instant credit, and points of access to accounts and financial services, the fix of quick cash and all the consumerist micro-vectors of pseudo-singularity as a risk profile, produced by an adaptable, flexible, creative, and subjugated cognitariat.[3] Marx vividly imagined credit as a 'humble assistant' who furtively creeps behind individual capitalists 'drawing into the[ir] hands ... by invisible threads, the money resources which lie scattered, over the surface of society.'[4] Today, in Canada, the point-of-purchase debit and credit payment processing network Interac advertises itself as a little yellow self-propelled truck that tags along behind one, like a humble assistant, unobtrusively enriching life's events.

Guattari attempted to develop the first semiotics adapted to the global information economies of the network society,[5] even though his untimely passing in 1992 did not permit him to experience the extraordinary accelerations of the 1990s towards and beyond the millennium of the burgeoning infotechnocultural era of digital capitalism; still, he was already attentive to the stirrings of the fusion of capitalism and informatics in his studies dating from the 1980s of the global economy of Integrated Worldwide Capitalism. It was on the information technology strand of the machinic phylum that IWC exercised its formidable integrative capacities, inaugurating 'the age of planetary computerization'; this has been developed at length by Manuel DeLanda in terms of the military machine's extractions, its taking hostage of operations and applications, from the information processing strand.[6] Guattari struggled against IWC's appropriations from the same technological strand for the sake of the production of certain kinds of subjects compatible with most of its values, stratifications, and disorienting visions of progress. For example, he thought that miniaturization was a way for capital to equip individuals with devices that would manage their perceptions by plugging them into strands of the machinic phylum concerned with consumer electronics, making them crazy for self-medicated highs of the kind that come from the aptly rechristened CrackBerry.[7] This drug of wired consumerism inserts subjectivity into incorporeal networks, sometimes requiring detox by disconnection. The courage to unplug became for Guattari a kind of ethical necessity that interrogated finitude and turned away from the affluence of signs – if email and texting and voicemail can be described this way – to the 'poetry of words' and 'the hope or nostalgia for a mythical time in which everyone would accede to the fullness of a bliss unlimited by the exigency of exchange,' in the words of anthropologist Pierre Clastres, whose work inspired Guattari.[8] Of course, the courage to unplug can have many resonances and, as Simon O'Sullivan reminds us, one of these includes rituals of meditation.[9]

Guattari sought to frame these issues in semiotic terms and to theorize a species of part-signs that expose salient features of informatized capital in whose networks they directly intervene by exploiting the potentiality materially present there. Guattari wrote of 'signaletic matter' in a manner similar to Deleuze in his cinema books, especially *The Time-Image*: the seething, dynamic stew of largely unformed but not completely amorphous matter out of which emerge part-objects (including part-signs), as well as more fully and creatively expressive and formed semiotic substances.[10] Basically, signaletic matter is defined as a-signifying. Both Guattari and Deleuze reverse the priority of form over matter inherited from the linguists Saussure and Hjelmslev, and in this way attempt to describe a process of teasing out what is already there in part and in varying degrees. With a-signifying semiotics, however, this work of teasing out never gets to linguistic formation; it is reticent, hesitant, working only with the parts and their intensities, without imposing on them further form: signification never culminates.

Material Molecular Revolutions

In a cluster of books published originally in 1977, the two editions of *La révolution moléculaire*, and *L'inconscient machinique*, Guattari elaborated a typology of semiotic systems framed in a Peirce–Hjelmslev hybrid conceptual vocabulary. Reading across these three books I want to flesh out a-signifying semiotics in relation to an infotech strand on the machinic phylum inspired by one of Guattari's favorite examples of the kind of semiosis put into play by a-signifying signs: credit and/or bank cards. Guattari's innovation was to develop a-signifying signs in a typology of sign types but with respect to the problem of the relationship between material and semiotic dimensions in the age of planetary computerization and globalization. Is there a semiotics adequate to the global information culture? Yes, just as there is an analysis of power of the same in the myriad of attempts to describe its features – for example, its non-linearity.[11] A-signifying signs, to the extent that they are at work there, bear some of its features, including superlinearity, which they operationalize. The very texture of the informatic strand of the machinic phylum upon which capital relies is populated – better, perfused – by a-signifying part-signs.

One of the main obstacles to thinking a-signification is that the promise of the prefix may not be kept by the base word, which clings stubbornly to signification despite an opening to elude it. So, a-signifying understood as non-signifying semiotics seems at best an oxymoron and at worst simply a species of signals. A-signifying signaletic matter may be non-signifying in the sense that signals directly transmit information without necessarily providing semantic content, on a slightly more progressive view than that of Eco.[12] This corresponds minimally to Guattari's sense of a-signifying signs, usually referring to non-linguistic information transfers. But more to the point is that no specific construal of that which emanates from the system is required in support of the action thereby triggered. The marginality of the conceptual dimension does not imply the absence of the action initiated by the triggering signal. Importantly, the absence of a semantic dimension is less pertinent than the non-representational and non-mental dimension. Guattari is less concerned about limiting the semantic than about underlining the strictness and precision of a-signification. In fact, a-signification operates by means of part-signs, that is, particle- or point-signs, as Guattari called them, and not through the fully formed signs of any tradition. But the restrictiveness of a-signification, the partial/particle/point-ness of such signs, and their non-representational character, entails for Guattari a micropolitical analysis of this kind of semiotics. So in this respect a-signifying semiotics differs from signaling, since the non-necessity of semantic content is not negatively construed as denying something to someone (e.g. to signal using higher animals) and does not entail some variant of behaviorism.

Let's begin with an apparently simple idea. A-signifying semiotics are defined relationally by Guattari against signifying semiologies. Guattari maintains the distinction between semiotics – Peircean–Hjelmslevian hybrid – and semiology – Saussurean, or dyadic and linguistic. There are of course many other ways to reinforce the distinction, for example with regard to the inclusion or exclusion of the referent, but the salient point is that a semiotics that is not dependent upon linguistics loosens, for Guattari, the hold that structuralism enjoys, in collusion with psychoanalysis, over the construction of the unconscious, that is, all the features of a formal description of its components – 'universals,' 'laws,' 'registers,' transcendent figures like 'lack,' etc. Guattari's great innovation was to conceive of the unconscious as a machine that was neither structured like a language nor conceptual-ized as an interior struggle within individuals indexed on static mythic figures or even mathemes: 'it was a grave error on the part of the structuralist school to try to put everything connected with the psyche under the control of the linguistic signifier!'[13] Correcting this grave error, and thus escaping from 'linguistic axiomatics,' involves bringing to the fore the machinic processes of a-signifying semiotics irreducible to semio-linguistic determinations. Guattari exhorts his readers to 'sortir de la langue' ('leave language'). Machines constitute according to Guattari a kind of 'changing matter'[14] that dynamically assembles as well as undoes components drawn from diverse domains and extracts from these their singularity traits (hybrid identities), not all of which will be constituted, some remaining virtual (pure potential).

Signifying semiologies concern well-formed substances situated on the stratified planes of expression and content, with the proviso that all such substances are linguistified; symbolic semiologies are a species of signifying semiologies and concern substances of expression that are neither completely translatable into linguistic terms nor may they be overcoded by any one substance of expression among them. This rule of non-translatability keeps at bay linguistic imperialism: 'the semiological linearity of the structural signifier which imposes itself despotically over all other modes of semiotisation.'[15]

Signifying semiologies are, as in Saussure, structured by the axes of syntagm and paradigm; the former is a series of terms in praesentia (co-present), supported by linearity, whereas paradigmatic relations are constellative, indeterminate, and in absentia (lacking co-presence); a-signifying semiotics, it has been suggested, elude these axes and 'add a third, diagrammatic axis.'[16] But what is the point of adding another axis? Simply put, it announces an attempt to break away from the horizontal syntagm and the vertical paradigm, that is, from speech and language; taken together these are the tools of a 'trans-linguistic semiology.'[17] This is a conservative maneuver, at best. Even Roland Barthes, one of Guattari's semiological nemeses, thought that 'creative transgressions' – 'structural scandals'[18] – can and do occur at the frontier of syntagm and paradigm, even if these are still glottic: puns, spoonerisms, rhymes, and the like. The Peirce-inspired diagrammatism elaborated by Guattari will be discussed later. The question for Guattari is not one of transgression but of the limits and controls on any semiotic deviation or deterritorialization.

So, is it enough to 'disturb'[19] by addition inherited binarisms like syntagm and paradigm? After all, disturbances do not persist with the same strength as the new over time and perhaps nestle comfortably into routines. It would be easy to trap a third axis in the production of a certain kind of subjectivity if it was always linked to a specific expression substance, like a despotic signifier. This despotism may be deposed if it is linguistic, but its relation to power, even the power of the psychoanalyst, is not vanquished.

Guattari is never done with signifying semiologies.

> Signification is always the encounter between the formalization [of both expression and content] by a given social field of value systems, translation systems, rules of conduct, and a machine of expression which by itself has no meaning, that is, which is a-signifying and automates the behaviors, interpretations and the responses hoped for by the system.[20]

Signification occurs in the conjunction of semiotic and semiological systems, marked by the stratifications of power actualized in informatic, economic, and social and political terms. For instance, Guattari reads the sign's arbitrariness as a 'basic' social and political demand: 'accept the systems of dominant encodings in which everything is done for you or you will end up with a repressive system.'[21] A-signifying signs 'automate' dominant significations by 'organizing a system of redundancy' on the levels of expression and content: automation entails normalization, invariance, and consensus. Guattari adds the further qualification of stabilization – what is arrested is wandering in textual space amid the mandalas of signification. There isn't any room for interpretation in the strings of numbers and characters on a typical magnetic stripe: the relevant system, bank, and account numbers are in fields of fixed length, separated by special characters and bracketed by start and stop sentinels, and are followed by a redundancy check; all of these are recognized automatically. In themselves a-signifying signs have no meaning, but for Guattari they operationalize local powers – here we see how he jumps from machinic trigger to political level and back again; they are akin to the 'role of the State in relation to different factions of the bourgeosie that consists in setting in order and hierarchizing the claims of various local factions.'[22] Sectoral interests and their lobby groups and regional political organizations with territorialized power bases are among such local factions whose claims are parsed and prioritized by a central power such as a board of trade or party apparatus in terms of political agenda setting, favor trading, and policy formation. These kinds of political decision are encoded in the magstripe, as we shall see shortly.

Signifying semiologies and their linear 'syntagms of power' combine with superlinear a-signifying automations. Guattari tended to compile lists of diverse encodings to explain the semiotic mixity of assemblages. But the conception is clear as far as the relations between signifying and a-signifying is concerned: the latter uses the former, puts it into play in some manner, as it were, only as a 'tool' and without itself functioning either semiologically or symbolically; in this way a-signifying semiotics are not subjected to semiological well-formedness, but to which they still have recourse in communicating in the way that dominant significations 'hope for' – which is to say if one wants to be taken seriously by semioticians, at the very least. But, Guattari boldly stated, a-signifying semiotics, like a physico-chemical theory, 'can do without this kind of crutch.'[23] He also claims that signifying semiologies are capable of 'deriving their efficacy from the fact that they rely upon a certain a-signifying machine.'[24] That is, they may find the deterritorializing tendencies of a-signifying semiotics helpful in blurring the territories of the body or certain institutional spaces. But in the very crossing between systems and generation of significations new territories are breached and powers engaged that perhaps lead to the imposition of a more rigid definition, or to claims of incoherence.

Plastic Cards, Magstripes, and Technomateriality

A-signification is essentially machinic. Guattari did not reduce his machines to technical devices; yet, his repeated description of how a-signifying semiotics triggers processes within informatic networks highlights the interactions initiated when a plastic card bearing a magnetic stripe activates access to a bank or credit account, engaging an elaborate authorization process, and makes it clear that we are dealing with a complex info-technological network. Here Guattari's part-signs 'give out start and stop orders.'[25] It is easy to think of such parts/particles as actual iron oxide particles on the tracks of the magnetic stripes of credit cards which are decoded – their polarities are immediately converted into binary digits – when 'swiped' through a reader with the appropriate software. As everyone knows, there is normally more to the operation than the gestural act. Of course, the use of 'particles' by Guattari tells us that the signs of a-signifying semiotics are just as much virtual – 'elementary' entities that are generated by machinic interactions like acceleration and mathematical prediction and whose existence is verifiable theoretically.[26]

Anyone who has received an error message in the process of inputting a PIN/password, which is usually the second step in the course of a debit transaction or log-in operation, understands the overt syntagmatic sensitivity of such part-signs (and in most cases the syntactical features – how many digits, upper and lower case sensitivity – of a password or PIN). Indeed, anyone who has had their card 'eaten' by a machine knows the vicissitudes of a-signification – perhaps this is just a jammed trigger, but it may be a security countermeasure triggered by the card's use in such a place for such a purpose against an established or even extrapolated pattern; moreover, when a card is, as one says, 'all swiped out' by intense usage after a shopping spree, the interaction between the oxide particles on its magnetic stripe and the reader head that converts the encoding into binary digits goes awry, because the magstripe is scratched or erased or demagnetized, thus introducing imbalance into the signal-to-noise ratio.

A-signifying part-signs do not slide; conversely, if they experience significant drift, they cease working (there are many homespun solutions such as swiping with a card wrapped in paper). Guattari provides a helpful description of the precise character of such signs:

It is as if [they] ideally sought to shed their own inertia and renounce completely the polysemy which can proliferate in symbolic and signifying systems: the sign is refined, there are no longer 36 possible interpretations but a denotation and an extremely strict and precise syntax.[27]

The '36' is of course a reference to Peirce's strategy of generating categories of signs by means of combining triadic divisions; today this is how we order overpriced coffee! The precision of the syntax is a more difficult issue to grasp. Whereas Deleuze considered a-signifying signaletic matter to be a-syntaxic, Guattari retains syntactic combinatorics of minimal units but without a necessary reference to a deep/underlying or high/transcendent semantics; he can maintain this because the primary context is not language. Further, part-signs work regardless of whether they signify something for someone or not. As Guattari specifies, they do not 'secrete significations' – whether these are 'thoughts,' 'psychical' entities, or 'mental representations'. Take a minimal definition of the sign – something that stands to somebody for something else – and incapacitate representation, and Guattari's position becomes a bit clearer: 'Signs "work" things prior to representation. Signs and things combine with one another independently of the subjective "hold" that the agents of individuated enunciation claim to have over them.'[28] However, having incapacitated a disempowering representation and brought signs and things, that is, the material and the semiotic, closer together, Guattari adds that this is the 'force of machinic assemblage' (as opposed to a disempowered semiology).

Whether they are randomly generated or carefully selected on the basis of paradigmatic clusters of birthdates, children's ages, former addresses, initials, nicknames, etc., PINS/passwords can, like the magstripe-reader encoding–decoding relation, do without mental representations; these latter may of course exist, but they are 'never essential' and no longer center signification.[29] Passwords just allow one to pass. With a-signifying semiotics there is no need, Guattari insisted, on passing through the summit of a typical pyramid of meaning, that is, through an already constituted referent, soul, substance, individuated subject's mental universe, etc. It is just as if, Guattari conjectured, physics 'renounce[d] any attempt to signify anything other than its own machinic articulations'[30] in generating particles it multiplies by means of signs (whose productivity is their only relevant property). Certainly, Guattari believed, one can create scientific representations of subatomic particles, but 'these cannot be taken into account by scientific semiotisation.'[31] The study of such representations is of interest to many technocultural theorists, philosophers, and sociologists of science, but Guattari underlines the limits of their pertinence and translatability.

The fallout for semiology is that new relations are established between form and matter by part-signs in as much as they skirt substance in some manner; there is a tendency in the information age for a-signifying semiotics to maximize its machinic force – to rapidly evolve, speed up, acquire greater mobility, miniaturize, and proliferate. In a-signifying semiotics, part-signs work 'flush' (*travaillent à même*) with the real, more precisely, with material fluxes. Guattari does not, however, uncritically valorize flushness as directness. At the same level as and in parallel is perhaps better. Directness has important qualifications.

The Diagrammaticity of Part-signs

Guattari explains how part-signs help to reconceptualize sign-referent relations. Modeling his conception on subatomic particles, like quarks, Guattari does not seek positive evidence of the existence of part-signs in referential anchors like space-time coordination and logical consistency, but notes how certain perceptions actualize them in specific ways; as Brian Massumi puts it, 'scientific perception actualizes a virtual particle.'[32] The problem of existence is imposed on them retroactively, and '[a] new type of relation is established between the sign and referent, no longer a direct relation, but a relation engaging [*mettant en jeu*] a theoretico-experimental assemblage in its entirety.'[33] Two points are worth making as, taking Guattari's advice, we work out the implication of the physics lesson in other domains. The first is that part-signs engage machinic material processes beyond the problem of referentiality, whose quandaries have always haunted semioticians. They are able to do so because such signs are creatures

of the *matière signalétique* – signalizing matter – they constitute
through machinic electromagnetic interactions, as in my magstripe
example. Secondly, Guattari suggests that entire experimental
assemblages are engaged, that is, IT networks of hardware and
software, international standards of practice and production,
requests for authentication from remote databases, supporting
the signalizations of part-signs, again in a credit-request situation.
In this immense information infrastructure, delimited for the time
being by the banks and their partners under many different kinds
of legislation (and calculi of profit rates), is the materially present
potentiality at and of the points of transaction triggered by part-
signs whose traces constitute raw data that may be transformed
for use in the security, promotional, gaming, etc. sectors through
mining operations. The discovery of new knowledge by data-
mining operations tends toward an increasingly speedy, cheap,
and analytically sophisticated category cross-linking independent
data records toward the construction of a 'virtual database' by
governments emboldened by post-9/11 anti-terrorist legislation.[34]
A virtual database results from a creative extrapolation from what
is known to what is unknown and most commonly is a profile. The
actions of a-signifying part-signs can be employed automatically
against models toward the generation of such a profile. 'Guattari
has imagined,' wrote Deleuze circa 1990,

> a town where anyone can leave their flat, their street, their neighbourhood,
> using their (dividual) electronic card that opens this or that barrier; but
> the card may also be rejected on a particular day, or between certain
> times of the day; it doesn't depend on the barrier but on the computer
> that is making sure everyone is in a permissible place, and effecting a
> universal modulation.[35]

Both Deleuze and Guattari alert us to the diagrammatic
modulations at precise locations of a-signifying part-signs and
how these work across, between and beyond barriers as data
reservoirs, not merely passively gathering but exploring, filling
in the vacuoles, according to constraints of models and analyses.
A 'dividual' is an informatic diagram pointing at the virtual but
dropping a line to an offline individual who is merely one of its

actualizations, because nobody totally corresponds to their data double or silhouette; this doesn't help when your debt is no longer deemed sustainably profitable for those holding it and your credit rating falls.

Guattari overwhelmingly advises against the deployment of the signifier in any way that would subordinate to it the formation of subjectivity. What Guattari wants to shed is the disempowered subject of Lacanian analysis, trapped by definition – 'a signifier is that which represents the subject for another signifier' – in a system of negative differential relations away from the real, arrested in its sliding only by *points de capiton* that allow anchor points from which selected signifiers may be seen, through analysis, to be retroactively attached to specific signifieds. But still no access to the real, Guattari claims, as the 'Lacanian signifier forbids us from entering the real world of the machine.'[36] Guattari clarifies that this 'real' is not so much symbolizable, against Lacan, but has a direct purchase on 'material machinic processes', like 'a credit card number which triggers the operation of a bank auto-teller' and 'activates' accounts and open access to resources.[37] A-signifying semiotics are an exit strategy from 'sliding signifiers' and the lack of 'ontological guarantees' of the structuralist signifier in general. The individuated subject's fate is released from the binds of the effects of the signifier, and to some degree from the human itself – Guattari occasionally describes the assembling of part-sign components as 'a-subjective and machinic,'[38] as taking place without the mediation of subjectification at all.

The triggering operations that Guattari identified with a-signifying semiotics have been appreciated by Jacques Derrida, among other members of the Tel Quel group. Guattari mentions Derrida's name in passing as someone whose work displays an acute sensitivity to the 'relative autonomy' of a-signifying textual machines. Consider the trigger (*déclenchement*). The trigger in both Guattari and Derrida is aligned with automatic and automated release – unclenching. Derrida finds this at work in the writing of Sollers' *Numbers*, in which the story is an auto-trigger: it releases 'the process of its own triggering.'[39] This is the work of machines with impressive recoil, adds Derrida, and it is unstoppable, incessant, irresistible, and plugs into 'you' via the numbers it calls forth and piles up; a self-reading and writing that plays on this self-presentation; a book-machine whose author's name is 'in the umbra' (shade), but put there having been 'assign[ed] a determinate place.' What makes this trigger a-signifying is the precision at work: the angles of the surfaces; the overall 'apparatus' that puts every term in its place, 'like all the parts of a machine,' so that the teeth of the gears mesh, Derrida concludes. Control and precision: without these a-signification goes awry. Such precision is made possible by recourse to numbers in various combinations – counting, sets, series, calculations, formulae, schema – and the self-explanations that pop up in the text. The deconstruction of the neutrality of representation and standard categories like author/reader described by Derrida is one example for Guattari of how to get at the non-human element of machinic self-production, with the proviso that this is a specific kind of textual machine.

Triggering is the key action of part-signs. This is Guattari's sense of the passage of molecular signs: machinic superempowerment and diagrammatization. Guattari extricates himself from the Peircean trap of subsuming diagrams under icons (within Peirce's logic, diagrams are graphic representations in mathematics – sketches, graphs, drawings, skeletons) and then gains the positive implications of losing aboutness as a criterion, bringing him into constructive coherence with a critique of representation. He separates the image and diagram; the former belongs to symbolic semiologies, and the latter to a-signifying semiotics (the domain of machinism). In shifting into a molecular-machinic modality of explication, Guattari highlights a tightly controlled repetition, whose deployment is open-ended, but whose operations are not, as a key aspect of the part-signs.

Part-signs 'support a mode of molecular semiotization of a nearly unlimited scope,'[40] with the proviso that they 'quantify the possible' and elude all signifying representations, to which they remain effectively 'blind.' Thus, Guattari continues, algorithmic, algebraic and topological logics, recordings, and data processing systems that utilize mathematics, sciences, technical protocols, harmonic and polyphonic musics, neither denote nor represent in images the morphemes of a referent wholly constituted, but rather produce these through their own machinic characteristics.

The concept of constraint should not be confused with a machine's degree of openness. Constraints modulate a diagram's movements, selections, and passages and temper its deterritorializations; otherwise part-signs are no longer 'able to cling to all the abstract spaces of machinic potentialities.'[41] Diagrammatic part-signs are dynamic and productive (capable of multiple articulations) but rigorously constrained – meaning is not essential in this activity, but specific codes, algorithms, materials, and standards are. To be sure, Guattari notes the 'production of unedited conjunctions'[42] in a-signifying assemblages, but this diverges from the uncontrollability of polysemy. Neither uncontrollable slippage and free play nor Peircean-syle multiplication of triads suffices to describe part-signs. Yet what is an unedited conjunction against these rather severe constraints presented by Guattari? 'There isn't anything to "comprehend" in the equations of theoretical physics,' Guattari boldly stated, which is to say that mathematical expression is tightly and technically circumscribed and not beholden to some qualitative content, metaphorical or otherwise. Guattari is not claiming that physicists don't have ideas or have nothing in mind when they are working out problems experimentally and mathematically.

Diagrammatism, in Guattari's hands, blazes a trail beyond the human and individuated subject (of the statement) into the collective machinic dimension. 'We leave the terrain of signification,' Guattari wrote, 'for that of the plane of machinic consistency,' that is, the continuum of interactions on which any machine is reducible to an individual only arbitrarily. There is no 'refolding' or 'returning' or 'reterritorialization' onto representation, or any kind of 'pre-signification' or even overcoding, by either consciousness or iconicity; instead, the part-signs work next to and creatively with the material fluxes; Guattari heralds 'a pluralism of articulations.'[43] With a-signifying semiotics one enters the 'more and more artificial' plane of the post-human. Guattari didn't shed any 'humanist tears' over this, rejecting anti-modern and anti-machine recapitulations of humanism.[44] It needs to be kept in mind, however, that not all machines are technical.

While it is relatively straightforward to appreciate Guattari's separating of diagrams from icons and his substitution of reproductive for productive force, his reconfiguration of Hjelmslevian linguistic terms is more complex. For Guattari, what he called an 'abstract machine' like a diagram was akin to the concept of form borrowed from Hjelmslev; unlike Hjelmslev, for whom forms are recognized in substance, even though he was ambivalent about which substance was at issue, Guattari used form independently of substance (formed matter) but linked it to semiological and symbolic signification stratified by the two planes of expression and content. And matter, unformed but not amorphous (or uninterrupted), was the site, for Guattari, of material intensities and the haunt of a-signifying part-signs in flux. For Hjelmslev, form was like a net whose shadow (substance) was cast on the surface of an unformed matter. For Guattari, abstract machines were conjoined with material fluxes and part-signs, but without producing well-formed expression and content substances like 'transcendentalized subjects,' or meanings 'embedded' in syntagmatic and paradigmatic chains and clusters, or affinity between subjects and substances of the statement.[45] Rather, the subjectifications at work here are collective – human and post-human. The articulations at issue do not obey, for example, the structuralist fetish for 'Chinese boxes' – hierarchically organized ever widening isomorphic systems all obeying the same rules. Guattari rejects this carefully cultivated sphere for the sake of semiotic intensities that he made to run the gauntlet of signifying propriety on the way towards more open and experimental machinic conjunctions of the formal abstract machines with various fluxes. Computer worms and viruses are abstract diagrammatic machines that conjoin with the digital strand of the machinic phylum and release tendencies of imperfect self-replication, that is, machinic mutation.[46] It is possible – even necessary – to hack a-signifying machinic part-signs and in so doing reveal the relations of power that condition them and perhaps even expose that the network itself is a system of representation that offers too much consistency and thus produces inertia.

Where Meaning Was, Technopolitics Will Be

Meaning may not be essential, but politics is (the requirement of meaning in politics is of course a complex challenge that cannot be adequately met here). All molecular phenomena display, for Guattari, a politics in lieu of a signified. The sign-particles are no different in this respect, though on the face of it the move to quantity and machinic interactions (automated triggers) belies it. Let's return to the magstripe. On the stripe, which is located in a certain position on the plastic card, there are several tracks. These are not neutral tracks upon which the particles are lined up. Rather, of the three tracks available, the first was developed for use by the airline industry, and the second is used by financial institutions. Each track's format was developed by and for specific interests. The cards meet a variety of international standards, and function by means of specific algorithms. A-signifying machines may be used to 'automate' the messages of the signifying semiologies that, in a capitalist system, begin stirring at a young age, especially around basic training in capitalist behaviors – credit, for example (a key facet of the capitalisitic subjective economy into which one is socialized). This is one reason why I have paid close attention to bank and credit cards

In a lengthy and stirring passage worth quoting in its entirety, Guattari exposed the place of a-signifying machines within capitalism's expanding frontiers:

> The very texture of the capitalist world consists of these fluxes of deterrito-rialised signs [a-signifying, diagrammatic, machinic]: monetary, economic, prestige signs, etc. Significations and social values (at least those that are interpretable) appear at the level of formations of power, but essentially capitalism relies on a-signifying machines (for example, the indexes of the Stock Exchange). Capitalist power, at the economic level, is not discursive; it

only tries to master the a-signifying machines and rotate the wheels of the system. Capitalism attributes a role to each of us: child, man, woman, queer. Each person adapts to the system of significations erected for them. But at the level of real powers, the type of role matters little because power is not necessarily confined to the level of the director or minister, but functions in the balance sheets and balances of power between influential groups. A-signifying machines recognize neither subjects, nor persons, nor roles, and not even delimited objects. That is precisely what confers upon them a kind of omnipotence; they pass through signifying systems within which individuated subjects find themselves lost and alienated. One never knows when or where capitalism ends.[47]

On the fringes of info-capitalism there are no bank machines that will take your card; networks are finite. The networked radiation of the a-signifying part-signs that automatically trigger anonymous at-a-distance verification processes find their machinic potentiality temporarily exhausted as the banking systems – Cirrus, Interac, Plus, and the rest – terminate until further notice. A-signifying semiotics are perfectly adapted to the networked banking systems we use on a regular basis. Their diagrammatic potential mobilizes for not-yet-actualized extensions of the cash networks, and new magstripe tracks to be colonized by the next corporate players.

Information precedes signification, the potentialities of which are in machinic systems, the site for the study of a-signifying semiotics. Repetitive machinic signaletic stimuli are the stuff of the info-capitalist technoverse. But these are not the signals of an older semiotics. Rather, Guattari's originality as a semiotic theoretician lies precisely in his innovative investigation of the characteristics of a-signifying part-signs and how they belong to the very texture of the informatic strand of the machinic phylum. He didn't forgo signifying semiologies and meaning-effects, but rather operated a displacement so that the unwarranted hierarchization of sign types inherited from structuralism could be retheorized; indeed, Guattari gave free rein to the overcodings and complexes in his analytic work. He certainly wasn't an apologist for automation, because he insisted on understanding the political dimension of the deployment of part-signs. After all, non-storage magstripe technologies are not 'smart' enough – do not store the data – to make independent decisions about your credit; but the potential for this completely automated and non-human practice remains, not as a standing reserve but as a tendency a glimpse of which one occasionally catches through the vague mists of virtuality and in the trial-and-error runs of new product actualizations to which such potential seems unassimilable – except in the eyes of an Orwell. Less extreme would be the exploratory visions of those, like John Willinsky, who imagine metanarratives in the form of virtual public corporations with the capacity to perform automated data mining of knowledge gleaned from all the social sciences.[48] Guattari regained signals towards the end of establishing the semiotics of the leading strand of the machinic phylum – informatics – more and more held hostage by corporations in what is known as the surveillance postindustrial complex.

The means of conceiving an alternative outcome, an escape from machinic enslavement by IWC, is still on the Guattarian agenda. The problem is: Does this mean that a-signifying semiotics simply and only obeys a network form? If so, must resistance to it take the network form? Would this mean the hegemony of the network (another master signifier)? – for even the state is thought to be an organizational and political network,[49] and the multitude is a distributed one too.[50] Obviously the key to overcoming this straightjacket of technological deterministic formal correspondence would be to look at the alternative ontological universes opened by a-signifying semiotics and the kind of subjectivities attached to them. Technically identical a-signifying declensions may unfold differently in the production of profoundly different universes and subjectivities – security professionals as opposed to hackers of various allegiances. Signaletic matter is not neutral; it is not waiting there passively to be formed, either. Beyond the myth of representation that injects and maintains passivity into semiosis, part-signs retain their plasticity and some of their intensivity; that is, they move onward rather than backward (merely receiving sense from their anchors), and for political ends retain a partial signifying sense in their multiple articulations. In this manner they may be nurtured in the non-linear ecologies of networked life by

diagrams that 'twist' their tendencies and 'blur' their encounters
with machine codes.

Where meaning was, technopolitics will be; and where technopolitics is, affect accrues. A-signifying semiotics as I have
presented it is not divorced from affect. In fact, Massumi, in
his work on former US president Ronald Reagan as an affect-
accumulator,[51] has posed the pertinent question of the relation
between politics and affect, and sketched answers to it by probing
the non-ideological means of ideology's production. What would
an a-signifying theory of affect look like when components of
informatic subjectivity are imbricated in the phyla of networks
marked by technopolitical striations?

Every insertion of a bank card into an automated teller,
every swipe of a point-of-purchase debit card, is a ritornello
of capitalistic subjectification, constellated by the a-signifying
part-signs unleashed and multiplying along the machinic phyla
of credit and banking systems, achieving consistency in the
mechanical stirring that produces a neat stack of crisp bills or
a tidy printed receipt; Guattari once wrote of an earlier version
of this process, but as a release of more abstract assonances of
power in relation to a signed paper banking slip, the signature
triggering a-signifying part-signs along a paper and prestige trail.[52]
The capitalistic subject of credit is another terminal, tributary of
the a-signifying machines, and the plastic cards that many carry
with them at all times are interfaces, existential operators that
provide access in sensory encounters at bank machines themselves
(and point-of-purchase card readers) with low-lit screens, keypad
tones made by repeatedly punched sequences, and more abstract
problematic affects as well, some archaic, like lingering affects
around socialization into saving – a penny saved is a penny earned
– while the entrepreneurial environment rocks us gently in its
fattened arms – occasionally dropping one flat onto the floor. If
the encounter with the ATM is an immediate scene rich in sensory
affect – several alt-rock musicians are transported beyond the
mundane by the colors of ATMs – the cash machine / is blue
and green / for a hundred in twenties / and a small service fee
(Wilco, 'Ashes of American Flags', *Yankee Hotel Foxtrot*, 2002)

– and more abstract affects take flight along evocations of ease, comforts of an obliging and faithful pet credit, modulated by forecasting in the forms of obligations, daily limits, and a quasi-seamless flow, a day of relays, then to bank on Guattari's lesson is to appreciate how sticky, suffocating affects accumulate around brandished plastic cards and the part-signs triggered by them, for capitalist subjects 'unfortunately' – to borrow Marx's ironic qualifier – enriched by the absence of meaning. Still, remember to ask about how the card works; don't remain subjugated to the micropolitical vectors buried in the infomachinic phyla. For surely, even before an ATM, one is not merely tributary of the specifically battle-hardened hardware and software of the 'empire of digital credit,'[53] but, rather, on the lookout for a hackable command prompt[54] on the monitor, or ready to excavate an offline vacuole,[55] or pursue anomalous (excess or dearth) affects of singularity alongside buyers of nothing and counter-surveillant assemblages, or reconfigure debt as a precarious palette for subjectivity's aesthetic explorations,[56] all of which are ways towards the reacquisition and retriggering of the means for subjectivity's own production at points along the silicon face where part-signs work flush with informatic technomateriality in a web of global debt in which finance capital feeds on its ordinary victims.

5

INFORMATIC STRIATION

In this chapter I want to explore another dimension of Guattari's conceptual arsenal that is especially promising in diagnosing the technomaterial and cultural conditions of information society. The conceptual coupling of striation and smoothness is useful for an investigation of a phenomenon I call, after Guattari, *informatic striation*: the instantiation of fluxes in binary code, the digitization of images and messages, and sequencing operations are all relevant examples. Informatic striation is a concept that identifies a complex communication between two kinds of space, smooth and striated, within the networking of society.[1] Generally, informatic means like administrative codings are deployed in order to translate smooth cultural practices considered ambiguously heterogeneous or 'nonformal' into a formally organized, manageable collection of distinct yet homogeneously coded data; the striation of smoothness by informatic means also effects a new smoothing operation in the ease with which files and data sets are compared, contrasted, and combined in novel ways. This is the moment when the contemporary dividual emerges. Striation has the aim of identifying and (in)dividuating otherwise unidentifiable persons; yet the combination of databases containing such information, by means of abstract operations and creative extrapolations from existing attributes, forges new classifications and identities that do not readily map back onto persons.

My hypothesis is that there are elements of smoothness in First Nations, Inuit, and Australian Aboriginal cultures that are an affront to state bureaucrats and lawmakers. Although this hypothesis remains problematic in many of its details, it is less an attempt to name an originary element than an effort to find a starting point that can adequately explain the conditions to which vast administrative sweeps and social sortings have been applied. Striation 'captures' through the imposition of criterial discernment derived from a shared grid; however, a striated space may be smoothed over or 'dissolved' by the discontinuation of a certain coding operation or by the reintroduction of smooth elements resisting containment or evading certain subordinations. Essentially, I am introducing into the discussion of the smooth-striated relation an informatic model of social sorting as it pertains to indigenous experience, using comparative data from Canada and Australia. This chapter consists of two case studies that illustrate how to apply and evaluate the related concepts of smooth–striated.

The context for this chapter was set in motion by Paul Patton's book *Deleuze and the Political*. Patton understands the war machine – the creative assemblage that brings about metamorphoses in the face of state forces to which it is exterior and resistant to the latter's apparatuses of capture and colonization by means of sedentarity – as a propagator of smoothings of all sorts.[2] Patton's insight is that it is possible to make smoothing useful in terms of understanding the dynamic and transformative work of Australian Aboriginal peoples in resisting and transforming the sovereign, colonizing settler state by means of jurisprudence. The emergence in both Australia and Canada of native title to land and resources otherwise previously transformed by law into the property of white settlers or 'Crown land' shows great potential and 'expresses a novel kind of right which opens up a smooth space in between indigenous and colonial law.'[3] What is accomplished by Aboriginal law in this smoothing is a deterritorialization of the judicial means of colonial capture; likewise, the latter comes to recognize another body of law, having a degree of uncertainty about whether Australia was settled or conquered, Patton concludes, and this troubles the Crown's sovereignty. At the basis of this smoothing is an assertion by native peoples of customary tribal practices hitherto not or insufficiently acknowledged by so-called 'settlers': contrary to the discriminatory doctrine of *terra nullius*, the land was not empty (uninhabited, lawless) when Australia was captured by the Crown; it was not a vast lack, and it was not striated with reference to an abstract, fixed grid of quantitative assessment (time zones, state boundaries, geometries of location, and all non-local parameters, including ownership of land).

The idea of applying concepts like smoothing and deterritorialization to indigenous cultures is also useful in describing how tourism and cultural appropriations of difference work: traditional practices such as ceremonial dances may be deterritorialized from their living matrices of meaning and authority and recoded or resignified as touristic spectacles in a marketplace of entertainments from which one may choose on any given vacation. In this context, smoothing accomplishes the production of equivalence – culture is no more than a commodity and has no other existence outside the market. Smoothing here is a process of naturalization of cultural difference as commodity.[4] However, what is at stake here is that deterritorialization has transformative effects both positive and negative: touristic simulacra of traditional practices have the power to offer a glimpse into an otherwise occluded world of non-market symbolic relations that may be personally transformative, and even contribute to the survival and intergenerational dissemination of some practices among indigenous persons themselves.

Disc Numbers

The history of disc numbers and their replacement by other systems, in addition to the perspective on contemporary redeployments of older, out-of-official-use systems in contemporary Inuit popular culture, centered on Iqaluit,[5] involves passages between, mixtures of, fixing and unfixing, smooth and striated informatic sortings. In this case study I want to mix historical and contemporary examples; the latter focusing on resignification of old and out-of-date informatic striations.

It is interesting to note that until 1967 all Inuit (formerly Eskimos) in the Yukon and Northwest Territories were identified by numbers imprinted on tags worn around the neck. Not surprisingly the Eskimos objected to the system and, in preparation for its abandonment, during the four years from 1967 to 1971 the Eskimos selected their own surnames which are now used in lieu of numbers. Neither the old disc-number files nor the new registry of names contain data other than that normally recorded at birth.[6]

What is remarkable about this passage is that the few, rather vague, details provide for a dramatic tension between rejection and remedy, from the alleged perspective of the Inuit themselves: they 'rejected' the disc numbering system (and the 'dog tag' technology) and then 'selected' a new system that permitted the choice of surnames. The sense of empowerment is undeniable, if illusory, and is at least as strong as the government's desire to exonerate its past practices.

The issue of rejection or even of the replacement of one striating governmental practice for another does not reach far enough into the reappearance and myriad reuses of disc numbers and the disc themselves, although it has been flagged by some of those directly involved in its justification. For instance, a longtime Arctic researcher, John MacDonald, director of the Igloolik Research Center, has maintained that

[a] more practical employment of disc numbers recently came to my attention. There's a man in Igloolik ... who always uses his E-number on combination locks and even on his banking access card because ... it's the only number he'll remember all his life.[7]

The question here concerns not only the long-lasting effects of striations but whether everyday redeployments of them after the life of the disc number program are in fact (re)smoothings and, if so, do these have a softly subversive dimension (without any need to believe that they 'suffice to save us,' as Deleuze and Guattari remind their readers[8]) rather than an adaptive one?

The context of the transformation of striated to smooth capital is central to the analysis of Deleuze and Guattari and is, as they put it, the 'essential thing.'[9] The resignification of striations like the disc numbers in a post-classical smoothed space of integration and control, a smooth capitalist space, seems on the one hand a moot point, considering the inevitability of the conclusion: reuses of disc numbers after the fact of the program merely participate in the new networked relations whose transversal flows are smooth, with provisos – that remote and sparsely populated regions still have less dense information networks, that telephone companies still own the lines used by Internet service providers, etc. Yet the interesting question concerns the 'necessity and uncertainty'[10] of such passages. The refloating of disc numbers in such a semi-smooth, semi-striated space (depending on one's level of analysis) of computer-assisted mediation suggests that no amount of bureaucratic striation could contain the smooth elements of Inuit culture that survive and which, in fact, counter-conquer the renaming regime of old by reinvention or (re)smoothing.

Deleuze and Guattari's formulations of smooth igloos and nomads and Eskimo ice space in *A Thousand Plateaus*, drawn from cultural anthropologist Edmund Carpenter, remain a matter of some import and contention.[11] Here what is at issue is less a space than a set of cultural practices in relation to striations and smoothings sponsored by federal and territorial governments (and crossing into personal security and systems security in commercial transactions) in dynamic centrifugal movement from center to periphery, finally sufficiently smoothed to translate and engage the flows of the information economy (circulation in remote and anonymous systems of verification), and partially refloated in creative productions (conversely, under which conditions they are not refloatable).

The debts of Deleuze and Guattari to Carpenter, while he did not count among their explicitly named 'models,' are worth asking after, among the many anthropological source materials in *A Thousand Plateaus*, since they help give definition to nomad thought. Unlike Christopher L. Miller, who reads the anthropological source materials of nomad thought as 'foreign to nomadology itself,'[12] Deleuze and Guattari, while skipping over the material borrowed from Carpenter, recast the idea of 'Eskimo space', not to criticize either Carpenter's enthusiasms for so-called 'Eskimo Realities' (his praise of 'great' documentary filmmaker Robert

Flaherty, director of Nanook of the North [1922], rekindles a kind of prototypical act of cinematic primitivism – noble, happy subjects in an ethnograpically thin drama set in the cinemato-graphic present) or his omissions (such as disc numbers, despite an acute sensitivity to the inauthenticity of governmental policies and the effects of the welfare state). Indeed, Carpenter's role as founding editor of what would become Canadian media guru Marshall McLuhan's famous journal of the 1950s, *Explorations* – the original series of which ended in 1959 with a special issue, 'Eskimo,' by Carpenter and Flaherty and Frederick Varley – makes clear the decisive influence of McLuhan on Carpenter's vision of Eskimo society as implosive, anindividual, auditory–tactile, haptic–close, non-optical, non-linear, non-nominal – in short, smooth. Deleuze and Guattari's heavily ellipsized quotation[13] from Carpenter runs together paragraphs from pages 20 and 25 on orientation and igloos, creating an 'intricated aggregate,' in words perhaps adequate to Carpenter's descriptions of Eskimo language as consisting of independent 'tight conglomerates, like twisted knots.' A language of felt, in Deleuze and Guattari's estimation, an anti-imperial language.[14] These examples of poetic anthropology settle on the same point: that there is something smooth about Inuit life that keeps issuing challenges to the self-appointed bestowers of names and number crunchers in state bureaucracies and elsewhere (churches, mining companies, etc).

One of the oddities of Inuit art in Canada is that it is art historians and curators who are perhaps most familiar with disc numbers, since they work with them every day. Most museum and gallery collections hold sculptures and prints 'signed' with disc numbers, often but not always in lieu of names. The compilation of a given Inuit artist's biography is a complex affair involving up to six different names: commonly known name; its various spellings; a surname (if one of the above is not such); nickname; baptismal name; and disc number.[15] Names, then, multiply and bureaucrats lose their bearings. Drift was arrested by the 'decisive striation' of the disc number, but not even it could hold the incipient smoothness that would escape from it. So the bureaucrats asked again: How do we contain Inuit names in the restricted spaces on our forms and documents? By 1970 a new plan of attack called 'Project Surname' was launched. This was a sponsored (Northwest Territories Commissioner) census-like, self-identification project in which Inuit could 'choose' surnames, even though they had not used them before; they could also have first names as long as these 'could be written in Roman script or English letters,'[16] as in the 'southern readers' for schoolchildren introduced into the government schools for Inuit in the 1950s.[17] First and last names are ordered in the standard last-name-first, first-name-last routine and semiologically subjected by Imperial language, linking the requirement of the form-fillable response to another national project, the issuing of Social Insurance Numbers (SIN) to all citizens, including Inuit, who were not yet included when the program was introduced in 1964, but who would be issued the springboard for dataveillance that is the Canadian Social Insurance Number.

The issue of contemporary 'Eskimo space' poses a problem of how to study its informatic striation and (re)smoothing and, despite severe criticisms, remains relevant. For example, in many far northern communities such as the aforementioned Igloolik, at one time houses had no street numbers: 'One occupies without counting,' to refocus a musical example from Deleuze and Guattari.[18] This is quite common in small communities in rural and remote Canada (e.g. in 'unorganized' municipalities). What happens when populations diversify and grow and new services appear such as taxi and other delivery services? Then, 'one counts in order to occupy,' if you will, so that deliveries can be made. Which numbering system is used? In some instances, it isn't a system at all, but a matter of personal choice. Some houses in Igloolik bear the disc numbers of their inhabitants.[19] This is a good example of 'melding' smooth and striated, of an impure intermixture, a Brownian street address. The challenge here is to grasp the 'tone' of the example. In which register is it to be understood: parody of street numbers? Probably. I will return to this because understanding the tone is key to what resignification communicates.

Administrative Convenience as Endocolonialist Violence

The imposition of disc numbers, sometimes referred to misleadingly and with unintentional irony as E-numbers (just why will be easy to appreciate shortly), dates from the 1940s. The first date of note is 1941, which was a census year in Canada. National census-taking occurred during this period every ten years. One of the typical methodological challenges facing census statisticians was the under-enumeration of First Nations peoples, as well as inaccuracies in the collection of personal information about them that skewed the official data. Midway between census years, then, government bureaucrats in the Departments of Indian Affairs and Natural Resources began to initiate changes that would address a variety of issues around identification and enumeration of First Nations. The need for this had been developing throughout the 1930s through parallel and complementary identificatory acts of 'cultural inscription'[20] aimed at Inuit. These included standardization of spelling of names adapted with difficulty for English pronunciation (above and beyond a missionary naming regime inscribed in baptismal certificates that reproduced redundancy in the proliferating Johns and Marys and Pauls and Davids); fingerprinting; imposition of surnames; and discussions of the appropriate model for the disc numbers systems (e.g. military dog tags bearing individual and unit numbers). In addition, a range of related issues was in play around the collection of reliable vital statistics, as well as policing issues, in what was then known as the Northwest Territories (for example, it was the responsibility of the Royal Canadian Mounted Police to update the lists, therein making their presence felt in outlying communities, and making it possible for them to identify individuals; especially, in some instances, in order to place them under arrest).[21] In a sense striation is precisely the practice of identifying individuals for the dual purposes of enabling and constraining them: for, on the one hand, delivering welfare cheques to them and, on the other hand, arresting them.

This general situation was exacerbated in the case of Inuit because of cultural naming practices in which many persons might

very well have the same name, of a great hunter, for instance; all
of those bearing the name would be connected with the ancestor
and embody the 'soul' of their namesake, a condition for his/her
resting in peace, even though not everyone bearing the name
would have the same intimacy with the deceased.[22] The fact that
Inuit names were genderless and without surnames, and that many
different persons had the same name, even Christian names, not to
mention that there could be a different spelling and pronunciation
of the same name in every colonial institution present in the
north, defined a local smoothness based on intensities of spiritual
affiliations that aggravated the search for viable models of
striation. Even animals could temporarily hold a name until a
new human birth occurred.

Personal names are my concern, but it is easy to appreciate the
politics of naming as it relates to toponymy by considering that
the place known since 1987 as Iqaluit, an Inuktitut word meaning
the 'place of fish [arctic char],' had been known since the late
sixteenth century as Frobisher Bay, after its so-called 'discoverer'
Martin Frobisher. The Department of Natural Resources has
authority over the Geographical Names of Canada system of
authorization and assigns its own imprimatur – unique identifier
codes – to official names. Dating from the late nineteenth century,
the Canadian 'Names Board' is a state apparatus of capture,
a machinic enslavement to official geography and cartography,
and it consolidates endocolonial assertion of sovereignty over the
territory it appropriates in its names (containing the name 'Iqaluit'
in brackets on older maps below Frobisher Bay), but also entails a
social subjection of Inuit to an 'exterior object,'[23] that is, entering
processes of statistical subjectification. Indeed, the process of
endocolonization, which turns processes of colonialist domination
inward on targeted groups of a given state's population within its
national boundaries, makes a 'subject' (loyal, beholden, captured)
who is a part of an inverted colonial machine (hence we can speak
of national–imperial subjectification). Resistance to the imposition
of external over indigenous names has gained immense ground
since the 1980s. A strong example of southern academic and
Inuit collaboration towards regaining place names is found in

the work of geographer Ludger Müller-Wille on Nunavik.[24] The rich gazetteer of place names that he produced in collaboration with Inuit elders reveals the uniqueness and subtlety of naming within oral tradition. Müller-Wille's project not only countered the erasure of cultural tradition carried out by machinic enslavement with the reinstatement of such names, whose specificity right down to the shore, dune, point, and line was remarkable, but provided energy for renewing bonds with the land.

Machinic enslavement, however, has been advancing and mutating with computerization in the society of surveillance; this generalized, networked enslavement[25] accelerated in the years of the Second World War before passing into the postmodern forms of control, with their distinct textures of modulation and flexibility. The 'list-form' catches up with Inuit peoples in Canada through the disc numbers scheme; but this is not unique. Since the mid nineteenth century, First Nations in Canada have been subjected to regimes of registration for the purposes of the construction of 'status,' as Indians in the Indian Register, maintained by the Department of Indian Affairs and Northern Development (DIAND), and subject to shifts in policy (dominated at one time by the principle of assimilation, then amended by expanding entitlement through reintroduction of hitherto excluded categories of persons determined through political positions taken on lines of descent); thus, legislation defined conditions of inclusion or exclusion (known during the assimilationist period as 'enfranchisement,' doublespeak for disenfranchisement from status or forced integration). The Indian Register and the Band Lists comprising it intersects with another register – reserve land entitlements administered through Location Tickets (until 1951) and thereafter Certificates of Occupation. These dense machinic striations of identity and location are linked to exterior objects, as they are in the case of the Inuit, because 'status' confers rights to federally administered benefit programs (specific tax exemptions, etc.). The Certificates of Indian Status or 'status cards' are no-tech paper identity cards produced by the First Peoples' bands ('nations') themselves and include a registration number with vital statistics (date of birth, height, weight, eye color, sex, band

name, and number) and a photograph.[26] 'Status' is the product of
a history of superfine bureaucratic striations of the welfare state
in concert with crude endocolonialist racism, still active today in
the constructions of health knowledge about First Nations peoples
(for example, the diabetes 'epidemic'[27]).

The politics of the erasure of personal names and their
renumbering for official purposes has been described as an
exercise in 'administrative convenience.'[28] It produced individually
identifiable bodies ('tagged') through a process of animalization,
the wearable fibre disks for hanging around the neck or attached to
the wrist; this 'taxonomic' strategy was done in the interest of 'good
administration,' thereby 'transform[ing] Inuit society into a more
manageable entity.'[29] The discs themselves were rich in semiotic
overcoding. Small, circular, and fibrous, they bore the stamp of the
Crown on the center of one side around which the words 'Eskimo
Identification Canada' turned (an icon of semiotic enslavement).
All lettering was in English (national or official languages are
one of the examples Guattari used to illustrate the semiological
economies of power that set the parameters of competence and set
the means for comportment and communication[30]) and syllabics
were disregarded. The reverse side held a sequence of letters and
numbers. The discs were not the unanimous choice of interested
state representatives, but they won out over identity cards. The
initial program of disc design and their distribution in the early
1940s used individual identification numbers on each disc of up
to four digits. In addition to semiological subjection through the
symbol of State authority, official language, and numerical code,
there is a social subjection initiated through taxonomic capture
and classification. Importantly, this social subjection merely meant
that 'classification preceded experimentation.'[31] The subjection
to an exterior object was renewed, this time in 1944–45 with the
introduction of the Family Allowance Program, then a universal
system of monthly payments to families with children under the
age of 16 years. This was the occasion for the revision of the
disc number protocol to include geographic/spatial identifiers
prior to the personal identifiers: twelve districts and two regions
segmented the Arctic – initially nine in the East and three in the

West; they grew to 14 in the 1950s.[32] These identification districts were represented in the form of E(ast) or W(est) and a number between 1 and 12 indicating place of birth, followed by a four-digit personal identifier ('E' is neither 'electronic' nor 'Eskimo'). The aforementioned Frobisher Bay was E7. Geographic striation into registration districts created manipulable categories (abstract placeholders) open to experimental combinatorics that accelerated during the 1950s (actual population relocations to bleak locations being the most severe). These were subjections to disciplinary calculations of federal welfare expenditures – rising – in relation to alleged sites of employment opportunities – falling – conceived with complex references to Cold War technological development; and earlier – for example, the landing strip at Frobisher Bay, built in 1941 as a stopover point for US military flights to Europe; and, specifically, Distant Early Warning Systems installations in Canada's Arctic, opportunities for resource extraction and geological surveys, livestock raising schemes (a steady stream of sheep and pigs went north in the 1950s, but livestock farming simply didn't work in the Arctic) art commodification programs, sovereignty jitters in Canada's North, and estimations of fluctuating game reserves, to name only a few.[33] The salient point is that the technical machines of the state shift enslavement to subjection.[34] Inuit were subjected to the technical machines of capitalist expansion in the North, with humanist apologies provided by the state's welfare policies and 'well-intentioned' experiments (during the 1920s 'confusion' reigned about who was responsible for Inuit;[35] it was in 1939 that the federal government assumed 'responsibility' for them, a Supreme Court decision that did not go down well; and in the 1951 and 1970 Indian Acts, Inuit were excluded[36]). Even today, the pollution from Second World War and Cold War militarization is bringing federal government 'remediation' money and short-term employment to the Arctic. It is not unusual to peer into the waters around Iqaluit and see a submerged parking lot of military vehicles.

The militarization of the Arctic in the 1940s and 1950s by the US Air Force and RCAF was the most important factor in the introduction of a historic striation, the temporary wage economy. Deleuze and Guattari explicitly link work to military organization, both through the appropriation of the war machine and the 'nullification of smooth space,'[37] but also through the state organization of armies and the production of surpluses in the form of stockpiles – weapons industries. In the case of the Inuit the link is incomplete. On top of traditional range patterns of Inuit groups (not strictly nomadic but structured by base camps and trap lines and shifting hunting groups), the clusterings produced by the locations of missions and trade posts, free or forced adjustments to trap-line patterns and locations, not to mention the centralizing influences of earlier whaling stations, the military installations created significant 'contractions' that were at odds with existing policies of population dispersal advocated by the Hudson's Bay Company at least from the 1920s to the 1950s, before forced relocation became a government policy by which state welfare could be administered (further, the residential school system was created, as well as vocational training programs for the minting of new proletarians). Pressures from federal welfare programs such as the Old Age Pension Act (1927) were not felt in the Arctic until decades later, due to uneven distributions of funds. The overwhelming evidence is of a policy cluster against the settlement of Inuit, despite the pressures for 'in-gathering' that had been building for decades. Paternal visions of 'native life,' supported by epidemiological worries about Inuit health amid the squalor around the bases, as well as the specter of post-construction unemployment in settlements around military and other installations and RCMP concerns about social instabilities, continued to 'discourage aggregations,' despite the effects of the wage economy at such places as Frobisher, Cambridge Bay, and elsewhere and, by the 1960s, the centralizations of populations produced by government welfare, loans, housing (the DEW Line brought subsidized housing with it, even if the housing consisted of styrofoam igloos, that is, simulated igloos[38]), health programs, and resource extraction of the so-called 'Diefenbaker vision' (John Diefenbaker was Canadian prime minister from 1957 to 1963).[39] Aggregation was necessary for population surveillance and efficient program delivery and administration. Aggregation, one might say, is space-time striation, on its way to generalized machinic enslavement, whose perfection and 'absolute speed,' in turn, is to be reconstituted as smooth capitalist space.

De- and Re-coded Flows

All apparatuses of capture release 'decoded flows.' Such flows are overflows or escape flows appearing beside and beyond the codes that give rise to them.[40] But the flows do not simply escape, for they are knotted together (conjoined, recoded, netted, determinate), and then in turn escape once more out the holes in the nets. The distinction between the conjoining of topical becomings and an abstract, generalized conjunction – the general axiomatic of decoded flows that is capitalism – is decisive, for a 'new threshold' is thus reached.[41]

This process is evident in the case of disc numbers: the subordination of Inuit cultural naming practices to administrative overcodings – capturing them by making naming functional, that is, regularizing naming, for bureaucratic sorts – in the form of the disc numbering and related systems that synthesize identity in new and bizarre connections (for example, personal numbers with their geographic striations are connected with estimates of shrinking caribou populations and thus groups were forcibly relocated from one place to another regardless of other considerations, including long-term survival). Resignification slips through the nets of overcoding.

Resignifications of disc numbers arise because the codes that created them can no longer contain them. The overcodings that gave rise to disc numbers were displaced by a new overcoding called Project Surname, and this was a scattering force because no collection for disposal of discs was undertaken; anyway, a molar injustice of the disc system was that the number remained in the memories of each and circulated with them, finding new referential materials with which to freely attach. Some call the power of resignification 'cultural reappropriation.'[42] The issue is that decoding is already in resignification linked to new recodings. The pertinent examples are all from the 1990s and after. The correlative decodings that undoubtedly arose prior to this time are less vivid than those that are available for scrutiny today, largely because these are tied to material recodings that circulate widely. The question of the 'rarity' of such recodings cannot be definitively solved. They are limited in their effects, in the same sense that smoothings do not in themselves suffice to liberate, and with respect to Patton's interpretation, necessitate going before the court with the confidence of having made something actionable but with few means to determine the outcome.

An example is in order. In 1991 a promotional activity was staged in Iqaluit, as a fundraising event for the Elders' Society, which featured the issuing of mock discs – Q-numbers and registration certificates – aimed at Qallunaat (white people) and signed by Abe Okpik, the Inuk originally hired to undertake Project Surname.[43] The parodic tone of these mock discs constitute smoothings that communicate new values of cultural becoming. Hence, decoding attaches to mimetic recoding in parodic mode that issues from the Inuit-initiated Quallunaat Registry. This registry, unlike the DIAND-controlled and -maintained Indian Registry, does not transform the identity of the white celebrities (actors, politicians, artists, journalists, and hockey players) who participated in it, except in as much as it occurs in a different space, that of becoming – temporary, semiotically disruptive, less an exact value that commands the tools of the informatics revolution in a countervailing fashion than a refloating of hand-inscribed artifacts embedded in a site-dependent locale where the stakes have been reconstituted and redirected.

Decoded flows are rather quickly attached to recodings. The touristic artifact is a good example. The Q-certificate is politically pointed, quite unlike most tourist art; it sends a message about the ridiculousness of disc numbers to visitors who may otherwise not know the history. Some recodings succumb more readily to imposed forms and thus to a limiting 'practicality' than others. There are music industry product recodings. In 1999 and 2002, two songs of note appeared on compact discs: Susan Aglukark's 'E186' and Lucie Idlout's 'E5-770, My Mother's Name.' Both CDs graphically reproduce original discs and run strings of E-numbers as borders or frames around the artwork and lyric sheets. Both Aglukark and Idlout have family roots in Nunavut and are well known, but neither live there today, pursuing careers elsewhere. Both singers make disc numbers the subject of songs and deliver criticisms of E-numbers as theft. However, the fury with which Idlout delivers her message of animalization ('cattled E') in a clanking machinic redundancy of the government 'farming' of 'name numbers' – the same background recitation of strings of E-numbers is used by Aglukark – is dismissed in some quarters as 'youthful radicalism,' since she was not old enough to have received a disc number, unlike Aglukark, for example.[44]

In music, storytelling, cultural geography reporting, the sculptural arts, and documentary filmmaking, the reclaiming of disc numbers is under way. Surely, this is an effect of the optimism and pride in the success of the land claims process that led to the creation of the territory of Nunavut in 1999. The most significant shift is that disc numbers have become integrated into the subject matters of various works. In addition to song titles, film titles and sculptures bearing the disc numbers of their sculptors, but not as signatures, have been noted in popular publications.[45] These artistic recodings only tell part of the story, even if they are far from the overcodings that separated 'right' from 'wrong' names and used numbers in lieu of names. This phenomenon, and its supposed corrections in Project Surname, have also become a subject of interest for the Nunavut Law Review Commission's attempt to correct the corrections to Project Surname in 'Project Correction': not only misspellings, but missed registrations that snarl due to bureaucratic processes (e.g. ineligibility for old age pension benefits due to lingering uses of disc numbers on birth certificates as a result of being overlooked during Project Surname), incorrect birthdates, and mismatches between pieces of ID.[46] Compared with a use of substitute names in legal discourse in, for example, the famous adoption case 'Deborah E4-789,'[47] the work of the current law commission is confronting head-on the obstacles of the intensive violence of the past. Resmoothings have the salutary effect of exposing lingering effects of striations across generational divides.

The problem is the emission of smoothings from striations. That is the release of decoded flows beside and beyond the imprisoning striations and overcodings of informatic impositions, and the recoding of these. The decoded flows are not free, in the sense that when Inuit regain cultural naming practices and in the process resignify disc numbers, new attachments to cultural products and information systems are made and hence new subjugations arise (e.g. to commodity forms, to music product formats). Yet there is an indeterminacy to the flight of decodings. When an Inuk uses a disc number on a snowmobile bib, as an email address, as a PIN number at a cash machine, as a house number, as part of the subject of a work of art, in short, when such a number is deployed in any instance requiring a personal identifier (but not exclusively, since a personal identifier, which is partially striating, is not necessary in many potential reuses of disc numbers, such as in the purchase of lottery tickets), there is a positive and enabling engagement existing between flight and (re)capture. This is precisely how surveillance resembles stratification: both are ambivalently enabling and restrictive, beneficial and unfortunate, as Deleuze and Guattari state.[48] When informatic striations are embedded in the memories of individuals and intersect with cultural naming practices, disc numbers are externalized and find new attachments. If Inuit names are points of transition that carry some values (inspiration, fear) while erasing other specificities (holding in abeyance the recipient's gender specificity until puberty, while carrying that of the previous owner), and disc numbers, despite their 'functional' and unfortunate histories, are regained in the field of this cultural practice, they, too, communicate and constellate and connect, often with the values of irony and parody, enabling the transit of individuals into informatic matrices.[49]

After all, as Guattari reminds us, transits–transformations between striated ontological functions constitute smoothing operations par excellence and possess the power to effect 'ontological conversions.' For instance, in passing from territories to universes, the subject in the world, existentially incarnated and *grasped*, takes flight into incorporeal universes of one's own self-definition. The initial hypothesis was of a smoothness that was then striated by disc numbers and further resmoothed with qualifications. As one Inuk, Jaipiti Nungak, E9-1956, exclaimed, using a redundancy full of irony, the punchline is this: 'I am seeking the right government agency to apply to renew my disk!'[50] So often laughter accompanies the contemporary mentions of disc numbers – the humor having a local inflection, such as the person who was an 'E1' – 'only 1' – or had an 'E6' but attended school in a differently numbered region and was ironically displaced. Although many of the discs themselves have been lost over time to all but memory, today surviving discs are reappearing as personal accessories, affixed to hats and coats as pendants, and worn with pride as a kind of jewelry.

In a time of cultural renewal and innovation, resignification of disc numbers is itself a cultural smoothing marking transits, real changes of direction, intensities of tradition and its multiple interruptions, into the new social flows of Integrated World Capitalism. As these transits proliferate, smoothness homogenetically emerges. The question is no longer or so much that of intergenerational resurrection through names, but a general, largely passive process in which the striations of discontinued disc numbers find new manifestations through resignifying attachments as linear strings of identifying letters and numbers, that is, as individual or personal identifiers, for the purpose of engaging pervasive machinic networks of computer-mediated communication, which are retained and reproduced and compared in ways not so far removed from their original usage. This is largely passive, because it is not a question of development or intensification in the fields of possibility as the pure potential of decoded flows passes into actual recodings but, rather, it is more a matter of their reinsertion for pragmatic purposes in everyday transactions and activities, a point underlined by Inuit today. Still, even here there are subtle explorations of fields of possibility in parody and humor, and in the laughter they can still elicit in interpersonal communication among Inuit (it is, after all, still quite laughter-provoking to refer to someone by their disc number), and, indeed, in the injustices they revisit in protest, even in the small acts of experimenting with disc and number in different contexts.

The resignification of disc numbers in contemporary Inuit popular culture effects displacements, not a global overcoming, of semiotic subjections and machinic enslavements, and is not a coherent subcultural, oppositional practice. Rather, today, disc numbers are viable and concrete subject matters for creative adventures of cultural self-reference.

Disorganized Informatic Subjugations of Australian Aborigines

Social control of Aboriginal populations by means of dependency on narcotics, especially alcohol, is perhaps as old as the Australian nation. Historical research in Queensland, for instance, reveals that during the nineteenth century alcohol was used to manage and manipulate the Aboriginal workforce (a misnomer, since wages for Aboriginals remained 'discretionary') because it was cheap (especially when offered in lieu of wages and contracts) and could be controlled surreptitiously by a cabal of publicans, magistrates, and police, at local and state levels, with interests in generating a network of dependents and informers. This was done in support of the state's policy of disconnecting federal agencies from local Aboriginal councils, thus ensuring the 'almost monopoly control over all aspects of Aboriginal life' enjoyed by state departments in charge of Aboriginal affairs.[51]

Alcohol's handmaiden was bureaucratic inscription of Aboriginal identities. In eighteenth and nineteenth century New South Wales, the politics of inclusion and exclusion of Aboriginal communities in official statistical constructions based on data collection in the state were not easily decodable: inclusion in law did not entail counting and exclusion resulted in the partial absence of official records. Data collection was fickle and often subject to the whims of local clerks. However, state interests were served by selective bureaucratic inscriptions, since the absence of officially recorded life events helped to support the thesis not only that the Aboriginal race was disappearing but also that breaks in the official historical record made it difficult for Aboriginal activists to establish ancestry and thus to ground any sorts of claims for services and recognition based on heritage.[52]

One of many clear expressions of this official erasure at the federal level was the infamous section 127 of the Australian Constitution of 1901 (not repealed until 1967), which spelled out in no uncertain terms that 'Aboriginal natives should not be counted' in the final numbers. Demographic blankness is one thing (officially addressed by statisticians only in the early 1970s), but the relatively recent intentional destruction of existing administrative files on Aboriginal families and individuals within the Department of Indigenous Affairs is another. The 'collateral damage' caused by the disposal of large quantities of archival material is easily appreciated considering their usefulness in claims to Native Title, since 'the files that remain form the backbone of evidential records for expert witness reports' in just such cases.[53]

This is not so much an informatic extension of *terra nullius* as a contingent social informatics of Aboriginal subjugation, a disorganized bureaucratic inscription of identity, which gave rise, however slowly and unevenly, to pernicious metonyms attached to Aboriginal rights. These are noted by Tim Rowse, among others: alcohol and cash (welfare) became metonyms for the ambiguous citizenship offered to Aboriginals.[54] Further, 'citizenship through assimilation' was a metonym for acquiring a dog license.[55]

It is worth exploring these connections in greater depth: alcohol–dog license–citizenship. Australian alcohol researcher Maggie Brady has collected first-hand accounts from Aboriginal interlocutors about when the 'grog' became available, and its disastrous consequences. A commonality in the reflections of Aboriginal witnesses is the connection between citizenship rights and legal access to alcohol: 'citizenship to drink'; 'citizenship came in and that's the reason I had to go and drink.'[56]

In her introductory overview to the works of artist Sally Morgan, whose screen print *Citizenship* (1987) visualizes the connection between citizenship for Aboriginals and the collaring and registration of dogs under legislative threat, Jill Milroy explains:

> Aboriginal peoples had to apply to become 'citizens' in their own country under the *Native Citizenship Rights Act* (1944). Strict conditions applied requiring Aboriginal peoples to prove that they lived like 'whites'. They were not allowed to associate with other Aboriginal people. Citizenship papers looked similar to a passport, containing a photograph and signature. The papers had to be carried at all times and could be easily revoked. As Jack McPhee recalls: 'we used to joke about the whole thing among ourselves ... We all called our papers a Dog License. We thought that was a better name for it than Citizenship.'[57]

The dog license or dog tags animalized Aboriginals in a specific way. The counter-term adopted by Aboriginals for these tags was of course derogatory and critical of discriminatory policies aimed against them, but also revealed the implicit assumption about how citizenship was applied to them as a form of domestication – they were made into pets of the Australian family of man. That is, those who held citizenship papers were 'civilized' and 'Europeanized' and thus 'whitened' and kept on an informatic leash. In other words, they could legally access alcohol, and thus their social worlds expanded to the extent that they were permitted entry (unevenly) into hotels and bars. Hence the idea of citizenship as a passport to white society, and the purity rules that prevented newly minted Aboriginal citizens from 'consorting' with other Aboriginals, sometimes even their own siblings and parents, under threat of revocation. Even the metonym (citizenship = alcohol) could be cancelled if an Aboriginal citizen shared alcohol with non-citizen Aboriginals. In essence, the conception of citizenship at play worked on negation: in order to become a citizen, one had to renounce Aboriginality, and hence the name 'exemption certificate' that was also applied to the dog license. The exemption was one's Aboriginality; one was exempt from treatment as a non-citizen and, hence, one was supposed to enjoy the rights of white Australians (e.g. social security benefits), but only by means of renouncing one identity and assuming another, even if bureauractic recategorization could not ameliorate troubles encountered in everyday life. The effects, as noted above, were at best 'ironic,'[58] but on the plane of everyday life inflicted 'a daily turn of slights and tacit exclusions.'[59] The removal of the exemption certificate in the late 1950s and the invitation to apply the benefits of the postwar welfare state to all Aborigines still involved exclusion on the grounds of the lingering idea of a domestic yet 'other' people – nomadic and primitive Aborigines would not enjoy state benefits such as pensions and maternity benefits.

The parallels with Canada in the field of informatic subjugation are striking: Australian 'dog licenses' and Canadian Inuit 'dog tags'; exemption is a species of 'enfranchisement,' a form of assimilation and loss of indigeneity by First Nations. As far as the surveillance of First Peoples in Canada and Australia is concerned (even in the case of the administration of the use of alcohol as a form of social control), the histories of the two countries dovetail even against the stark contrasts of the former's treaty-based political history of Crown-tribal nation relations and the latter's very late recognition of native title and land rights. This is not the place to compile a list of the comparative colonial miseries of Aboriginal and First Nations experience in their respective countries.

Gorgets

Rather, the salient comparison between Canada and Australia is that informatic striation is historically tied to naming and stratifying gifting practices. The historical material concerns the practice of awarding decorative gorgets to Aboriginals both as rewards for services rendered to various branches of the government, or for special achievements and demonstration of skills, but just as often as a strategy for building alliances with reliable informants. The crescent-shaped metal plates were worn around the neck on a chain and bore inscriptions that bestowed a 'fictitious title' on the wearer, most often 'king' or 'chief,' as well as a transliterated name or invented English first name linked to an anglicized place name ('King Billy'). Although clearly implicated as an informatic inscriptive practice of an expanding endocolonialist administration throughout the century, the common use of colonial icons (emu and kangaroo) on the gorgets (as well as the coronet) also made them signifiers of imperial power. The bestowal of 'fictitious titles' has been recoded from an Aboriginal perspective not as an emblem of ridicule (mock aristocracy) and interpellation of manipulable foreign hierarchies (tools for social disorganization), but as real indicators of leadership and strength, especially under the duress of invasion: 'the "fictitious" titles were incorporated by Aboriginal people into their own language and culture'[60] in positive ways because they confirmed the power of certain individuals. This was not always the case, as undeserved titles left some open to ridicule. Although self-appointed Aboriginal leaders and self-nominated 'kings' may have been granted some authority by white officials, this did not translate into credibility within Aboriginal communities, in which the sobriquet needed a real foundation.

The ability of Aboriginal cultures to absorb and resignify informatic striations like the disc numbers and gorgets by recoding them in meaningful ways is evident in the work of contemporary self-identified Aboriginal artists like Treahna Hamm (of the Yorta Yorta clan), whose zinc breastplates (another common word for the gorgets and king plates) with sedge fringes recode significations of oppression and annihilation (gorgets were sometimes awarded to those believed the last of their kind), because they offer valuable, sometimes the only, material link to lost figures, specific places, and family members. The genealogical value of the gorgets for Aboriginal self-understanding of family, community, and place, like an 'Aboriginal heritage site' (regained, for example, in Hamm's 2005 *Barmah Forest Breastplate*[61]), cannot be underestimated in the context of the disorganized destruction and representation by the state of material evidence of Aboriginal history; evidence, that is, that would enhance the actionability of Aboriginal claims on territory and resources in the present and future tenses. Hamm's design work on the crescent plates evokes living forms, but also turns around the object's function as a stratifying distinction, at one time a death watch,[62] into a vehicle of cultural presence and survival. Moreover, the aesthetic and symbolic recodings stand over and against the official collection and display in museological contexts of genuine 'heritage' items and the state's protection of them against their auction and sale on the shifting winds of the open antiques market.[63]

With the example of Australian gorgets it is once again possible, as was the case with disc numbers, to appreciate the movements of striations and smoothings as indeterminate passages affecting mutations between heterogeneous and homogeneous domains of manifestation and possibility. In this chapter, smoothings are positioned prior to the imposition of state striations, and some of these latter are resmoothed through acts whereby autochthones regain and reinvent artifacts of endocolonial subjugation, new cultural possibilities, themselves constrained by the fields in which they intersect (the art market, music industry, administrative surveillance systems, legal struggles, etc.), each with their own striations and smoothnesses. The originary smoothness corresponds to nomadism (outside the state, and about which the latter is suspicious, wants to repress, but can't do without as a source of innovation) and not to romanticism or to primitivism. Deleuze scholars working on Australian themes have been careful to emphasize the mutual pressures of nomad and state, of smooth and striated, desert (nomos) and city (polis), rapidity as opposed to gravity; indeed, nomadism is not a racial category.[64] Recall Guattari's suggestion that when striations are smoothed, a passage from one ontological function to another takes place; resignification is regained by artists and activists even if this ends up among a variety of other striations and smoothings in the intersecting registers of contemporary global network society: the traffic engineer and the jaywalker, the systems security analyst and the hacker. The point to hold onto is that smoothings and striations are always in process (they are like passages between active and passive states), whether the passage is apprehended in terms of synchronic and diachronic temporalities, or instantiation and abstraction, manifestation and potentialization.

6

MINOR CINEMA

Guattari's most sustained comments on cinema consist of several interviews and occasional pieces dating from the 1970s gathered together in the 'Encres' edition of *La révolution moléculaire* under the title of 'Cinema: A Minor Art.'[1] While the minor is a widely discussed figure in the Deleuzo-Guattarian conceptual arsenal, it is largely confined to literature and language. All too typically, when the topic is broached in the *Deleuze Dictionary* entry 'Minoritarian + Cinema,' Guattari's independent work is completely ignored and none of his interest in militant cinema, especially its anti-psychiatric pedigree, is discussed.

For Guattari, cinema is a privileged medium for minoritarian becomings that show a specific orientation towards the progressive goals of alternative psychiatric practices linked to multiple progressive social and political movements. Guattari's approach to cinema through the minor is generally consistent with Deleuze's deployment of the anti-colonialist, revolutionary Third Cinema, which is distinguished from the first cinema of Hollywood and US finance capital and the second cinema of the auteur, which is assimilable to the first cinema's industrial model – its much vaunted independence is only a miniature version of what it seeks to escape. Third Cinema is broached in terms of how it is loosened from the shackles of representation and the yardsticks of regional authenticity, irreducible to Third World cinema (yet grounded in Latin American experience in anti-colonial struggles applicable to developed and developing and underdeveloped countries) and even to the aspirations of national cinemas.[2] While this helps to clarify the link between progressive political goals and artistic experimentation in the minor (the counter-power of variations against constants, heterogeneous deviations from homogeneous impositions of largely abstract, empty, and static redundancies), it says little about which elements of Third Cinema are relevant for Guattari's minor cinema; he did not accept the typological distinction in Third Cinema between Hollywood's industrial model and auteur cinema. In explicating the minor in Guattari's writings on cinema, critical attention will be paid to the applicability of positions articulated in Third Cinema.

Indeed, although the minor is not usually affixed to oppressed minorities (who might on a restricted view of identity author only marginal works), this does not change the fact that many people struggling with mental illness and poverty and racism – some treated in the films favored by Guattari – are, in fact, oppressed and socio-economically and psychically ghettoized. Guattari does not conflate minor and marginal. He is not of course making a socio-demographic claim, although the basis to do so surely exists in some cases. Marginal is distinguished from minor in Guattari's thought in as much as a minority (e.g. first wave gay-rights activists in the United States) refuse their marginality because it is tied to repressive recenterings on normative models (often medicalized) of sexuality and lifestyle.[3] Again, the transition from margin to minor may be used to describe numerous social movements that make significant gains for themselves and on this firmer ground are able to explore minoritarian and other becomings in the creation of new alliances. Guattari cites the example of the occupation of Lincoln Hospital in the Bronx neighborhood in New York City in the summer of 1970 by the Young Lords – a local Puerto Rican group advocating self-determination and engaging in coordinated health activism with allies like the Black Panthers, among others. Although the occupation of the long-condemned facility lasted only a few weeks, the protest action had the goal of reorienting practice away from university research and training towards serving neighborhood (rather than university) interests, agitating for a new building, linking housing and health, and reinventing the marginal as a vital force of social change and expression of collective values and tactical deterritorializations (e.g. using former drug addicts to run the detox unit). At Lincoln Hospital, the residues of marginal-become-minor would be realized later in the 1970s in the progressive and creative use of acupuncture in detox treatments.

Guattari did not elaborate a comprehensive theory of the cinema. In fact, he discusses few films in depth. The few he did treat in detail tell us that his approach cannot be contained by all of the categories of Third Cinema – he mixed and matched Hollywood with examples of European auteurs on the basis of critical psychiatric concepts while cleaving to some key ideas of militant filmmaking, even while implicitly criticizing the Third Cinema's unanalyzed pretentions of the 'selective detachment'[4] of an intellectual vanguard which discovers cinema's liberatory potential and demystifies it for the masses. Still, there is something of this spirit of politics in Guattari's working out of the minor's connectivity in a progressivist voice, indeed, in film's ability to give voice to workers themselves; but he doesn't explicitly discuss the Third Cinema theory or films of Fernando Solanas and Octavio Getino, and how they take up favorably Chris Marker's experiments in France to empower workers to film their own realities: 'the goal was to have the worker film [using 8mm equipment after some basic instruction] *his way of looking at the world, just as if he were writing it.*'[5] There are, however, similar examples at play in Guattari's thinking about cinema.

Guattari is interested in how minor arts assist in connecting those not usually considered to be oppressed with subjugated groups, and thus in defining a minor line of flight that goes somewhere and not only gets the word out but is heard – and eventually brings supportive people back with it. However, this doesn't reduce cinema to recruitment, either, for the connectivity at stake can be to the molecular features of film – sounds, colors, rhythms, etc. – that are not bleached and dissipated, but allowed to multiply and connect and serve as relays between hitherto non-communicating groups, even progressive groups, that have not yet found a mutual consistency. Of course, political consciousness-raising is a basic feature of both Third and minor cinemas. Solidarity building is not, however, reducible to making art politically functional, although the foundation of Third

Cinema is the unity of politics and culture in the service, not of a passive representation of events, but of activist interventions that emphasize experimentation (new forms of expression) and transformation (of a situation) that are not readily recuperable within the terms of a dominant power's need for manageable examples of negativity adequate to its artificial reproduction. This is not a demand for meta-critical reflection, but an opportunity that emerges through situations and conditions and is seized upon by actors, audiences, and filmmakers alike.

Minor cinema's affinities with Third Cinema need to be taken with care. There is some continuity at the level of film praxis with a *cinema without bosses*, that is, of 'total filmmakers,'[6] as Solanas insisted, not directors, stars, studio mandarins, and long lines of specialists, but revolutionaries prepared to tackle all of the dimensions of film production. To the extent that Guattari valorized a democratization of production and responsible documentation, he is in line with Third Cinema objectives. While Solanas theorized that Third Cinema could not be fictional – like the bourgeois preoccupation with love that he criticized in the French cinema, displaying a classic leftist puritanism[7] – he did debunk the fiction/documentary opposition, by allowing for the introduction or re-creation of situations in documentary works. Guattari did not take this route, instead selecting from a mixture of films and styles and directors, having no compunction about noting his favorites – Lynch, Bellochio, among others. For Solanas, Third Cinema was ideally a *cinema without signatures*, in which works in progress, and anonymous masterpieces, were not weighed down by names. Guattari liked to drop names, but was consonant of their impact; on one occasion he even regretted lumping an old militant together with right-wing politician Le Pen.[8] The point here is not to expose Guattari's weaknesses, but simply to point out that his tendency to list names, as he does with both film titles and directors, necessitates critical parsing and in no way corresponds to the imported categories of Third or any other cinema.

Deleuzean film critics point out that the major statements of Third Cinema by Solanas and Getino, as well as Julio García

Espinosa's 'For an Imperfect Cinema,' are 'movements' in which nomadic cinema participates,[9] not in terms of representation, but along political lines of becoming, inside of colonial situations, working against mastery, towards imperfection, carving out sites of struggle whose effects make beautiful, celebratory, commercial cinema with stars in its eyes, and imported abstract standards take flight, peeling back commercial cinema's layers of self-sufficiency and narcissism.[10]

Fifteen years after publishing 'For an Imperfect Cinema,' Espinosa clarified that one of the stakes of imperfection in a cinema of struggle was to find an audience not yet formed and that perhaps never will be denumerable, but will hopefully 'become conscious and participate with those who are making changes.'[11]

Always changing shape, deviating, experimenting, giving the slip to dominant representations – what if Freud would have accepted Mr. Goldwyn's offer of $100,000 to put his case histories on the screen? asks Guattari in horror.[12] A minoritarian audience, following Espinosa, 'isn't the one that is participating in the changes, or isn't even potentially able to do so';[13] it is an audience in formation, that still needs to be invented, that cannot be counted nor counted on in advance, but is becoming through contact with the vital part-signs of minor cinema's explorations of madness and commitment to struggle. Deleuze confronts the same problem as Espinosa: the people are missing in modern political cinema. This is political cinema's minor condition and the condition of minority's political predicament, and the task of the filmmaker is to sow the 'seeds of the people to come,' to 'prefigure' a people.'[14] In Deleuze the minor erases the distance between the private and political. This is especially the case in films concerning mental health in which the social character of illness, and the state of the family, is immediate. The political multiplies with the private, and people multiply to infinity; so the filmmaker becomes a movement amongst other movements with no unifying consciousness. Yet the prefiguration of a people is carried by the filmmaker's work, which, Deleuze explains, catalyzes by expressing potential forces and collectively assembling movements (because there is no divide between the private and political); and in Third Cinema this is accomplished by exposing the dual impossibilities of living under the yoke of colonialism and raising the consciousness of a unified people, because neither unity (undifferentiated) nor a people to come (multitude) exist.

Guattari did not straightforwardly valorize documentary cinema, even though he cites a significant number of such films. His interest in a wide variety of documentary works within the stream of the anti-psychiatry movement leads him to criticize the same defects in them that he found in the movement itself and its stars – a creeping familialist analysis (Oedipalism), reformist sentiments, a reactionary countercultural abdication of concrete struggle, and a taste for spectacle. Even this level of criticism was tempered by exceptions, such as the cinematic works dealing with the Italian situation of the movement and the institutional experiments of guerrilla psychiatrist Franco Basaglia.

Thinking the Minor

Let's turn to the theorization of the minor and then consider how it conjoins with a cinema whose overt content is anti-psychiatric in the broadest sense of the term.

From *A Thousand Plateaus* we learn that minorities are opposed to axioms. An axiomatic describes how a system like capitalism works directly on decoded flows (the condition in which capital can become anything without regulatory reference points) regardless of their specific characteristics, domains in which they are realized, and relations between such elements. The axiomatic is thus immanent (and not transcendent or perfect and thus closed) to the decoded flows and thus more flexible than coding operations, which are attached to specific domains and establish rules for relations among their elements. An axiomatic is aligned with the models of realization through which it is effectuated; the models differ widely but are all isomorphic with such an axiomatic (e.g. all the different types of states and capitalisms). In this sense the axiomatic capitalism may add new axioms in response to events or in order to master certain kinds of flows, and also subtract axioms. The nation state, in all its remarkable diversity, is one model of realization for the capitalist axiomatic, which Deleuze and Guattari note has the task of 'crushing' its own minorities in an effort, for instance, to manage nationalist aspirations.[15] Minorities are not easily quashed, but they are captured in the name of an axiomatic of the majority that is countable and modeled by a standard form. A minority is not countable and thus has nothing to do with the smallness or largeness of its numbers, but rests on the production of connections between its elements. To the extent that the axiom of the majority manipulates countable elements, non-countable minorities elude its grasp. Minorities are not definitively non-axiomizable. New axioms are introduced in order to translate them into majoritarian clusters (e.g. granting them some political autonomy and thereby integrating them as entities in a political union). The power of minorities rests with the multiplication of connections among their elements and the forging of lines of escape and errant trajectories, even though the assertion of such powers through demands against the countable (e.g. rights, territory, self-government) generates new axioms. It is not only a question of managing minorities at some point on a continuum between two extreme poles (extermination or integration), but also of the axiomatic's constitution of them, of that which remains just beyond its grasp in asserting the power of the countable. In abstract terms, the opposition that Deleuze and Guattari posit is between *revolutionary connections* of becoming minor available for all and the *conjugations of the axiomatic* that inflect and fix the flows.[16]

For Guattari, cinema is a minor art that

> perhaps serves the people who constitute a minority, and this is not at all pejorative. A major art is at the service of power ... A minor cinema [is] for minorities ... and for the rest of us, too, since all of us participate in these minorities in one way or another.[17]

A minor cinema precipitates minoritarian becomings in the mass. The minor is a 'universal figure'[18] in the sense that everybody becomes and becoming minor is universal.[19] And to become minor is not to be in a minority or the representative of a minority, or even to formally acquire the characteristics or status of a minority through some such affiliation as spouse, expert, or even informant. It is not a question of mimesis or membership.

Minorizing the Cinema

How is cinema minorized? How does it produce becomings which summon a people with whom it connects? The fundamental theoretical problem here is at the heart of what it means to summon a new people outside of a political or messianic telos.

In order to answer this question, we need to turn to some of the films that Guattari discussed within the terms of both the European anti-psychiatry movement and under the general heading of a cinema attuned to mental illness. But a mad cinema does not have a clinical, criteriological character, to be sure; rather, it can open up the exploration of anyone's anoedipal becomings and in the process transform normopathic subjects into the molecularly and inclusively, but non-specifically, mad – not in accordance with a model, but by getting in touch with certain affective intensities made available through specific cinematic works. Guattari lamented what he described as the popular 'taste for morbidity' that brought psychiatric patients to the big screen in the early 1970s. This sudden interest in madness was for him subsumable under the same impulse that made pornography and cop stories so successful. Less dejectedly, though, he thought that non-spectacular (not on the order of May '68) molecular disturbances – 'soft subversions' – across the socio-political spectrum were causing primary institutions of socialization to decay and reorganize themselves, and this was picked up on by filmmakers, some of whom caught wind of developments in the anti-psychiatry and other social movements and took them beyond the discourses of professionals (analysts, doctors, and nurses) as well as psychiatric survivors. In this Guattari didn't pay much attention to Hollywood hits like *Catch-22* (Mike Nichols, 1970) that staged madness as a volatile category to be occupied – even with its attendant dangers – but did not themselves work with its potentialities. To be fair, a film such as *One Flew Over the Cuckoo's Nest* (Milos Forman, 1975) did connect the denizens of the ward – who were under the deathly Oedipal manipulations (the imprint is so unbearable that it leads to one character's suicide) of Nurse Ratched and the violent electroshock 'treatments' and lobotomies authorized by Doctor Spivey – with an outside in a remarkable bus and boat ride; it is upon returning from an interrupted fishing trip that trouble really starts, because the reality that was gained during the adventure was lost.[20] Yet both of these films only play at becoming mad through calculable odds, another of R.P. McMurphy's – actor Jack Nicholson's memorable ne'er-do-well – wagers.

Guattari triumphed any cinema that provided the means for the multitude to connect with the struggles it communicated, but not in the form of an ideological conversion or the dictates of a leadership caste; in the same spirit, I look at cinematic political work in social context, without privileging specific genres or styles or directors or films of sociological interest, and without excluding the popular, no matter how unappealing this may be for some film purists.

This approach simultaneously involves demystifying big-studio representations of social issues (reduced to an order word like the classic 'catch-22' – a general description of the knots of bureaucratic reason that bind the becoming mentally ill of Captain Yosarian) and the pseudo-objectivity of cinema verité, which puts the struggles of minorities under its lens instead of putting the combatants and agitators themselves behind the camera lens. This is key to understanding Guattari's favorable mention of films like Martin Karmitz's *Coup pour coup* (1972), in which non-professional actors who were engaged in a protracted labor struggle in a textile factory created a document of their own actions. Guattari is comfortable, then, with a core idea of militant cinema: democratization of the means of production, specifically overcoming the barriers of specialization, technical, and cost challenges – putting cameras into the hands of workers. A film camera is a machine for proletarian subjectivity's continuous reinvention of itself. Guattari did go further and conceive, as Solanas and Getino had, of spectatorship in an active mode as a vehicle of alternative distribution, making each screening an opportunity for participation.[21]

A further example of this democratization and autonomization of the means of cinematic production in the service of summoning a people to come is found in Guattari's short reflection on hyper-dense urban life in the Sanya district of Tokyo, where foreign and day laborers live under the yoke of organized gangs. In 'Tokyo, the Proud,' Guattari notes in passing that he received an invitation from the Aid and Mutual Action Committee of Sanya and took a guided tour 'to the place where the Yakuzas assassinated Sato Mitsuo, and paid homage to this progressive filmmaker who investigated the Japan of the disenfranchised, precarious and rebellious.'[22]

Many of Sanya's foreign and day laborers may be counted as part of a growing homeless population; others dwell in cheap rooming houses, although the degree of permanence varies. Those who find temporary employment in the construction industry or as longshoremen are ruthlessly exploited. The neighborhood is divided into territory controlled by the Kanamachi family gang (though this is not the only gang), which exploits the cheap labor and the ways in which earnings are disposed, and the Sanya Dispute League, which supports the workers, and engages in militant anti-yakuza activities.[23]

The cinematic significance of Sanya is that Mitsuo, a Japanese documentary film director known for his social activism, was murdered during the making of his 1985 film *Yama: An Eye for an Eye*; the colloquial name for Sanya is Yama. The film follows the struggles of the district's day laborers to organize themselves, and the clashes they had with the local yakuza family, which led to the stabbing to death not only of Mitsuo. Yamaoka Kyoichi was a labor activist who took up the reigns of the project and saw it through to its completion after Mitsuo's murder. The tragic situation that unfolded is recounted in an interview about Sanya with Japanese media activist Ueno Toshiya, conducted by journalist Krystian Woznicki.[24]

Toshiya explained that his first visit to Sanya was with Guattari in 1985. He met Guattari through his involvement with the 'free' mini-FM station Radio Homerun, and an entourage of activists, artists, and public intellectuals toured key sites in Tokyo. However,

> our guide was Yamaoka Kyoichi, who, after the assassination of Sato, continued the production. I remember him very vividly. He was very kind and helpful in explaining the history of Sanya, its importance in the urban landscape, etc. Unfortunately he was also killed by organized crime.

The double murder of *Yama*'s two directors – the second before the film's premiere – at the hands of killers contracted by local mobsters reveals the danger of a kind of documentary film that is deeply embedded in local struggles. Mitsuo himself declared that

> it will take two years to complete this film. During that period we will stay in the *yoseba* [gathering place for urban day laborers; in yakuza slang the word means 'prison'[25]], making a living from day labor as you do. It is not our intention to film you with an irresponsible attitude.[26]

This strategy of immersion into the struggles of day laborers in order to ethically grasp their marginality, extortion by labor brokers and middle-men illegally extracting their fees, black marketeering yakuzas dealing in unemployment insurance stamps, the ravages of winter for the homeless, and murderous violence, answers Guattari's idea of establishing through film praxis a direct connection with concrete social realities, even if the stakes can be very high. A becoming minor may be effectuated in this instance through an ethics of film praxis that is built around respect for subjects and responsibility for the creation of documents.

Guattari illustrated his positions on cinema with reference to selected films that transcended their overt representational content – being about mental illness – but showed in their very modes of expression a schizo sensibility in direct touch with the real. This is not a matter of technical prowess, but an acute awareness of the textures of psychosis. For instance, Guattari, in a highly contentious interview, discusses at length Terence Malick's *Badlands* (1973) as a film displaying the effects of *amour fou*: 'the story is only there to serve as support for a schizophrenic journey.'[27] This position does not correspond with Malick's own views, which Guattari acknowledges, and in addition flies in the face of its critical reception and modeling of characters on 'lost children in a state of nature', or more obviously on the mythological hero – James Dean – 'Kit' played by actor Martin Sheen. Perhaps Edgar Morin was right that James Dean's immortality survives in a 'thousand mimetisms.'[28] This would entail that the character Kit was trapped by an image, an identity that preceded him, and in pursuit of which he went off the rails. There are undoubtedly better examples. Instead, Guattari rejects the mimetic reading and insists that Kit did not evolve into madness but was from the outset plugged into pre-personal flows of desire already located in a becoming the intensity of which could not be managed. In this respect Kit was an abstraction from the intensities of *amour fou* released by Holly (actress Sissy Spacek), and the film is marked by vivid a-signifying part-signs – intense blues, bizarre behaviors, border crossings – in support of the schizo journey. Guattari does not provide many examples; he does not present a full reading of the film, because he is too busy defending himself against an unsympathetic interviewer. Still, his few observations are astute: the blue skies of the prairie appear throughout the film and are at times, as he insisted, 'distressing' in their intensity;[29] Kit displays bizarre behaviors all along the voyage – shooting a football (and unsuccessfully shooting at some fish) with his revolver; constantly collecting and throwing stones; he stands on top of a dead cow and tests the springiness of its bloated body; when he and Holly retreat to a hideaway in the woods, the broken toaster that Kit found earlier, after dragging the dead body of Holly's father into a basement room, is seen abandoned in the grass behind a makeshift chicken coop. Kit brought this toaster with him as they fled from Holly's family home, which he had set ablaze; it is one of the little machines that gets him on his deterritorializing way into marginal spaces. Kit is wrapped up in these perversions – these desiring connections that appear throughout the film – but he gets them to work with Holly (e.g. by throwing stones at her, or by bringing the toaster along to their hideaway, built in a tree in a cottonwood grove and with no electricity). A totally non-functional item is connected with a tree house and a campsite and a chicken and a revolver and a rifle and Holly, too, in a great meshwork of productive breaks and flows – an aggregate schizomachine of disparate parts.

A-signifying Cinematic Part-signs

Guattari's sense of minorization rests on the capacity of a-signifying part-signs. For Guattari, commercial cinema not only serves the interests of corporate power, as a vehicle through which docile models of subjectivity are communicated by means of dominant signifying semiologies, but it also reveals beyond its dominant features (star system, studio moguls, static genres) militant becomings in the socio-political effects of its technological organization. Guattari sought a direct and efficacious contact between semiotic and material fluxes, which he found in the free-radio movement, for instance, or in the promise of super-8, inexpensive video cameras, easy to use editing software programs, etc.[30] The directness between semiotic and material fluxes (intense and multiple) is not diverted into a sphere of representation or signification (psychical quasi-objects like the Saussurean sign consisting of sound image and concept) that results in their mutual cancellation, which is how Guattari characterizes the condition of the subject in both structuralism and psychoanalysis; instead, the a-signifying particles, the most deterritorialized types of signs (not fully formed but part-signs), provide lines of escape from the snares of representation, and they '"work" things prior to representation.'[31]

In the Lacanian formula – 'a signifier represents the subject for another signifier' – a signifier is haunted by the latency of the paradigmatic (associative) relations of terms in opposition. Following Žižek,[32] on its own a signifier means nothing; but in addition its presence is tempered or set against its own possible absence and thus the presence of its opposite, with the proviso that this presence is not direct, because, vice versa, the opposite term is set against the background of its possible absence, which is occupied by the presence of its opposite. This is for Guattari a 'duplicitous' conception of the subject, because a signifier represents another signifier by holding open a void space in which its possible absence is filled by its opposite (another signifier), and this lack is the subject barred (simultaneously represented and not-represented by a signifier to infinity if all signifiers reveal this lack – at least until a master phallic signifier appears that represents the subject's failure of representation in all other signifiers).

Guattari wants to outflank representation and its failures predicated upon language altogether by focusing on a-signifying semiotics. And these signs play an important role in cinema. Guattari writes:

> It it equally important to underline and insist on the independent status of what are called a-signifying semiotics. This will allow us to understand what permits cinema to escape from semiologies of signification and participate in collective assemblages of desire.[33]

First of all, recall that signifying semiologies are based on dominant systems of encoding, such as non-verbal codes, speech, and writing and thus constitute stable 'centering' codes of fully formed substances indexed on individuated subjects (even if the non-verbal is, it is claimed, universally translatable into a linguistic-based semiology, and the letter insists in the unconscious!). Guattari clarifies that a-signifying part-signs 'break the effects of significance and interpretance, thwart the system of dominant redundancies, accelerate the most '"innovative," "constructive," and "rhizomatic" components.'[34] While signifying semiologies want to find meaning everywhere, and therein refuse any independence to a-signifying semiotics, which can function without them (but may make tactical use of them), Guattari resists embalming cinema in meaning, that is, in transcendent narratives and syntagmatic/paradigmatic chains of relations and clusters. Instead, he proposes that these incomplete part-signs, which are not interpretable and centered on the signifier, but are expressive of the unformed signaletic matter of cinematic images, trigger a becoming minor in those sensitive to their encounter with them. Dynamic cinematic part-signs trigger minoritarian becomings in the same way thought is forced or shocked in an immanent encounter. This is perhaps the most innovative dimension of Deleuzean philosophy of film: his focus on what arises or is produced in a subject's encounter with signs, this 'shock to thought' speaking to the continuity between mind and matter as bodies are forced to think and this thought is itself real, not merely about reality.

A-signifying fragments populate the cinema as colors (or in black and white), non-phonic sounds, rhythms, facility traits, in short, in manifold modalities and expressive matters that are open, Guattari specifies, to 'multiple systems of external intensities.'[35] One doesn't connect with these ideologically, but rather is transported by them, moved into new universes of reference, because one's existential territory has been enriched by them. Such expressive matters, claims Guattari, quoting Christian Metz, have unbounded matters of content or 'semantic tissue' that run beyond the reach of signifying semiologies and the dominant values that their encodings presume, such as stereotypes (e.g. 'normal,' likeable, characters, and model families) and behaviors (e.g. going to school, cooperating with authority).[36] By the same token, Guattari adds that the textures and traits of expressive matter at the disposal of filmmakers elude stabilizing codes or deep syntaxes that might still the restless deployment of heterogeneous semiotics and their creative constellations.

Cinema emits a-signifying part-signs that trigger the desire to follow their leads. But what does this mean for film criticism? A good example is Laleen Jayamanne's discussion of Spike Lee's *Do The Right Thing* (1989).[37] Jayamanne displays acute attention to non-narrative rhythms and textures through the work of a-signifying signs in the film's visual and aural fluxes, focusing on the staking of territories by means of a sonic motif – blasts of Public Enemy's 'Fight the Power' from Radio Raheem's boom box – and the dilly-dallying of Mookie in the sinuous everyday life on the block. These a-signifying particles have the power to throw one into minoritarian becomings that cannot be captured by the stock discourse of racial violence that took the film hostage shortly after its premiere. The analysis of Hollywood liberalism, which both Jayamanne and Guattari undertake, exposes its latent racism.

Cinema, Guattari wrote, 'intevenes directly in our relations with the external world'[38] and influences the semioticizations of viewers. But these interventions also happen imperceptibly, behind the scenes, as it were. Dominant values can be attacked in a variety of ways within film praxis.

Guattari selected key early films by directors whose importance has grown over time as vital to minoritarian cinematic becomings. He enthusiastically endorsed David Lynch who, in *Eraserhead*, has made 'the greatest film on psychosis, alongside *Fists in the Pocket* by Marco Bellocchio. I find these two films overwhelming.'[39] Neither of these films qualified in their time as strictly 'commercial'; for Guattari this degraded form of cinema was reactionary – a drug whose trip is adaptation.[40] Guattari's focus on the minor within a diverse range of engaged cinemas runs all the way from the emotional textures of collective creation in *Germany in Autumn* (Alf Brustellin, Hans Peter Cloos, et al., 1978), which exposes the role of the mass-mediatic machine in distributing subjugating affects, through its reportage of acts of armed struggle in Germany in the late 1970s, staging the Manichean confrontation between a 'monstrous state power and pathetic politico-military apparatuses,'[41] to the documentary style of Raymond Depardon in *Urgences* (1988), which in 20 sequences shot at the emergency psychiatric service at Hôtel-Dieu in Paris not only interpellates viewers into the alienations and deceits of intake interview situations with psychotherapists and those suffering from everything from dereliction to psychosis, but Guattari believed that 'the spectacle of these existential ruptures works directly upon our own lines of fragility.'[42] Indeed, while struggling with his own depression, Guattari was deeply moved by the suicide of the *soixante-huitard* in Romain Goupil's *Mourir à trente ans (Half a Life)* (1982).

Cinemas of Anti-psychiatry

Guattari's overt interest was in a cinema of madness. During the late 1960s and early 1970s, a number of films were produced which were loosely aligned with the progressive goals of the anti-psychiatry movement that crossed genres and even called into question anti-psychiatry itself as a reformist endeavor bewitched by representations of its schizo-superstars (Mary Barnes), infatuated by the next moves of its sages (R.D. Laing), and the legacies of its failed experimental communities (e.g. Kingsley Hall and Pavillon 21 in London). Although Guattari was frustrated by Laing's retreat from real psychiatric struggles, he did not completely eschew him; Laing's insight into schizophrenia as a breakthrough into an excess of reality remained vital to Guattari's and Deleuze's sense of the possibilities of a materialist psychiatry and a critique of psychoanalysis. By the same token, Guattari preferred David Cooper's authenticity to the countercultural veil many other anti-psychiatrists drew over their real analytic interests, and once praised Cooper to the effect that he 'did not in any way deny madness,' that is, did not attach a regressive ball and chain to it.[43] Guattari also qualified his praise by pointing out that psychotic production is arrested by a creeping familialism *even in Cooper*.[44] Despite Guattari's criticisms, he participated in projects with both Laing and Cooper and was active in the European Network of Alternatives to Psychiatry during its heyday in the early 1970s.

Let's consider some filmic examples mentioned by Guattari. Peter Robinson's film about Laing, *Asylum* (1972), is included in a list of films headed by the important *Fous à délier* that inaugurates something new – a minor cinema. *Asylum*, Guattari thought, found a significant audience and 'indirectly revealed an anti-psychiatric current.'[45] Minor cinema probes a potential public, a public yet to come, with which it attempts to connect by bringing its a-signifying part-signs flush with sensibilities not yet entangled in dominant modelizations of identity and social relations. The study of how subjectivity is modeled, Guattari noted, is really the sole question of schizoanalysis. Guattari enlisted minoritarian becomings – which can be called 'affective contaminations'[46] – released by the cinema of anti-psychiatry for schizoanalysis's criticism of standard systems of modelization, but not toward the erection of a general model; rather, 'as an instrument for deciphering systems of modelization in diverse domains, in other words, a meta-model' of subjectivity's autopoietic formation in context, through the assemblage of heterogeneous coordinates and the discovery of consistency among its components by means of refrains – those felicitous 'existential communicators' (any iterative compositions) catalyzing passages into new universes of reference.[47] Minor cinema can and must contribute to a practical self-enrichment that comes through some of the features already outlined above in terms of semiotics and film praxes.

The documentary *Asylum* undoubtedly impressed Guattari because of the intimacies of the household dramas it revealed in true verité style, right down to the exposed microphones, in the context of Laing's post-Kingsley experiment in community care, Archway House. The commitment of the filmmakers was evident in as much as they stayed in the therapeutic community for six weeks during the filming (echoing Mitsuo's commitment), and over this period they not only recorded but played active roles in the group problem solving sessions. This community was itself questioning existing models of community and family and struggled with its own alternative auto-modelizations through the episodes of its key denizens: Julia's reversion to childhood, her departure and return; David's efforts to dominate the household through incessant verbalization and violent outbursts. One psychiatrist tries to get through David's defensive stream of nonsensical verbalizations with a Freudian incantation about his dislike of all the younger brothers' access to him, which understandably creates frustration and leads to his violent outbursts. This wears David down. In the final scene we see a discussion with David, who has dropped his incessant talking, and he answers questions about his past (his job as a computer programmer, and designer of switches for power stations, which contextualizes some of his ramblings about ohms), the failed community of friends in which he was involved that precipitated his hospitalization before coming to Archway, etc. This is not so much an abstract resolution as an accomplishment of the group, who together insisted that David take personal responsibility for his actions in the house they shared and ran together – this is a component that emerges and forms an important part of the social pragmatics of the schizoanalytic approach of the generative type aiming at the production of new competencies, exploiting what Guattari dubbed 'situational potentialities',[48] by breaking the wall of clichés and fragments of speech that assisted David in not listening. The quiet dialogue at the kitchen table with David, brilliantly contrasted with an earlier night scene shot in an empty kitchen, but filled with David's loud yelling and thumping and arguing, shows the simplicity of the new transformation without assigning its diagnosis to the taboo around a central figure, for instance; although *Asylum* is not a didactic schizoanalysis, it does follow a schizoanalytic process of assisting in the discovery of passages between assemblages by releasing blockages (rather than, in transformational schizo-analytic mode, of creating new assemblages altogether).[49]

Guattari was most interested in the Italian strain of anti-psychiatric activity, particularly the work of Basaglia and members of the Psichiatrica Democratica movement, who remained committed to a public system of healthcare rather than a retreat into private facilities, despite the cornerstone of 'the negation of the institution.' Anti-institutional struggle in Italy was necessary owing to the archaic nature of the asylum system and absence of patients' rights. An institution is negated, Basgalia explained, 'when it is turned upside down, and when its specific field of activity is called into question and thereby thrown into crisis.'[50] While Guattari remained suspicious of this strategy, not because he believed that the hospitals in Gorizia and Parma were not totally repressive, but because negation was not sufficiently anchored in extra-institutional social reality and tended to result in a denial or suppression of madness – in short, that negation overwhelmed madness, too.[51] Yet to read Basaglia is to acknowledge immediately that the institutional experiments in 'negative thinking' undertaken by him parallel those of Guattari and Jean Oury at La Borde. Certainly the daily collective assembly at Gorizia, in which patients and staff met voluntarily in a dehierarchized environment in which roles and uniforms were abandoned and topics for discussion came from the floor, were disorganized and at times confrontational; they were not as tightly semioticized as the table of work rotations on display at La Borde – the abstract machine that diagrammed that clinic. Notwithstanding this chaos, this was for many the first occasion they had to voice their concerns and needs and have them heard. It was the translation of these individual demands into a collective assumption of responsibly that could be addressed by changes in the institution itself. This assumption of responsibility was not abstract, because the assembly was empowered to make decisions about discharges and work placements, and took collective responsibility for problems relating to the criminal actions of those whose discharge it had authorized (even if this was unusual).[52]

Guattari praises the 'exceptional' film *Fous à délier* made by the March 11 Collective (Silvano Agnosti, Marco Bellocchio, Sandro Petraglia, Stefano Rulli, 1976) about the hospital in Parma – to which Basaglia had moved in 1969.[53] Guattari focuses largely on the youth and women in the film, because their recounting of experiences of psychiatric repression in the hospital and triumphs in everyday life on the outside are the most moving; but he also notes how labor activists have come to integrate the psychiatricized and ex-patients into their political projects. This connection between mental health and industrial workers and patients was for Guattari one of the most remarkable features of the documentary, because it provided evidence of new alliances across otherwise non-communicating sectors of the progressive political spectrum; Guattari later clarified his opinion: 'the idealist character of these experiments makes one smile these days, considering the development of increasingly computerized and robotized industries, yet the global aims of the Italians remain sound.'[54] Further, Guattari considered the film as demonstrating that 'a militantism of everyday life ... undoubtedly constitutes the only way to move public opinion in the direction of supporting a radical transformation of "state" psychiatry.'[55]

What is also interesting is that Guattari's praise for *Fous à délier* is marked by provisos that he adds near the end of his short discussion. These should be read as general comments about how he tempers his enthusiasm for progressive documentary work in the anti-psychiatric milieu – that 'truth' doesn't always come from the people, even if he is convinced that repression almost always comes from the caregivers; that good intentions and community actions are not enough to ameliorate the suffering of the mentally ill; and that there are pressing issues within psychiatric hospital practice that need urgent revision. Moreover, for Guattari, *Fous à délier* continues the earlier work of Bellocchio in *Fists in the Pocket (Les poings dans les poches)* (1965). Together these films register and fling centrifugally traces of the molecular disturbances of the status quo underway throughout the network of alternative psychiatric practices throughout Europe and, to a lesser extent, North America. I want to return to *Fists in the Pocket* in Chapter 7.

Guattari's minor cinema is catalyzed by the schizo process. His high but, unfortunately, passing praise for Lynch's *Eraserhead*, for example, is evident enough in Henry Spencer's molecularizations – the 'psychotic multiplicities of dispersion'[56] in the eraser shavings that swirl around him; these same shavings are brushed off the desk of the operator of the machine in the pencil factory that mounts erasers on pencil ends using material extracted from Henry's head. Henry passes through the radiator in his room onto the stage of a singing lady and is pursued by the worms that live in the heaps of dirt in his room, and find their way into his bed, even dropping onto the stage of the lady in the radiator; she at first gingerly steps around them, but then begins to crush them underfoot, just as Henry flung them at the wall of his room (his own precious little worm that he kept in a ring box even danced for him!). Henry's delirium puts his flows into circulation through the subterranean passages of the planet around which he orbits, until he no longer returns to his room at all, where his schizo energies were bound by the mutant infant imposed upon him by his partner Mary, his planet having exploded and his love being returned only by the lady in the radiator.

Guattari doesn't divide minor cinema into cinemas that either display worker struggles or explore madness in documentary or fictional forms. Like Deleuze, Guattari sees political film's task in terms of the multiplication of connections among disparate fragments – between, for instance, anti-psychiatric struggles and the labor movement; between the family as a domain of containable private problems and dramas, and as an already social and political entity. But at the core of Guattari's minor cinema is the idea that cinematic investigations of everyday struggles precipitate changes in those hitherto uninvolved in them, reducing the distance that separates private from political, issue from issue, and ameliorating the many ways in which problems are swept from view and cleansed of complexity in being simplified and compartmentalized. Guattari elegantly expresses this in terms of Depardon's *Urgences*, but he also investigated a similar phenomenon in Jean Schmidt's film *Comme les anges déchus de la planète Saint-Michel* (1978). Guattari is struck by the immediately political effects of the homeless speaking freely about their lives; Schmidt 'takes things as they come; he has not selected from their remarks in order to obtain the best effects of montage.'[57] Instead, he includes tirades, racist outbursts, and clichés alongside passionate and poetic statements. Guattari enumerates several kinds of dependencies that structure the lives of these marginal people subsisting in the center of Paris: physiological (drugs, cold weather, and alcohol); psychological or ethological (precariously occupying territories populated by many different homeless and transients, but also by tourists – the square before the Centre Pompidou, for example); institutional labyrinths (the social services, jails, hospitals, shelters – benevolent organizations peddling hope); and the spectacles of street youth. No easy solutions are proffered; groups are shown to coalesce toward collective projects and then decay into atoms of loneliness and delirium and violence. For Guattari, there is no point in handing issues over to specialists; there is no way to take one's distance from the myriad of challenges on display; Schmidt 'is not content with denouncing a scandal: he squarely puts the blame on sensibilities dulled, "drugged," and infantilized by mass media, and by a public opinion that "does not want to know about it".'[58]

Another anti-psychiatric film that caught Guattari's attention was René Feret's *Histoire de Paul* (1974). Using professional actors in an asylum setting, the effect is realistic, documentary-like, but causes a double take. Foucault reacted by rubbing his eyes: those are actors, not psychiatric inmates, yet the setting is not *like* an asylum, it *is* an asylum.[59] Everything orbits around a patient named Paul, and how he is swallowed by the institution, and in turn ingests it. The effect that Feret sought was based on 'playing mad by the rules of the asylum in order to better show their effects.'[60] This film illustrates that minor cinema is not dominated by one genre, but crosses and mixes and confounds its expectations.

What Guattari wanted to be understood by minor cinema was its ability to promote, through a-signifying part-signs and ethically responsible film praxes, the release of minoritarian becomings in the masses (or a strain therein); or, at least, to precipitate a move towards this utopian goal that he shared with Espinosa, the means to which were otherwise encysted in dominant models and meanings, and beholden to many contingencies and false immutabilities foreclosing them. By promoting the release of creative potentialities, by extracting and loosening them, Guattari hoped they would mutate in a way that would allow them to emerge as components in new auto-modelizations of subjectivity open to establishing existential coordinates that include the ethico-political imperatives of an engagement with madness and poverty, as well as following forward the references they trigger, intimately and in terms of potential praxes.

European anti-psychiatry movements were dominated by leading radical psychiatrists and theorists whose ability to speak in the language of Michel Foucault's *History of Madness* (2006), appropriated for anti-psychiatry when it was originally published in 1961, often took precedence over making concrete interventions. A sophisticated social-realist work on schizophrenia like Ken Loach's *Family Life* (1971) was brilliant at exploring the contrast between progressive small group therapy within a hospital devoted to sedation and electroshock, and the production of case histories, but was still short on concrete reforms, according to Guattari – 'not accompanied by a single concrete proposition for reforming the situation.'[61] Guattari makes no mention of classic anti-psychiatric documentaries such as Fredrick Wiseman's 'reality fiction' about the conditions in the State Prison for the Criminally Insane in Bridgewater, Massachusetts, *Titicut Follies* (1967). However, 'popular' works like these held promise because of the potential publics they catalyzed, which, Guattari hoped, would make new demands on the dominant commercial film industry to deliver radically different messages.

7

AFFECT AND EPILEPSY

In Chapter 6 I deferred my discussion of Bellocchio's film *Fists in the Pocket* in order to place it in the context of Guattari's original insight into one of the most influential aspects of theory today – the philosophy of affect. In this chapter I present a detailed study of how a phenomenological psychiatric conception of epilepsy shaped Guattari's theorization of existential affects, and explain how this illness informed his delineation of different kinds of affects. Guattari's overriding concern was with the production and composition of subjectivity in a pathic mode, and my critical task is to show how epilepsy contributed to this theorization, and to explore it through select cultural materials, namely, the films by Bellocchio and Corbijn I mentioned in the introduction.

On the face of it, epilepsy may seem to be the kind of thing that befalls a body and has the effect of diminishing or at least restraining the power of such a body to act. The capacity of a body to be affected by an epileptic event would appear to lessen it in some measure, and thus decrease its joy by increasing its sadness, at least in the terms given by Deleuze's Spinoza.[1] Modified by epilepsy, affect then becomes the kind of transformation that careens towards decomposition – this is what I call affect's void. By the same token, the challenge of thinking affect together with epilepsy is to avoid jumping to conclusions about the inevitability of the void, and how it jeopardizes affect by putting it on a one-way street to what is lesser; one might also claim that a body's capacity to live with epilepsy makes it more powerful, for this experience increases the diversity of the ways in which it can be affected, and enhances its sensitivities: 'the sum total of the intensive affects it is capable of at a given power or degree of potential.'[2] In the cinematic examples I shall discuss, affect as an intensity linked with epilepsy ends badly; but this is not inevitable because the potential embodied by an epileptic may indicate other, even incompatible passages. Affect's much discussed autonomy is its openness and excess that escapes functional anchoring. Yet the epileptiform coloration of affect also suggests that escape is not a perception of vitality at all, and not thereby intrinsically positive. Thus, Guattari adds an important reminder about how important it is to follow the negative effects of affect on a body's capacity to endure, how its constitution is affected, and how such a body in turns affects others. The problem that this chapter grapples with is the absence of a reflection on Guattari's contribution to the theory of affect, especially in Deleuzean thought, but also in Massumi's candid recognition that in the unscripted potentiality of the virtual the problem of the void will need to be addressed at some point in the future.[3]

Glischroidy

Like many intellectuals of his generation, Guattari read Eugène Minkowski's important book on *Lived Time*, first published in 1933 but reprinted in the late 1960s. *Lived Time* is one among many intersections between psychiatry and phenomenology. There are traces of this reading in Guattari's challenging essay on 'Ritornellos and Existential Affects,' in which he suggests at the outset that, borrowing from Minkowski's writing on epilepsy, affect adheres to the subject in a 'glischroidic' manner.[4] Affect is sticky; it is also non-discursive and pre-personal and has a transitivist character that makes it transferable or sharable between subjects, but not bound to dyadic representations such as speaker–listener or tied down to a specific emotion (or other functional anchors). In fact, as Massumi has clarified, emotion is subjectively 'owned,' whereas affect is an 'unowned' intensity.[5] 'Somewhere,' Guattari wrote, 'there is anger' that is available communally as it circulates through a dimension that may work itself out through, by analogy, objects of value that an individual's or clan's influence ('mana') finds to express itself.[6]

What is significant is that the search for philosophical precedents for this view of affect in Spinoza, Bergson, and elsewhere has underplayed Minkowski's contribution and overlooked the fact that some of the character given to affect is borrowed from epilepsy. What I propose to do is excavate glischroidy in Minkowski in order to expose epilepsy's role in Guattari's thinking not only of affect, but of how it works in the cinema as well. Of course, one could say that the intersection between Guattari, Minkowski, and affect is found in Minkowski's precursor Henri Bergson, as Minkowski's psychiatric phenomenology of time was, with a number of important qualifications and deviations, Bergsonian in inspiration.[7] While this is undoubtedly accurate as far as line of influence is concerned, I want to emphasize that Guattari's path was different than Deleuze's – and he notes as much, referring to the effect on his thinking of affective 'atmospherics' (hazy yet comprehensible) borrowed from phenomenological psychiatry; specifically, Guattari gleaned this from Arthur Tatossian's overview *Phénomenologie des psychoses*. While this tradition is not well known, it is decisive for Guattari's construction of affect with reference to pathology, which will be somewhat familiar to readers of Maurice Merleau-Ponty's *Phenomenology of Perception*, in which case studies of the brain-damaged patient 'Schneider' were used to describe the body's spatiality and motility. Merleau-Ponty borrows this example from Kurt Goldstein's studies of brain-injured soldiers during the 1940s, in this instance a man in his twenties, whose vision and ability to perform abstract movements were impaired by a shell splinter in the back of his head.

In Massumi's writings on virtuality, one finds epileptoid phenomena of gaps, lags, and missteps ('something that happens too quickly to have happened') that have always concerned the thinking of infolding, psychopathological or otherwise. I am not suggesting in these remarks that affect, in being ascribed to individuals as clinical entities, has been psychopathologized. On the contrary, one of the hallmarks of Minkowski's approach is that he considers the epileptoid character in the context of a world of objects and others, especially families (within which illnesses are unevenly distributed), social situations, intergenerational relations, and biological issues around heredity. Readers of *Anti-Oedipus* are familiar with the non-clinical entity – the schizo process – that involves a dismantling of the ego, escaping the imposition of a breakdown by the capitalist mode of social production: 'society is schizophrenizing at the level of its infrastructure.'[8] Deriving affect from epilepsy, like creating schizoanalysis from the ruins of capitalism's schizophrenia, is turned into a 'positive' task, but one with attendant risks.

Merleau-Ponty reflected on his use of Schneider in terms of the role of pathology in phenomenological analysis of the body in movement and in space: he argued that normality could not be deduced from pathology. It did not suffice to grasp lack and then recover it in the normal. For Merleau-Ponty, the world of illness is no less a world than that of a so-called normal person. The role of the pathological case 'has enabled us to glimpse a new mode of analysis – existential analysis – which goes beyond the traditional alternatives of empiricism and rationalism, of explanation and introspection.'[9] In other words, for Merleau-Ponty there is something more basic at issue than a description of Schneider's failures (of representation, of objectifying schemas, and in his misapprehension of symbolic intermediaries of experimental simulation), and it is that the intentional arc of consciousness that unifies our sensory world, intelligence, and motility '"goes limp" in illness.'[10] Although Merleau-Ponty is not discussing epilepsy, his approach to the pathological is foundational within the phenomenological tradition.

In his discussion of glischroidy, Minkowski relies upon the family-centered research of Françoise Minkowska on epileptic character. Minkowski first rejects the older view that epilepsy, that is, grand mal delirium, is intimately linked with thoughts of death, God, ecstasy, and mysticism brought on by the trauma of the seizures. The problem with this view is that, for Minkowski, there is a false transposition between the trauma's 'brutality' and the reaction taking the form of 'morbid religiosity.' Minkowska's research, published in the 1920s, showed, on the contrary, that 'explosive reactions' to trauma are secondary to a more basic disorder described as 'a slackening and a particular viscosity.'[11]

Minkowska further filled out the epileptoid constitution (glischroidy) as involving: loss of mobility; incapacity to remove oneself from one's environment; lack of initiative; lack of productivity; clinging to what one has; unattractiveness of change; love of order, especially details, to the detriment of the 'big picture'; admiration of stability; concentration of emotional energy on one's family or general ideas (world peace); intellectual slowness; and morally informed missionary zeal. She specified that the 'viscous affectivity' of this constitution appears in the epileptic's inability to detach him/herself from objects when change requires it. Thus: 'the epileptoid is the paradigm of the affective personality ... this emotion is viscous and lacks mobility.'[12] Ultimately, the suffocating stasis and immobility eventually combust and the consequent explosion leaves an anguished psyche beset by delusions. This, I shall suggest, is precisely the atmosphere evoked by Bellocchio in *Fists in the Pocket*.

Minkowski reads this characterization of a 'general slackening' and saccharine emotional life through a three-pronged strategy of backgrounding trauma and its effects (the 'falling sickness' of the pre-moderns), rejecting single causation (inability to interact), and resisting reduction to certain unexamined expectations (squandering an opportunity to emigrate; denigration of a strong cultural attachment to native soil; or praiseworthy tenacity). Instead, he recalls the difficulty of interpreting viscousness, as it may erroneously show as insincerity; or, again falsely, as egotism. While viscosity steers clear of explosiveness and mysticism, it runs into other phenomena such as contemplation, which is only allegedly immobile and 'completely different from real immobility.'[13] There is a 'syntonic' element of epileptoidism that suggests the nuances of thinking through any kind of unity with the environment as sympathy, which, for Minkowski, has a viscous side. So, just as the personal elan (the withdrawal from reality that the accomplishment of a personal project requires before re-engaging with becomings beyond the subjective) has a schizoid element, contemplation and sympathy have epileptoid nuances in their characteristics of engagement.

Types of Affect

Guattari separates affect (open and full of potential) from emotional anchors (limits of embodiment). This separation is relative, because although affect lacks an obvious origin and destination, it can and does find an existential footing in intersubjective phenomena like commiseration, where it is sharable. Affect still retains a vagueness, a qualitativeness against efforts to bind it to a quantity (this is its virtuality, its openness and autonomy – unassimilable and unanchorable). Affect has the capacity to fade out and escape from its most intense footings.[14] But it also has the capacity to invade, disorient, and break down subjectification, carried by a death-dealing ritornello of sound and seizure.

In order to characterize sharable affect as an extra-personal phenomenon that 'speaks through [one],' Guattari borrows from the anthropologically tinged phenomenological psychiatry of Hubert Tellenbach the idea, developed in the late 1960s, of an 'atmospheric diagnostics' relevant to schizophrenia. Guattari quotes Tatossian's overview on this point about diagnosing schizophrenic alienation, not symptomatically, but through phenomena that are embedded in a communicative situation of intersubjective encounters, and are thus 'atmospheric'; unlike the symptoms which, for Tellenbach, an illness itself displays, and which thus are not present but must be diagnostically inferred, phenomena revealed by the bracketing of the empirical are given directly and fully, not through inference or interpretation. The characterization of phenomenological diagnostics involves 'ascertaining the dissidence between the atmospheres proper to two partners.'[15] For his part, Tatossian wonders whether phenomenological diagnostics is pre-semiological, and thus naive and non-psychiatric, or simply post-semiological, thereby 'integrating but moving beyond the cataloguing of symptoms.'[16] Guattari would reject a dyadic construction of Being and situate affect as pre-personal, choosing, as he put it, a 'polyvocity of components of semiotization which, however, are still not on the way to their existential anchors.'[17]

Guattari is indebted to the conceptualization of vitality affects in the work of psychologist Daniel Stern, and it is the non-categorical or non-discrete character of such elusive qualities to which he turns in particular for important clues about expression without specific categorical colorings and sensory specificities.[18] For instance, a vitality affect like soothing need not be experienced by an infant (whose sense of self is still emerging) as linked to a specific modality of expression (vocal or gestural) or even anchored in a response to discrete stimulus categories (fright or sadness). The supra-modal character of vitality affects makes them rich in transversal potential for matching, transferring, and assembling sensory experiences between and among different modalities of expression and behavior. Freeing affect from arousal and how it is experienced enhances its transversality. For Guattari, not only is affect pre-personal, literally experienced before a category of person may be used to describe selfhood's integrated networks organized under identifiable principles, for instance, as Stern describes the emergent self in an infant immersed in vitality affects; but such affects also consist of multiple transferences (across sensory domains, for instance, prior to the hierarchies of semiology, with language at the center and all other semiotic modes subject to translation by the central mode, but not vice versa) whose origins (and destinations), or the stimuli and categories from which they are abstracted, are not locatable. Transference, transitivist, transversal: these terms, employed by Guattari in rapid succession, indicate the dynamic and abstract features of affect, whose semiotic polyvocity remains incomplete, thus not yet yoked to one semiotic–sensory modality: 'somewhere there is anger ...' It circulates, thought Guattari, like 'spirit' which is under collective 'ownership' and in its own right a sort of medium through which its influences are distributed or shared. Affect is far removed from its analysis as discourse, and from extensional categories in general. Affect is collective. It 'speaks to and through me,' Guattari wrote,[19] yet it is not language.

Affect sticks to a subject in production, a processual subject defined provisionally: 'the ensemble of conditions which render possible the emergence of individual and/or collective instances as self-referential existential territories, adjacent, or in a delimiting relation, to an alterity that is itself subjective.'[20] Guattari describes an existential territory in which his subjecthood is given shape as a tributary of the following scene:

> The somber red color of my curtain enters into an Existential constellation with nightfall, with twilight, in order to engender an uncanny Affect that devalues the self-evidences and urgencies which were imposing themselves on me only a few moments earlier, plunging the world into a seemingly irremediable void.[21]

Guattari qualifies this example by distinguishing it from the lingering influences (emotive and cognitive) of affects that reach beyond the confines of a localized and immediate scene like that involving his red curtain and twilight. The base line is the apprehension of a chaosmotic (grasping chaos by osmosis) territory to which lines are added – these are other sorts of affects, called *problematic*, as against immediate *sensory* affects; problematic affects are spatio-temporally ungrounded and in flight (more than just associative, but fading and thickening) and for Guattari they are more ontologically basic than situationally bound sensory affects in terms of the latitude given to their influence; the residues of signifier and signified are evident enough, and Guattari reinscribes them as sensory (ritornello) and problematic affect (abstract machine), or form of expression and form of content (their mutual relationship is what Guattari calls the sign function, and this becomes the existentializing function when form finds substances of expression and content). For subjectivity as a tributary of a number of diverse components assembled in a 'scenic disposition' announces a relation of dependency:

> I find myself subject to a multi-headed Assemblage of enunciation: the individuated subjectification which in me is authorized to speak in the first person is no more in fact than the fluctuating intersection, and the conscious 'terminal,' of these diverse components of temporalization.[22]

This subject is composed from heterogeneous components that achieve a certain consistency, but it is not an effect of structure (signifying operations), Guattari having displaced the signifying chain of linguistics and reinscribed the scene in terms of non-discursive affects, retaining semiotic heterogeneity in the process. The attainment of consistency in subjectification through a heightened affectivity is achieved without threatening the latter's autonomy. But affect sticks to subjectivity nonetheless. It is a 'glischroid matter' that gives texture to the existential constellation of components and the temporalities that cross and catalyze them (like iterative ritornellos understood as emergent motifs that cluster the components and adhere them to the subjectivity in process). Further, in order to describe the 'inchoate dimension' of affects that have not achieved consistency (but have not lost the capacity to influence), Guattari turned to a cluster of concepts borrowed from phenomenological psychiatry and psychopathologies of temporality – for example, reversals (history bathed in guilt) and shrinkages of time (classic symptomatology of disruptions in lived continuity) in melancholia and autism. He makes a point of not, however, producing a distinction between orderly and harmonious temporal components of subjectification and discordant com-ponentialization, which would erroneously uphold a further distinction between normal and abnormal (one wouldn't deny the profound difference between the pathic temporalizations of a manic whose accelerations fan out and an obsessive whose inhibitions retain and circumscribe); instead, diverse, livable temporal modes which are crossable constitute normality, while only one mode (a '"hardened representation" like an obsessive ritual'[23]) dominates in abnormality. This is not a diagnostics, but a way of presenting a more general perspective on problems of enunciation, not to mention an appreciation of its precariousness, irreducible to both psychopathology and linguistic semiology (the tyranny of the signifier becoming in this light abnormal with regard to enunciation).

Reiterative phenomena like ritornellos congeal by giving substance to sensory affects, in music or intonation, for instance, and open the fields of reference of problematic affects, as in the feeling of ambiance or atmosphere for those attuned to such environmental features. In terms of semiotic functions (sensory affects), ritornellos concern the relations between enunciation and the form of expression, and abstract machines (problematic affects) concern the relations between enunciation and the form of content. In these terms, semiotic functionality involves the existentializing function of enunciation engaging both 'functives' of the sign, understood as two mutually presupposing forms – expression and content – which are projected onto unformed matter in order to create substances – expression and content substances. Substances are ordered or subsumed by form, with the expression substance finding a medium like sound, and content substance performing conceptual labor. Guattari advocated for greater attention to be paid to how ritornellos 'fix [that is, extract or detach something from the significational chaos and congeal it in a substance] the existential ordering of the sensory environment and ... prop up the most abstract meta-modelizing scenes of problematic Affects.'[24] For Guattari, ritornellos intersect both types of affects, just as abstract machines involve sensory affects as well. Enunciation is not anchored to a speaking subject, but exhibits a certain degree of autonomy and 'foliatedness' (*feuilletage*) – exhibiting growth as in an arrangement of leaves – in consisting of a number of heterogeneous voices (social and pre-personal) in which semiotic components are assembled in an open-ended way and through which subjectivity takes and changes shape, pursuing becomings that place it in 'zones of indetermination' in which it is no longer human, but contiguous with colors, sounds, smells.[25] The entire territory of subjectification is pathically perfused. The existential function of enunciation opens a territory for subjectification to emerge through the imperfectly and non-structurally and multi-centered (multi-headed layout) intersecting affects.

Sound and Seizure

Bellocchio's first film, *Fists in the Pocket* (1965), is set in an isolated family villa in a small Italian town. The story revolves around the interactions of the adult children – three brothers and their sister – and a blind mother. Although considered crazy by the townspeople, the children struggle for independence in a claustrophobic environment over which hangs the terrible legacy of the family illness, a debilitating epilepsy, distributed unevenly among the children; Alessandro is in between attacks and seems to have his epilepsy under pharmaceutical control, even if the rest of his actions lack such control, while brother Leone is brain-damaged and subject to uncontrollable seizures. Elder brother Augusto's narcissism seems manageable enough for him to contemplate marriage, while Giulia's fragility threatens to disintegrate at any moment. The film catalogues the misplaced enthusiasms of the split Ale/Sandro (a familial schizo splitting of the name, not not unlike Guattari's hyphenated first name, Pierre-Félix) as he plots and executes the murder of his mother and brother Leone, attempts to seduce and/or smother his sister, arranges a suicidal car ride to his father's graveside for his siblings, and even follows in Augusto's footsteps beyond the family with hopeless schemes. It is the final scene of Ale/Sandro's massive and deadly seizure that features the work of a notable ritornellizing expression-substance, Verdi's *La traviata*. Throughout the film Bellocchio has Ale/Sandro retreat to his bedroom and play his Verdi record, to which he moved and mimed and performed strange signal-like gestures, sometimes simulating suicide, other times gleefully play-singing an aria like a massive baritone. His bedroom has hitherto served as a protective, infantile territory, the soundtrack to which is always the same. The Verdi ritornello shapes the final bedroom scene and fills it with sound, yet it is not the only expressive substance, as Ale/Sandro's gestures and movements – singing, miming, dancing, bouncing on his bed, laughing, and thrashing – agglomerate and induce in him a kind of ecstatic experience. Bellocchio shows us in one violent edit – a blurry close-up of Ale/Sandro's mouth followed by a quick cut – what is about to occur, as he has throughout used, as one critic astutely observed, 'aggravated editing, with sequences jerking spasmodically from one to another ... like epilepsy itself.'[26] This edit drags us across a threshold and intersects with problematic affect – that glischroidic affect that oppressed the household, coloring everything, until the film's climactic scene. The seizure that kills Ale/Sandro enters upon the scene from 'somewhere' and reorganizes it, turning ecstasy inside out, reconnecting ecstasy with its Neoplatonic twin – epilepsy.[27] Suddenly the rapturous experience animating Ale/Sandro's gestures becomes unbearable as he thrashes violently on the floor, and the aria changes face as a new component introduces itself beyond the music – the seizure clashes with the singularizing effects of the music, and the scene becomes tense and disharmonious – heightening and prolonging his suffering. What happens to a ritornello whose content is a seizure? Time can no longer be kept, a vast gulf opens up between the record that plays on and the seizure that continues but turns the drama in a different direction and brings it to a brutal end. This is not all external; from inside the seizure, Ale/Sandro calls his sister for help – 'hold my head,' a request he used earlier when he felt a seizure coming on and sought comfort from her. But Giulia remains in her bed and does not move, listening with a certain satisfaction to the horrible events, as the massive seizure opens a territory with which she is familiar and which she permits to run its course, because through it she explores her own share of atmospheric immobility in relation to her murderous brother.

If Bellocchio dramatically cultivated the psychotic episodes that sometimes accompany and alternate with epileptic events – in this case inter-ictally, or between seizures, as Ale/Sandro's behavior becomes more and more bizarre[28] – then Corbijn works the post-ictal terrain, where the resulting psychopathology not only increases the risk of suicide, but exemplifies it.[29] The final scene of Control – in which Ian Curtis hangs himself in his kitchen on the support rope of a clothes rack after a night of heavy solitary drinking and failure to reconcile with his spouse, to passages from Werner Herzog's Stroszeck (1977) on a black and white television and Iggy Pop's (and not Dostoevsky's) The Idiot on the turntable – is shaped by the seizure that announces itself with an auratic hand tremor that loosens the suicide note from his hand, as his body follows the note to the ground. All the components of territorialization and temporalization at play in the final scene – night gives way to morning (by which time he 'will be gone'), the television broadcasting day ends in static, his passing out accompanies a fade out, the record ends – constellate around an impending end, his suicide, which is never seen, only heard in a muffled sound behind a black screen. The black screen is the threshold across which the suicide, pushed by the seizure, carries the viewer. And with his spouse Debbie's discovery of the body, the hollow, insistent strains of Joy Division's 'Atmosphere' emerge to count off the final moments of the film, her pleas for help giving way to the black smoke rising from the chimney of a distant crematorium.

In *Control* the ritornellization is accomplished by means of the recurrent and unpreventable seizures that haunt Ian Curtis's private and public lives (his on-stage seizures are remarkable for the confusion they create in his band-mates and audiences). He slows down, cannot accept change in his family situation, and the atmosphere with his partner is complicated by his heavy drinking, nicotine loading, and emotional inability to accept that his spouse wants a divorce because he has taken a lover, whose capacity to stick to him he rather lethargically laments. The Joy Division soundscape of pain, disillusion, and persecutory energy catalyzes the existential affects that assemble like ominous clouds waiting to strike discords – the unpredictable seizures whose debilitating effects earlier led Curtis into an attempted suicide by means of overdosing on his medication. Between Bellocchio and Corbijn, there are at work in the two films under discussion complementary intersecting ritornellos of sound and seizure, each in a different order of priority – in *Fists* the ritornellos of *La traviata* are subject to the contingent emergence of the final seizure, which finds Ale/Sandro in a state of paroxysmic joy whose content is revealed as the unpreventable, final crushing seizure; while in *Control* the seizures repeatedly experienced by Curtis shape numerous sensory scenes, finally becoming intolerable and precipitating suicide. Both filmmakers insert the somewhat residual, gendered technology of the record player as one vector along which subjectivation takes place (the vinyl record serving as a controllable palette for subjectivity's self-positioning, even if what is put on does not make a sound) in, as Guattari put it, 'eventful compositions' of sounds and seizures that create damaged subjects.

Epilepsy's Potential

In the cinematic examples under discussion, the self-enunciative potential of the key characters is put at risk by their seizures, as the components of partial subjectivation seem to indicate that only an action undertaken to conquer what is unmanageable is valid, in the case of Curtis's suicide; but in Ale/Sandro's situation, the sonic ritornello cannot guard against the threat of a seizure, whose convulsiveness is final, but the effects of which have already hardened into psychotic violence directed against his family. In *Control* Curtis's final episode intersects with a musical ritornello by delay because, unlike *Fists*, the seizure carries us into an intensive time in which the record, while apparently playing (the needle is first seen in the lead-in groove and later found in the lead-out area), is not heard; whereas the music in Ale/Sandro's bedroom is heard all too well. In both films, the content affects – Ale/Sandro's seizure and Curtis' suicide – give a definitive consistency to the sensory affects, but one whose hopelessness is brutal. Affect tonally colored by epilepsy attaches to what ends badly. One way or another, the result of epilepsy is death. It deterritorializes rapidly and effectively: the joy and comfort of Verdi reverses and Bellocchio reveals its capacity to abolish: 'music,' wrote Deleuze and Guattari, 'has a taste for destruction.'[30] Epilepsy deterritorializes the ritornello towards death, unwinds it too quickly and with ferocity, and Giulia refuses the line it sends out for help. And in Curtis's situation, his epileptic ritornello ter-ritorializes with precision, as we see in his relationship with his child, whom he cannot pick up and hold, but only stare at through the playpen's bars; and in his relationship with his band-mates, whose gigs his seizures violently interrupt (and carry forward, as his stage presence had seizure-like elements). It is only when all the lines of flight and fields of reference converge/collapse on the same content that the ritornello contracts intensely around a single reference and the subject plunges down into suicide – lost in affect's void.

It is worth noting that the distinction between the sensory and problematic affects, in which the latter is more determinative, because more transversal, disappears sometime during the period between the *Cartographies schizoanalytiques* and *Chaosmosis*,[31] these affects together becoming hyper-complex ritornellos/refrains – the first crystallizing existential and territorial assemblages and the latter catalyzing transversal connections among incorporeal universes – reinserted into an ontology that remains organized around expression/content among other pairings (both universes [virtual] and territories [actual] occupying the content side of ontological functions). Therefore the pre-eminence given in the cinematic examples to ritornellos that shut down enunciation and hurl subjects into the void, presenting epilepsy as a kind of death sentence, one among a crowd of incipiences jockeying for position to be actualized. To be the tributary of a layout or assemblage that is epileptoid creates heterogeneous implosive temporalizations ('missing time') which eventually snuff lifelines. Period. Can this end point be turned into a pause?

Epileptic Affect's Promise

If affect is epileptoid, then we are all perhaps epileptics[32] to the extent that our bodies have the capacity to be affected by seizures, and to have epileptoid incipiences[33] of varying intensities jostling for completion, but not necessarily toward the actualization of a final extreme event, and not always at the level of conscious awareness.[34] My cinematic examples are extreme for the purpose of reinjecting sadness into the apprehension of affect, yet admit of lines of differentiation distributed in directions that lead to other outcomes, with non-actual remainders.

What an expanded investigation of the response of a body to the loss precipitated by an epileptic event would need to account for is how this transformation of consciousness is experienced and what forms it might take or give rise to. The loss or 'missing' dimension would need to be interrogated and, no matter how elusive, understood as a disorienting intensity, perhaps on the amodal model (not belonging to any one sense) that Guattari borrowed from Stern: the question concerns non-specific experience of moving aliveness around the fringes of conscious perception. An aesthetic apprehension of the epileptiform as an elusive, abstract change in relation to the fading/phasing and return of consciousness is the subject of Australian artist Isabelle Delmotte's work 'Epileptograph: The Internal Journey,'[35] an ongoing work of sound and vision based on her efforts to attune herself to internal changes during seizures and to sense what cannot be sensed, in the process inventing new senses, she suggests. Aesthetically and therapeutically, Delmotte tries to bring sensation back to thought, to feel what was not felt during the episode, but was nonetheless registered, and with tangible effects, during which consciousness and perspective were adrift in chaotic change, and her body was disorganized by seizure. Her goal is to regain body knowledge in order better to manage her seizures, feeling them before they occur. Affect in this regard increases sensitivity to discontinuity of self, and the perception of a pure relationality between a borderline subject and borderless object. Delmotte does not passively endure her seizures, but excavates their material and energetic complexions – Guattari's terms for the fluxes: blips of energy, bits of discourse, part-signs, and hues – that provide the real traits of the stasis of epileptoid experiences. Delmotte trains herself to enter and inhabit the chaotic opening and closing of her seizures and develop a new sensitivity to their complexions.

The cinematic examples I have discussed, taken in the context of minor cinema built around alternative visions of psychiatry, may at best be said to precipitate minoritarian becomings that set off from the visual degradations of seizures and their consequences (violent psychosis and suicide) on a journey into the depths of a ruptured universe whose features await release. Guattari was careful not to run together psychosis and epilepsy, maintaining the plurality of these 'deficit alterations,' and 'unindulgently' balancing their unique potential for providing, from the depths of their facticity, source material for subjectification.[36]

CONCLUSION

Guattari's original intuition about the machine was that it exposed the relationship between subjectivity and desire (the unconscious subject of desire and the machinic order are indistinguishable) by introducing disequilibrium into structure – not merely as a formal disruption of homeomorphism, but 'a radical ontological reconversion' that escapes into universes of reference far from the imprint of signifying semiologies, syntax, space, and time.[1] The machine was an impure element in an otherwise pure system, which smothers subjectivity, which captures it in a reverberation of interdependent, repetitive differences, and keeps it from the real. Guattari resuscitated speech, for instance, which in structural analysis receives unity from language, and stands in a relation as an accessory does to what is essential, in support of this invasion of structure.[2] Getting structure to shift exposes subjectivity. The loosening of the subject from structure takes an event of the revolutionary historical order of the Bolshevik revolution, which Guattari attributes to the 'audacious Leninist [machinic] cut' that ruptured historical causality (it is inattention to subjectivity and desire that provides an opening for Stalin).[3] In his early writings, Guattari sees the machine as the way to keep plugged together the subject, history, desire, and the real, signs and matter. He never loses the connection between large-scale events and how they are connected with molecular perturbations of subjectivity.

As the machine expands in Guattari's thought into an evolutionary phylum containing numerous kinds of devices, some abstract, some mechanical, a range of which obsolesce and are replaced, while others stall and later restart at some point along their 'phylogenetic line of infinite, virtual extension,'[4] the problem of structure falls away, and the question of whether or not the machine is a metaphor is completely eclipsed. As the phylum assumes the role of creative historical force (without succumbing to linear progressivist or dystopian illusions), its rhizomically assembled objects, processes, and diagrams display the power to manufacture subjectivities. Guattari's typical strategy is to provide a restrictive example – the subjectivity of a child fixated on a technical object like a television – and then a more expansive and mutational vision, in which technical progress and 'the ever more artificial processes of subjective production can very well be associated with new social and creative forms. That's where the cursor of molecular revolution is located.'[5] Molecular revolution lies at the heart of the interface between subjectivity and technological (and socio-collective) transformations, which is analyzable by means of the hybrid semiotics (signifying and a-signifying) that cross the heterogeneous components out of which subjectivity is engendered. No one knows what the results will be. But the urgency of the matter is underlined by Guattari with reference to the information revolution, which is the strand on the phylum where the real stakes are. For Guattari, relations of a human subject with alterity must account for the impact of a machinic, non-human enunciation.

Changes in mentalities and everyday practices connect transversally with large-scale challenges like climate change, and in this subjectivity might either enter into a self-modeling, by forming a resistant shell of disempowerment and falling back on established patterns of behavior and consumption as 'rights,' or by transforming practices and planning across the life world, achieving a kind of autonomous understanding of the problem and assuming some element of responsibility for it in relation to complex forces on a variety of levels. Subjectivity (re)singularizes itself by taking the complex interactions between the molecular and molar scales of such challenges as opportunities for realizing autonomy in terms of relations with thoughtful transportation choices, informed food and lifestyle decisions, expanding recycling practices, a rebirth of political curiousity, changing media, etc. This kind of singularization is not merely happening at the level of personal choice, but before (pre-verbal, emergent self, amodal perceptions) and beyond (collective determinations, machinic entanglements) the category of person. Social and technical machines impinge upon (models and maps for subjectification arrive from everywhere and at all times) and are (re)appropriated by subjectivity (extracting an object, content or affect from the dominant models and testing its creative potential) in a way that introduces non-human elements into its assemblages. Subjective processes of singularization engage a politics that can learn as much or more from poetry, especially spoken performance – a torpor-reducing 'vitamin of meaning'[6] – as from economics, even though many of today's leading ecologists are economists and not poets. Revisiting the structure-upsetting voice, Guattari calls for a machinic orality of the MC or rapper,[7] not the computer voice, not the telemarketer, but a semiotically complex speech whose subtle features survive the flattened interactions of the marketplace, and exude affects which effortlessly transport one into universes of longing (a welcome voice from the past), of pain (a voice bearing the weight of suffering), and of healing (empathic listening and understanding).

If there was a constant in Guattari's restless, life-long chaodyssey, it was the centrality of collective production of journals by transdisciplinary editorial assemblages. He first went down this road in his teenage years, when he engaged in a collective auto-unfolding of a peripatetic youth group dedicated to far-left politics in one of the splinter groups within the youth hostelling association. In Chapter 1, I discussed the importance of Freinet's innovative pedagogical methods of the school printery, which Guattari praised as an example of a machinic process that modifies subjectivity in collective, scholarly settings.[8] Guattari worked out human–machine relations through the social ecologies of publishing machines: a broad strand on the phylum for collective subjectification and innovation that he repeatedly entered into as a component part, assembling heterogeneous elements, drawing and cutting transversal lines between distinct parts, without a unifying whole.

The journal is a choice micro-institutional matter produced by editorial assemblages seeking to collectively realize their projects and create new worlds of reference, fabricate affects in the manner of artists, and summon a readership and participants yet to come. *Recherches* catalyzed the collective self-production of the micro-institution CERFI (the Center for Study and Research into Institutional Functioning).

CERFI may be described as a freelance research group that managed to solidify a core membership in affective communion around the production of collective objects, primarily funding research projects leading to journal issues. It was created by Guattari in 1967 and replaced the two-year-old predecessor organization, FGERI, which began by publishing *Recherches* at La Borde. CERFI also enjoyed a community of experiences through the work of many of its members at La Borde as *stagiaires* or trainees. CERFI was an extra-academic assemblage that was funded by the civil research contracts under the budgets of the French ministries (for example, by the Ministère de l'Équipement). It provided salaries to its members and financed its projects. Eventually it was edged out by professional academic bodies as budgets shrank, governments changed, and research became more university focused. Eventually, the state's strategy was to co-opt some of the core CERFI researchers, a move that failed. The lack of funding – the failure of what Anne Querrien called 'a ministerial godsend' – became an issue after 1974, causing internal strife and protective restructuring.[9] Eventually, by the end of the 1970s, CERFI turned its back on the radicals who had prepared its most notorious issue (*Recherches*, No. 12, 'Trois milliards de pervers: Grande Encyclopédie des Homosexualités,' 1973), and the blending of affective and political dimensions imploded.[10] Originally, CERFI legitimated its marginality through the participation of leading intellectuals in its streams; thus, Foucault was research director of the Généalogie des équipements collectives stream, which resulted in a number of issues of *Recherches* on a variety of topics, including architecture, psychiatric hospital planning, safeguarding vernacular languages, and power. CERFI also collaborated with other independent groups, which opened up pathways for the explorations of its members, and invited other groups to occupy its space. Although Guattari sometimes makes light of his many criminal and other charges,[11] he never ceased mentioning the 'Three Billion Perverts' issue, and his fine of 600 francs for affronting public decency.[12] Indeed, it is an irreplaceable discussion point for anyone interested in the history of CERFI.[13]

It is 1973 and CERFI is at its 'zenith' – flush with cash, full of the success of *Anti-Oedipus* published the previous year, flirting with the prospects of communal life in the Parisian suburbs, drawing the brightest-burning intellectual stars into its orbit, not merely in its pages but in its living, editorial auto-productions.[14] Then No. 12 appeared. By 1974, CERFI had changed fundamentally under a variety of pressures (change in government, internal reorganization), and Guattari took his distance at the moment when CERFI took off in the direction of professional publishing (developing the 'Encres' series of books, re-editing *Trois milliards de pervers*, joining forces with Éditions 10/18 to reprint issues of *Recherches* as standalone books, abandoning under pressure from new members an older set of radical causes, etc.), finally ceding his directorship in 1981.[15] Was 1973 the beginning of the end of CERFI?

Publishing machines, like all machines, break down, yet continue to function. This is merely one dimension of their process of production. Parts of broken-down machines may be cobbled together to produce wonderful devices, as Rube Goldberg demonstrated in his comic drawings. Something of the molecular texture of a machine is revealed when it is idle; its micropolitical potentialities come into view perhaps for the first time. In this case, CERFI joined forces with Hocquenghem's FHAR (Front homosexuel d'action révolutionnaire) to produce a volatile cocktail of an issue, largely because Hocquenghem had been given a free hand by Guattari to create what he wanted, beyond the confines of academic respectability and scientist neutrality. For Hocquenghem the important point was about 'group creativity because we in fact occupied another journal. It is very important to occupy someone else's terrain.'[16]

For Guattari, however, the social and political predicament was very much a matter of the opportunities and consequences of 'giving voice' to a ghettoized minority. Guattari rejected or, rather, reformulated this issue in a twofold manner: first, he rejected the 'formal and Jesuitical' version of 'giving voice' to one's 'research subjects' under the guise of a problematic pseudo-objectivity; second, he wanted to use the special issue to 'create the conditions for a total, indeed a paroxysmic, exercise of that scientific enunciation.'[17] These conditions would entail a decentered scientificity in three senses: against the logic of the survey à la Kinsey; beyond psychoanalytic prejudices (sameness fixation); and outside the isolated conditions of a classical union-based militancy that did not yet connect with the burgeoning social-liberation movements. Indeed, for Guattari, the problem of militancy is its (in)ability to connect with other progressive movements and currents. This was the institutional task that CERFI attempted to ameliorate by engaging the expressive desires of FHAR and MLF (Mouvement de libération des femmes) during this period; in fact, CERFI put at Hocquenghem's disposal its infrastructural resources and the assistance of Querrien. By the same token, this did not mean that Guattari was hyper-valorizing the figure of the gay activist: 'Incidentally, for the deaf: the gay, no more than the schizo, is not *of himself* a revolutionary – the revolutionary of modern times!'[18] Rather, Guattari considered the potential of what the gay activist could become to constitute a critique of sexuality as such, to the extent that homosexuality 'concerned all normal sexual life.' In this expanded field of becoming, 'homosexuality would be, thus, not only an element in the life of each and everyone, but involved in any number of social phenomena, such as hierarchy, bureaucracy.'[19] Not an ethnographics of a marginal people, but a non-uniform becoming in which opportunities are pursued and tendencies mined across the social field. In the process, for Guattari, homo- becomes trans-sexuality: 'From this perspective, the struggle for the liberty of homosexuality becomes an integral part of the struggle for social liberation.'[20]

The emission of molecules of homosexuality is, then, the desire in this publishing machine; and the activation of minor homosexual becomings in those who read the issue. Overall, CERFI managed to interrupt its state cash flow in the process, but, as a flow itself connected with other machinic entities, such as the FHAR and MLF and GIP (Groupe Information Prison, from which post-1973 CERFI publisher Florence Pétry came), eventually tapped a new energy source through three syntheses: *connecting* with book publishing, and *disjunctively* subdividing into speciality and regional groups (music, film; CERFI Southeast); introducing difference in connective repetitions (the burden of serials publishing) by means of renewal and breakage (learning how to distribute itself and its products); finally, *conjunctively* extruding a collective subjectivity about which histories may be written: 'So *that's* what it was?'[21]

The molecular revolutionizing of machinic subjectivity is a permanent process. Guattari's own lifework was remarkably consistent on this point, from the period of his youthful peregrinations, institutional experimentations, and machinic ecological investigations of techno-semiosis and the promise and perils of informatics. The real ontological textures which formed his own process of subjectification were social-group machines that networked subjectivities and the formation of experimental institutional matters accomplished by forging tools for transversality. His belief in the power of the machinic phylum to provide, through 'technological evolution ... new possibilities for interaction between the medium and its user, and between users themselves'[22] was firm and unwavering. Of course, machines have the capacity both to subjugate and to liberate subjectivity as an individual and collective phenomenon, crossed by any number of processes and corporeal and incorporeal, non-human components. In spite of the risks of subjugation by a homogenizing mass media and neo-liberal Integrated World Capitalism, the very thing that Guattari thought gave some hope was a new alliance with machines; and, most importantly, alliances to come, particularly through new cinematic minor becomings. It is not so much a matter of choice, and especially not a question of party policy. Information, Guattari claimed, is not to be understood objectively, but in terms of the production of subjectivity and its consistency: 'The truth of information refers to an existential event occurring in those who receive it.'[23] There is already an intermingling of human and machine, and as a result subjectivity continuously mutates through its machinic components; the challenge is to ensure that on the terrain of its creativity, subjectivity is guided by ethico-aesthetic, democratic, eco-praxic values that carry it to and fro amongst molecular and molar obligations. Watch out for the highs machines can deliver, Guattari warned,[24] as there are also lows on the horizon once the thrill of existential affirmation in extreme sports or in the creative commons wears off. At the same time, information subjugates, by ascribing quantitative identities that integrate more intensively, and thicken, subjectivity's ecology in the web of machinic enunciations by means of a-signifying part-signs (which requires a remarkable technical knowledge to manage, if not outwit). The lure of 'empty stakes' is subjectivity's challenge to meet and overcome: 'Refusing the status of the current media, combined with a search for new social interactivities, for an institutional creativity and an enrichment of values, would already constitute an important step on the way to a remaking of social practices.'[25]

Machines intrude with seductive systems of valorization and imaginary solutions; subjectivity multiplies its components and blazes aberrant paths between components, wholly artificially drawing rhizomes, speaking in heterogeneous voices, subverting to create and singularize by agglomeration, and steadying itself. 'Subjectivity is the real.'[26]

NOTES

Introduction

1. Marie Depussé, *Dieu gît dans les détails: La Borde, un asile*, Paris: P.O.L. Éditeur, 1993, pp. 144–5.
2. François Dosse, *Gilles Deleuze and Félix Guattari: Biographie croisée*, Paris: La Découverte, 2007, pp. 44–5.
3. Quoted in Michael Goddard, 'Bifo's Futural Thought,' *Cultural Studies Review* 11/2 (2005): 50.
4. Félix Guattari, 'Raymond et le groupe Hispano,' in *Psychanalyse et transversalité*, Paris: Maspero/La Découverte, 1972/2003, p. 268. 'Hispano' refers to the Hispano-Suiza automobile plant in Bois-Colombes in suburban Paris and 'Raymond' is organizer Raymond Petit, one of Guattari's earliest mentors in the leisure/labor ligature, who formed the Groupe jeunes d'Hispano. The group primarily served the leisure and cultural needs of workers under 20, but branched out into the suburb of La Garenne to include young people like Félix.
5. On this point see Jean Baudrillard, *Fragments: Conversations with François L'Yvonnet*, trans. Chris Turner, London: Routledge, 2004, pp. 15–16.
6. In Lacanian psychoanalysis a 'matheme' is a notational symbol, the combination of which, in pseudo-algebraic statements, expresses the relations between the smallest and most fundamental conceptual units in the analysis of the unconscious.
7. Félix Guattari, 'Machine et structure,' in *Psychanalyse et transversalité*, p. 240.
8. Félix Guattari, *L'inconscient machinique*, Fontenay-sous-Bois: Recherches, 1979, p. 190.
9. Sigmund Freud, 'Recommendations to Physicians Practising Psycho-Analysis,' *Standard Edition of the Complete Psychological Works of Sigmund Freud*, vol. 12, London: Hogarth/Vintage, 2001, p. 115.
10. Jacques Lacan, 'The direction of the treatment and the principles of its power,' *Ecrits: A Selection*, trans. A. Sheridan, New York: W.W. Norton, 1977, pp. 229–30.
11. Félix Guattari, 'Nous sommes tous des groupuscules,' in *Psychanalyse et transversalité*, p. 284.
12. Slavoj Žižek, 'Introduction: Alfred Hitchcock, or, The Form and Its Historical Mediation,' in *Everything You Always Wanted to Know*

About Lacan But Were Afraid To Ask Hitchcock, London: Verso, 1992, p. 4.

13. Guattari, 'Machine et structure,' p. 244.

14. Ibid., p. 243.

15. Ibid., p. 241.

16. Félix Guattari, 'On the Machinic Interpretation of Lacan's "a",' in *The Anti-Oedipus Papers*, trans. K. Gotman, Los Angeles: Semtiotext(e), 2006, p. 153.

17. Gilles Deleuze and Félix Guattari, *Anti-Oedipus: Capitalism and Schizophrenia*, trans. Robert Hurley, Mark Seem, and Helen R. Lane, New York: Viking Press, 1977, p. 285. 'Desire is not in the subject, but the machine in desire.'

18. Ibid., p. 244.

19. Ibid., p. 73.

20. Félix Guattari and Antonio Negri, *Communists Like Us: New Spaces of Liberty, New Lines of Alliance*, trans. M. Ryan, New York: Semiotext(e), 1990, p. 17.

21. Maurizio Lazzarato, 'Semiotic Pluralism and the New Government of Signs: Homage to Félix Guattari,' *Semiotic Review of Books* 18/1 (2008): 9–12.

22. Paul Bains, 'Subjectless Subjectivities,' in *A Shock to Thought*, ed. B. Massumi, London: Routledge, 2002, p. 103.

23. Franco Berardi, *Félix Guattari: Thought, Friendship, and Visionary Cartography*, trans. G. Mecchia and C. Stivale, London: Palgrave Macmillan, 2008, see ch. 9.

24. Félix Guattari, *Chaosmosis*, trans. P. Bains and J. Pefanis, Bloomington: Indiana University Press, 1995, p. 60.

25. Félix Guattari, 'Institutional Practice and Politics,' interview by J. Pain, in *The Guattari Reader*, ed. G. Genosko, Oxford: Blackwell, 1996, p. 122.

26. Guattari, *Chaosmosis*, p. 61.

27. Ibid., p. 14.

28. Guattari, 'Institutional Practice and Politics,' p. 133.

29. Ibid., p. 136.

30. Guattari, *Chaosmosis*, p. 18.

31. Félix Guattari and Suely Rolnick, *Molecular Revolution in Brazil*, trans. K. Clapshow and B. Holmes, Los Angeles: Semiotext(e), 2008, pp. 357–63. This short section bears the title 'Schizoanalytic cases.' Guattari bequeathed few of these.

32. Ian Buchanan, 'Deleuze, Gilles and Félix Guattari,' in *The Johns Hopkins Guide to Literary Theory and Criticism*, 2nd edn., eds. M. Groden et al., Baltimore: Johns Hopkins University Press, 2005, p. 248.

33. Slavoj Žižek, *Organs without Bodies*, New York: Routledge, 2004, p. 83.

34. Ibid., p. 191. See undocumented and vague claims such as: '(Guattari once directly ...).'

35. Michael Hardt and Antonio Negri, *Empire*, Cambridge: Harvard University Press. pp. 290 ff.

36. Félix Guattari, 'Capital as the Integral of Power Formations,' in *Soft Subversions*, New York: Semiotext(e), 1955, p. 212.

37. Michael Hardt and Antonio Negri, *Multitude: War and Democracy in the Age of Empire*, New York: Penguin, 2004, p. 336.

38. Hardt and Negri, *Empire*, p. 406.

39. Félix Guattari, *The Three Ecologies*, trans. Ian Pindar and Paul Sutton, London: Athlone Press, 2000 (orig. *Les trois écologies*, Paris: Galilée, 1989), p. 68.

40. Guattari, 'Institutional Practice and Politics,' p. 132.

41. Guattari, *Chaosmosis*, pp. 35–6. Note the elaborate contrast drawn between tools and machines: the former as extensions of humans, the mutual adaptability of humans and tools, and the evolutionary progress of tools into machines, as well as the latter's betrayal of their makers; whereas machinic assemblages bring together heterogeneous components (including certain humans and not others) based on recurrence and communication rather than contact and projection. See also Félix Guattari, 'Balance-Sheet for Desiring-Machines, in *Chaosophy*, New York: Semiotext(e), 1995, pp. 121–2.

42. Félix Guattari, 'Microphysics of Power/Micropolitics of Desire,' in *The Guattari Reader*, p. 175.

43. Ibid., p. 181.

44. Guattari, *Chaosmosis*, p. 7.

45. Félix Guattari, 'Entretien avec Félix Guattari,' interview by E. Videcoq and J.-Y. Sparel, *Chimères* 28 (Spring/Summer 1996): 20; and see L. Margulis and J.E. Lovelock, 'Gaia and Geognosy,' in M.B. Rambler et al. (eds.), *Global Ecology*, Boston: Academic Press, 1989, pp. 1–30.

46. Guattari, 'Institutional Practice and Politics,' in *The Guattari Reader*, p. 126.

47. Guattari, *Chaosmosis*, pp. 93–4. 'Jazz ... is simultaneously nourished by its African genealogy and by its reactualisations in multiple and heterogeneous forms. As long as it is alive it will be like that. But like any autopoietic machine, it can die for want of sustenance or drift towards destinies which make it a stranger to itself.'

48. Ibid., p. 133.

49. In this respect I agree with John Marks when he writes 'it seems unjustifiable to read Deleuze and Guattari as cyber-enthusiasts *avant*

la lettre' as they do not offer 'a blueprint for a utopian, disembodied cyberspace,' John Marks, 'Information and Resistance: Deleuze, the Virtual and Cybernetics,' in I. Buchanan and A. Parr (eds.), *Deleuze and the Contemporary World*, Edinburgh: Edinburgh University Press, 2006, p. 40. Still, Guattari was explicitly enthusiastic, but cognizant of the limits of the very machines – computers – that permitted him to pursue his interests. After all, he was not one to refuse a machinic buzz.

50. Félix Guattari, 'Typescript of an Interview with T. Wada of the *Asahi Shimbun*, London Bureau,' October 2, 1985, Fonds Félix Guattari, L'Institut Mémoires de l'Édition Contemporaine (IMEC), Saint-Germain-la-Blanche-Herbe, file I02-21.
51. Félix Guattari, 'Towards an Ethics of the Media,' trans. J. Watson, *Polygraph* 14 (2002): 19.
52. Gilles Deleuze and Félix Guattari, 'Treatise on Nomadology: The War Machine,' in *A Thousand Plateaus*, trans. B. Massumi, Minneapolis: University of Minnesota Press, 1987, pp. 353 and 360.
53. Ibid, pp. 388 and 389.
54. Félix Guattari, 'La Borde: A Clinic Unlike Any Other,' in *Chaosophy*, p. 196.
55. Nicola Spelman, 'Reversing us and them: anti-psychiatry and "The Dark Side of the Moon",' in R. Reising (ed.), *'Speak to Me': The Legacy of Pink Floyd's 'The Dark Side of the Moon'*, Aldershot: Ashgate, 2005, pp. 123–42.
56. If anti-psychiatry had a core, it was articulated by David Cooper in his comments on his work in the early 1960s on an experimental unit in a psychiatric ward, Villa 21, as a critique of the conventional mental hospital's 'institutional irrationality' (staff and patient fantasies were analyzed through collective meetings and role changes). This experiment in anti-psychiatry is described in David Cooper, *Psychiatry and Anti-Psychiatry*, London: Tavistock, 1967, pp. 83–104.
57. Guattari, *Chaosmosis*, pp. 92–3.
58. See Brian Massumi, *Parables for the Virtual*, Durham, NC: Duke University Press, 2002, p. 36.
59. Guattari and Rolnick, *Molecular Revolution in Brazil*, pp. 196–7.

Chapter 1

1. Félix Guattari, *Psychanalyse et transversalité*, Paris: Maspero/La Découverte, 1972/2003, p. 154.
2. François Dosse, *Gilles Deleuze et Félix Guattari: Biographie croisée*, Paris: La Découverte, 2007, p. 37.

3. Félix Guattari, *The Anti-Oedipus Papers*, trans. K. Gotman, Los Angeles: Semtiotext(e), 2006, New York: Semiotext(e), 2006, p. 303.

4. Félix Guattari, 'La Borde: A Clinic Unlike Any Other,' in *Chaosophy*, New York: Semiotext(e), 1995, p. 189.

5. Guattari, *Anti-Oedipus Papers*, p. 307.

6. Ibid., p. 307.

7. Jean Oury, 'Une dialectique de l'amitié,' *Le Monde* (1 September 1992): 11. 'He [Guattari] began studying pharmacy. That did not please him at all ... I encouraged him not to continue.'

8. See Tom De Coster et al., 'Emancipating a Neo-Liberal Society? Initial Thoughts on the Progressive Pedagogical Heritage in Flanders since the 1960s,' *Education Research and Perspectives* 31/2 (2004): 156–75.

9. Nicholas Beattie, *The Freinet Movements of France, Italy, and Germany, 1920-2000*. Mellen Studies in Eduation, vol. 74, Lewiston: The Edwin Mellen Press, 2002, p. 229.

10. Ibid., 232.

11. Catherine Bédarida, 'Disparitions: Fernand Deligny – Un éducateur et un écrivain au service des enfants "anormaux",' *Le Monde* (21 September 1996).

12. Liane Mozère, 'In Early Childhood: What's Language About?' *Educational Philosophy and Theory* 39/3 (2007): 296.

13. Dosse, *Biographie croisée*, pp. 95–6.

14. Pierre Boiral, 'Introduction,' in *Deligny et les tentatives de prise en charge des enfants fous: L'aventure de l'aire (1968–1973)*, Ramonville Saint-Agne: Éditions Érès, 2007, pp. 15–17.

15. Nicholas Beattie makes this point, but in so doing incorrectly limits Jean Oury's adaptation of Freinet techniques like the school printery to 'work as a therapeutic tool'. See Beattie, *Freinet Movements*, p. 228.

16. Piet Kimzeke, 'The Educational Function of the Youth Hostel,' in Graham Heath (ed.), *The International Youth Hostel Manual*, 2nd edn., Copenhagen: IYHA, 1967, p. 97.

17. Anton Grassl and Graham Heath, *The Magic Triangle: A Short History of the World Youth Hostel Movement*, Bielefeld, Germany: International Youth Hostel Federation, 1982, p. 47.

18. Graham Heath, 'The Growth of the Youth Hostel Movement,' in *International Youth Hostel Manual*, p. 19.

19. Grassl and Heath, *Magic Triangle*, p. 58.

20. Ibid., p. 85.

21. Ibid., p. 58.

22. Ibid., p. 105.

23. Jean Oury, 'Finalités conscientes et inconscientes des institutions,' in *Onze heures du soir à La Borde: Essais sur la psychothérapie institutionnelle*, Paris: Galilée, 1980, p. 259.
24. Félix Guattari, 'L'intervention institutionnelle,' typescript of an interview (1980), Fonds Félix Guattari, L'Institut Mémoires de l'Édition Contemporaine (IMEC), Saint-Germain-la-Blanche-Herbe, file ET09-26, pp. 135–6.
25. Félix Guattari, 'Du Zen aux Galeries Lafayette', interview with Jacky Beillerot, typescript dated November 23, 1986, Fonds Félix Guattari, IMEC, file I02-22, pp. 6–7.
26. Ibid., p. 15.
27. Félix Guattari, *Chaosmosis*, trans. P. Bains and J. Pefanis, Bloomington: Indiana University Press, 1995, p. 65.
28. Aida Vasquez and Fernand Oury, *Vers une pédagogie institutionnelle*, Paris: François Maspero, 1968, pp. 43 and 200.
29. Vasquez and Oury, *Vers une pédagogie institutionnelle*, p. 243.
30. Célestin Freinet, *La méthode naturelle. 1. L'apprentissage de la langue*, Neuchatel and Paris: Delachaux et Niestlé, 1968, p. 146.
31. Célestin Freinet, 'L'éducation du travail,' in *Oeuvres Pédagogiques*, vol. 1, Paris: Éditions du Seuil, 1994, p. 309.
32. Freinet, *La méthode naturelle*, p. 122.
33. Ibid., p. 122.
34. Ibid., p. 123.
35. Ibid., p. 124.
36. Célestin Freinet, 'L'École moderne Française,' in *Oeuvres pédagogiques*, vol. 2, Paris: Éditions du Seuil, 1994, p. 59.
37. Ibid., p. 60.
38. Vasquez and Oury, *Vers une pédagogie institutionnelle*, p. 82.
39. Félix Guattari, 'La grille,' typescript dated January 29, 1987, Fonds Félix Guattari, IMEC, file ET04-13, p. 6.
40. Vasquez and Oury, *Vers une pédagogie institutionnelle*, p. 82.
41. Guattari, 'La grille,' p. 9.
42. Vasquez and Oury, *Vers une pédagogie institutionnelle*, p. 242.
43. Ibid., p. 243.
44. Freinet, 'L'Éducation du travail,' pp. 252–3.
45. Guattari, 'La grille,' p. 3.
46. Freinet, 'LÉducation du travail,' p. 252.
47. Freinet, 'L'École moderne Française,' p. 47.
48. Guattari, 'La Borde', p. 193
49. Ibid., p. 194.
50. Guattari, *Psychanalyse et transversalité*, p. 80.
51. See Célestin Freinet, 'Rapid Growth of School Magazines in Various Parts of the World,' in *Cooperative Learning and Social Change:*

Selected Writings of Célestin Freinet, ed. and trans. David Clandfield and John Sivell, Toronto: OISE Publishing, 1990, pp. 34–5.
52. The schedule is presented by Beattie, *Freinet Movements*, pp. 22–31.
53. Guattari, 'La Borde', p. 190.
54. Michel Foucault, *Discipline and Punish*, trans. A. Sheridan, New York: Vintage, 1977, p. 149.
55. Félix Guattari and Suely Rolnick, *Molecular Revolution in Brazil*, trans. K. Clapshow and B. Holmes, Los Angeles: Semiotext(e), 2008, p. 380.

Chapter 2

1. Félix Guattari, 'I Am An Idea-Thief,' in *Chaosophy*, New York: Semiotext(e), 1995, p. 39.
2. Félix Guattari, 'Beyond the Psychoanalytic Unconscious,' in *Soft Subversions*, New York: Semiotext(e), 1955, pp. 196–7.
3. François Dosse, *Gilles Deleuze and Félix Guattari: Biographie croisée*, Paris: La Découverte, 2007, pp. 66 and 81.
4. Ibid., p. 73.
5. Félix Guattari, 'Transversalité,' in *Psychanalyse et transversalité*, Paris: Maspero/La Découverte, 1972/2003, p. 75.
6. Félix Guattari, 'The Transference,' in *The Guattari Reader*, ed. G. Genosko, Oxford: Blackwell, 1996, p. 63.
7. Gilles Deleuze, 'For Félix,' in *Two Regimes of Madness*, trans. A. Hodges and M. Taormina, New York: Semiotext(e), 2006, p. 382.
8. Guattari, 'Transversalité,' p. 79.
9. Ibid., p. 80.
10. Ibid., p. 80.
11. Guattari, 'The Transference,' p. 62.
12. Guattari, 'Transversalité,' p. 76.
13. Guattari, 'Transference,' p. 63.
14. See my *Félix Guattari: An Aberrant Introduction*, London: Continuum, 2002, pp. 87–90.
15. Freud, 'Neurosis and Psychosis,' *Standard Edition of the Complete Psychological Works of Sigmund Freud*, vol. 19, London: Hogarth/Vintage, 1964, pp. 151–2.
16. Freud, 'An Outline of Psycho-Analysis,' *Standard Edition of the Complete Psychological Works of Sigmund Freud*, vol. 23, London: Hogarth/Vintage, 1964, pp. 206–7.
17. Félix Guattari, 'The Best Capitalist Drug,' in *Chaosophy*, p. 215.
18. Guattari, 'The Best Capitalist Drug,' p. 219–20.

19. Dosse, *Biographie croisée*, pp. 36 and 89.
20. Ivan Illich, *Tools for Conviviality*, New York: Harper & Row, 1973, p. 17.
21. Ibid., p. 191.
22. Michel Foucault, *Discipline and Punish*, trans. A. Sheridan, New York: Vintage, 1977, p. 152.
23. Deleuze, *Foucault*, trans. S. Hand, Minneapolis: University of Minnesota Press, 1988, pp. 34–7.
24. Félix Guattari, *La Révolution Moléculaire*, Fontenay-sous-Bois: Recherches (Encres), 1977, p. 271.
25. Stephen Zepke, *Art as Abstract Machine: Ontology and Aesthetics in Deleuze and Guattari*, London: Routledge, 2005, pp. 189–92.
26. Zepke astutely emphasizes that building an abstract machine is a do-it-yourself project, ibid., p. 2.
27. Illich, *Tools for Conviviality*, p. 37.
28. Deleuze, *Foucault*, p. 22.
29. This glossary is found on the clinic's web site under 'Repères,' <http://www.cliniquedelaborde.com>.
30. Le Club Laborde, 'Le feuille de jour: traverses les cloisonnements,' listed under 'Quotidien,' at <http://www. cliniquedelaborde.com>.
31. CERFI, 'La grille: 1958–1973,' originally published in *Revue perspectives psychiatriques* 45 (1974)' and available under 'Réflexions' at <http://www.cliniquedelaborde.com>.
32. Félix Guattari, 'La "grille",' *Chimères* 34 (1998): 18–20; and Félix Guattari, 'Entretien avec John Johnston: Vertige de l'immanence,' *Chimères* 38 (2000): 14–15. Guattari explains very briefly that transversality changed from his early deployments of it in the 1960s as a passage between heterogeneous poles, through the concept's use to describe what happens to events and forces as they escape stratification by signs, identities, or other coordinates, and then, finally, as chaosmotic transversality, the concept indicates the risk of altogether exiting from meaning.
33. Deleuze and Guattari, 'Balance-Sheet for Desiring Machines,' in *Chaosophy*, p. 136.
34. Foucault, *Discipline and Punish*, pp. 164 ff.
35. Guattari, 'Subjectivities: for Better and for Worse,' in *The Guattari Reader*, p. 201.
36. Richard K. Ashley, 'Living on Border Lines: Mass, Poststructuralism, and War,' in James Der Derian and Michael J. Shapiro (eds.), *International/Intertextual Relations: Postmodern Readings of World Politics*, Lexington, MA: D.C. Heath, 1989, pp. 296 ff.
37. David Campbell, 'Political Prosaics, Transversal Politics, and the Anarchical World,' in Michael J. Shapiro and Hayward R. Allier

(eds.), *Challenging Boundaries*, Minneapolis: University of Minnesota Press, 1996, p. 20.
38. Roland Bleiker, *Popular Dissent, Human Agency and Global Politics,* Cambridge: Cambridge University Press, 2000, p. 119.
39. Michael Hardt and Antonio Negri, *Multitude: War and Democracy in the Age of Empire*, New York: Penguin, 2004, p. 88.
40. Ned Rossiter, *Organized Networks,* The Hague: NAi Publishers, 2006, pp. 208–9.
41. Michel Foucault, 'Afterword: The Subject and Power,' in Hubert L. Dreyfus and Paul Rabinow, *Michel Foucault: Beyond Structuralism and Hermeneutics*, Chicago: University of Chicago Press, 1982, pp. 211–12.
42. Félix Guattari, 'Microphysics of Power/Micropolitics of Desire,' in *The Guattari Reader*, p. 174.
43. Ibid., p. 176.
44. Félix Guattari, 'Réinventer la politique,' *Le Monde*, March 8, 1990.
45. Félix Guattari, 'La revolution moléculaire,' *Le Monde*, December 7, 1990.
46. Félix Guattari, 'Ecologie et politique: Un nouvel axe progressiste,' *Le Monde*, April 6, 1992.
47. Félix Guattari, 'Capitalism: A Very Special Delirium,' in *Chaosophy*, pp. 61–2.
48. Hardt and Negri, *Multitude*, p. 222.
49. Ibid., p. 358.
50. Félix Guattari, *The Three Ecologies*, trans. Ian Pindar and Paul Sutton, London: Athlone Press, 2000 (orig. *Les trois écologies*, Paris: Galilée, 1989), pp. 68–9.

Chapter 3

1. Félix Guattari, *The Three Ecologies*, trans. Ian Pindar and Paul Sutton, London: Athlone Press, 2000 (orig. *Les trois écologies*, Paris: Galilée, 1989).
2. Félix Guattari, 'Les fondements éthico-politique de l'interdisciplinarité,' handwritten text, April 1991, Fonds Félix Guattari, L'Institut Mémoires de l'Édition Contemporaine (IMEC), Saint-Germain-la-Blanche-Herbe, file ET10-24.
3. Ibid., p. 15.
4. 'De la pluridisciplinarité à la transdisciplinarité,' written with Sergio Vilar, Barcelona and Paris, Sept. 1992, Fonds Felix Guattari (IMEC), file ET05-13, p. 6.
5. Jean Chesnaux and Roger Gentis, 'Félix, Our Friend,' trans. M. McMahon, in G. Genosko (ed.), *Deleuze and Guattari: Critical*

Assessments of Leading Philosophers, vol. 2, London: Routledge, 2001, p. 544.

6. See François Dosse, *Gilles Deleuze and Félix Guattari: Biographie croisée*, Paris: La Découverte, 2007, pp. 449 ff.
7. This is a dominant theme in Berardi's writings about his friend Félix.
8. See 'Summit of Radicals,' in my *The Party without Bosses: Lessons on Anti-Capitalism from Félix Guattari and Luís Inácio 'Lula' da Silva*, Semaphore Series, Winnipeg: Arbeiter Ring, 2003.
9. Félix Guattari, *Chaosmosis*, trans. P. Bains and J. Pefanis, Bloomington: Indiana University Press, 1995, p. 128.
10. Félix Guattari, 'Une autre vision du futur,' *Le Monde*, February 15, 1992.
11. See 'La preparation des elections régionales: Les Verts de Paris proposent une referendum sur l'aménagement de l'Ile-de-France,' *Le Monde*, February 27, 1992.
12. Félix Guattari, *La Philosophie est essentielle à l'existence humaine*, interview with Antoine Spire, Michel Field and Emmanuel Hirsch, Paris: Éditions Aube, 2002, p. 42. Also, Félix Guattari, 'L'intervention institutionnelle,' Fonds Félix Guattari, IMEC, typescript of an interview, 1980, file ET09-26, p. 146.
13. Guattari, *La Philosophie*, p. 47.
14. Guattari, 'I am an Idea-Thief,' pp. 46–7.
15. Ibid., p. 47.
16. Félix Guattari, 'La grand-peur écologique,' handwritten MS, Fonds Félix Guattari, IMEC, file ET10-03.
17. Guattari, *The Three Ecologies*, p. 34.
18. Ibid., p. 29.
19. Félix Guattari, 'Remaking Social Practices,' in *The Guattari Reader*, ed. G. Genosko, Oxford: Blackwell, 1996, p. 264.
20. Ibid.
21. Ibid., p. 268.
22. Guattari, *The Three Ecologies*, pp. 41–2.
23. Ibid., p. 35.
24. Ibid., p. 36.
25. See Steve Baker, *The Postmodern Animal*, London: Reaktion Books, 2000, p. 63.
26. Guattari, *The Three Ecologies*, p. 49.
27. Félix Guattari, 'Introduction,' in *George Condo*, Paris: Daniel Templon, 1990, p. 5. See also Guattari, *Chaosmosis*, pp. 6–7, and Gary Genosko, *Félix Guattari: An Aberrant Introduction*, London: Continuum, 2003, pp. 49 ff.
28. Guattari, *The Three Ecologies*, p. 45.

29. Ibid., p. 52.
30. Guattari, 'Subjectivities: For Better and for Worse,' in *The Guattari Reader*, pp. 199–200.
31. Félix Guattari, 'Les Ritournelles du temps perdu,' in *L'inconscient machinique*, Fontenay-sous-Bois: Recherches, 1979, pp. 239 ff.
32. Guattari, *Chaosmosis*, p. 90.
33. Guattari, *The Three Ecologies*, p. 46.
34. Guattari, *Chaosmosis*, p. 91.
35. Guattari, *The Three Ecologies*, p. 52.
36. Guattari, 'David Wojnarowicz,' *Rethinking Marxism* 3/1 (1990): 76–7.
37. Ian Wallace's large-format photographs of the anti-logging protest at Clayoquet Sound in 1993 in British Columbia were exhibited at the Vancouver Art Gallery in 1995.
38. Guattari, *The Three Ecologies*, p. 66.
39. Félix Guattari, 'Les machines architecturales de Shin Takamatsu,' *Chimères* 21 (Winter 1994): 127–41.
40. Hear his remarks in Ben Wright's film, *Slavoj Žižek: The Reality of the Virtual* (2004).
41. Gilles Deleuze and Félix Guattari, *What is Philosophy?* trans. H. Tomlinson and G. Burchell, New York: Columbia University Press, 1994, pp. 183–6.
42. Guattari, *The Three Ecologies*, p. 66.
43. Félix Guattari, 'Regimes, Pathways, Subjects,' in *The Guattari Reader*, p. 103.
44. Guattari, *The Three Ecologies*, p. 69.
45. Gilles Deleuze, *Francis Bacon: The Logic of Sensation*, trans. D.W. Smith, Minneapolis: University of Minnesota Press, 2003, p. 70.
46. 'I refuse transcendent judgements.' Félix Guattari, 'Entretien avec Félix Guattari,' interview by E. Videcoq and J.-Y. Sparel, *Chimères* 28 (1996) (Spring/Summer 1996): 22.
47. In the view of A. and M. Mattelart, *Rethinking Media Theory*, trans. J.A. Choen and M. Urquidi, Minneapolis: University of Minnesota Press, 1992, pp. 20–7.
48. Several participants in the colloquium on transdisciplinarity at L'Abbaye de Royaumont call for a 'transcendent language' or 'transcendent explanatory power.' M. A. Somerville and D. J. Rapport (eds.), *Transdisciplinarity: Recreating Integrated Knowledge*, Oxford: EOLSS, 2000.
49. Famously, E.O. Wilson wrote about the 'path back from chaos,' and this is picked up as a definition of transdisciplinarity by one of the editors (Rapport) of the volume *Transdisciplinarity* previously cited, p. 135.

50. Guattari, *Chaosmosis*, p. 80.
51. Ibid., p. 133.
52. Ibid., p. 129.
53. Arne Naess, *Ecology, Community and Lifestyle*, trans. D. Rothenberg, Cambridge: Cambridge University Press, 1989, p. 38.
54. Ibid., p. 86.
55. For example, see Warwick Fox, *Toward a Transpersonal Ecology*, Albany: State University of New York Press, 1995.
56. Guattari, 'I am an Idea-Thief,' pp. 47–8.
57. Guattari, 'Remaking Social Practices,' p. 268.
58. Hans Jonas, *The Imperative of Responsibility: In Search of an Ethics for the Technological Age*, Chicago: University of Chicago Press, 1984, p. 9; Guattari, 'Remaking Social Practices,' p. 271.

Chapter 4

1. Umberto Eco, *A Theory of Semiotics*, Bloomington: Indiana University Press, 1976, p. 20.
2. Ibid., p. 33.
3. See Maurizio Lazzarato, 'Immaterial Labor,' in Paolo Virno and Michael Hardt (eds.), *Radical Thought in Italy: A Potential Politics*, Minneapolis: University of Minnesota Press, 1996, p. 143.
4. Karl Marx, *Capital*, vol. 1, trans. S. Moore and E. Aveling, Moscow: Progress Publishers, 1986, p. 582
5. Manuel Castells defines the material foundations of the network society in five ways: information is the raw material upon which technologies act; the new information technologies are pervasive; these technologies obey a logic of networking; this logic is characterized by its flexibility; and it is characterized by the convergence of old and new technologies; Manuel Castells, *The Rise of the Network Society*, Oxford: Blackwell, 2000, pp. 70–1.
6. Manuel DeLanda, *War in the Age of Intelligent Machines*, New York: Zone, 1991. DeLanda cites two meanings of 'machinic phylum': the first is borrowed directly from Deleuze and Guattari as the 'flow of matter-movement'; the second concerns the processes by means of which 'order emerges out of chaos' (p. 20). The 'phyla' are the lineages of technologies whose emergence interests DeLanda to the extent that they are operationalized for military ends and defined scientifically. Guattari simply defines the phylum as the 'continuum of possibility' of machinic interactions modeled on the libido as an abstract matter of pure possibility striated by the fluxes of desire (drives, objects, stages, etc.), but not these alone; Félix Guattari, *Cartographies schizoanalytiques*, Paris: Galilée, 1989, pp. 42–4.

7. Félix Guattari, 'Machinic Junkies,' in *Soft Subversions*, New York: Semiotext(e), 1995, p. 103.
8. See Guattari, 'Révolution informationnelle, écologie et recomposition subjective,' *Multitudes* 24 (2006), <http://multitudes.samizdat.net/spip.php?article2390>; and Pierre Clastres, *Society Against the State*, trans. R. Hurley, New York: Zone, 1987, p. 47.
9. O'Sullivan presented this reading of subjectification at the First International Deleuze Studies Conference in Cardiff, August 2008 in a paper titled 'Non-sense and Indeterminacy in Contemporary Art.'
10. Deleuze, *Cinema 2: The Time-Image*, trans. H. Tomlinson and R. Galeta, Minneapolis: University of Minnesota Press, 1989, p. 29. For Guattari, on the phylum the particle-signs attest to its smoothness and abstractness, as they are not fully formed, but concrete enough. But the phylum is striated already by rhizomes. The signaletic matters and energies come into play as the abstract and continuous domain of the phylum is manifested in space-time-bound, discontinuous, striated fluxes in terms of (libido, capital, semiotics, labor) multiple articulations. One could say, after Guattari, that the phylum is to whole numbers as fluxes are to fractions.
11. For instance, on this point see Scott Lash, *Critique of Information*, London: Sage, 2002, pp. 18 ff.
12. Michael Ruse, 'Signal,' in Paul Bouissac (ed.), *Encyclopedia of Semiotics*, New York: Oxford University Press, 1998, p. 576.
13. Félix Guattari, *Chaosmosis*, trans. P. Bains and J. Pefanis, Bloomington: Indiana University Press, 1995, p. 5.
14. Félix Guattari, *L'inconscient machinique*, Fontenay-sous-Bois: Recherches, 1979, p. 13.
15. Guattari, *Chaosmosis*, p. 49.
16. Bruno Bosteels, 'From Text to Diagram: Towards a Semiotics of Cultural Cartography,' in C.W. Spinks and J. Deely (eds.), *Semiotics 1994*, New York: Peter Lang, 1995, p. 353.
17. Roland Barthes, *Elements of Semiology*, trans. A. Lavers and C. Smith, New York: Hill and Wang, 1967, pp. 11 and 86.
18. Barthes, *Elements of Semiology*, p. 87.
19. Inna Semetsky, 'Semiotics' in A. Parr (ed.), *The Deleuze Dictionary*, Edinburgh: Edinburgh University Press, 2004, p. 243.
20. Félix Guattari, *La Révolution Moléculaire*, Fontenay-sous-Bois: Recherches (10/18), 1977, pp. 230–1. This is the '10/18' edition.
21. Ibid., p. 234; and Félix Guattari, *La Révolution Moléculaire*, Fontenay-sous-Bois: Recherches (Encres), 1977, p. 243. This is the 'Encres' edition.
22. Guattari, *La Révolution Moléculaire* (Encres), p. 243.

23. Ibid., p. 281.
24. Guattari, *La Révolution Moléculaire* (10/18), p. 236.
25. Guattari, *Chaosmosis*, p. 49.
26. Janell Watson, 'Guattari's Black Holes and the Post-Media Era,' *Polygraph* 14 (2002): 35.
27. Guattari, *La Révolution Moléculaire* (10/18), p. 235.
28. Guattari, *La Révolution Moléculaire* (Encres), p. 282.
29. Guattari, *L'inconscient machinique*, p. 224.
30. Félix Guattari, *The Anti-Oedipus Papers*, trans. K. Gotman, New York: Semiotext(e), 2006, p. 387.
31. Guattari, *La Révolution Moléculaire* (10/18), p. 235.
32. Brian Massumi, *A User's Guide to Capitalism and Schizophrenia*, Cambridge, MA: MIT Press/Swerve Edition, 1992, p. 53.
33. Guattari, *La Révolution Moléculaire* (Encres), p. 244.
34. See Oscar Gandy, 'Data Mining, Surveillance, and Discrimination in the Post-9/11 Environment,' in K. Haggerty and R. Ericson (eds.), *The New Politics of Surveillance and Visibility*, Toronto: University of Toronto Press, 2006, pp. 363–84.
35. Gilles Deleuze, 'Postscript on Control Societies,' in *Negotiations 1972–1990*, trans. M. Joughin, New York: Columbia, 1995, pp. 181–2.
36. Guattari, *Chaosmosis*, p. 48.
37. Ibid., p. 49.
38. Guattari, *L'inconscient machinique*, p. 55.
39. Jacques Derrida, *Dissemination*, trans. B. Johnson, Chicago: University of Chicago Press, 1981, p. 292.
40. Guattari, *L'inconscient machinique*, p. 224.
41. Ibid., p. 223.
42. Guattari, *La Révolution Moléculaire* (Encres), p. 259.
43. Ibid., p. 259.
44. Ibid., p. 264.
45. Ibid., p. 267. See also Gilles Deleuze and Félix Guattari, *A Thousand Plateaus*, trans. B. Massumi, Minneapolis: University of Minnesota Press, 1987, p. 129.
46. Jussi Parikka, *Digital Contagions*, New York: Peter Lang, 2007, pp. 260 ff.
47. Guattari, *La Révolution Moléculaire* (10/18), p. 237.
48. John Willinsky, *Technologies of Knowing*, Boston: Beacon Press, 1999.
49. For Castells, Europe is a 'network state'; *End of Millennium*, Oxford: Blackwell, 2000, pp. 338 ff.
50. Michael Hardt and Antonio Negri, *Multitude*, New York: Penguin, 2004, p. 88.

51. Brian Massumi, *Parables for the Virtual*, Durham, NC: Duke University Press, 2002, pp. 46 ff.
52. Félix Guattari, 'Ritornellos and Existential Affects,' trans., Juliana Schiesari and Georges van den Abbeele, *Discourse* 12/2 (1990): 74.
53. After Eric Alliez's beautiful phrase 'empire of digital capitalism.' Eric Alliez, 'Anti-Oedipus: Thirty Years On,' in M. Fuglsang and B.M. Sorensen (eds.), *Deleuze and the Social*, Edinburgh: Edinburgh University Press, 2006, p. 165.
54. Acidus, 'NCR ATMs – Aurum Ex Machina,' *2600* 19/2 (Summer 2002): 18–19.
55. On the minor strategy of 'willed poverty' as a 'deferral of subjective plenitude,' see Nick Thoburn, 'Vacuoles of Noncommunication: Minor Politics, Communist Style and the Multitude, in I. Buchanan and A. Parr (eds.), *Deleuze and the Contemporary World*, Edinburgh: Edinburgh University Press, 2006, p. 44.
56. For example, see the work of Sharon Kirksghard, who mapped her personal debt in a flow chart in a becoming-deliquent in the work '2.8.99'; Sharon Kirksghard, 'Performer turns credit card debt into art,' STTF.org (South to the Future), <http://sttf.org/wires/1999/03/22/performer-turns-credit-card-debt-into-art/>.

Chapter 5

1. Gilles Deleuze and Félix Guattari, *A Thousand Plateaus*, trans. Brian Massumi, Minneapolis: University of Minnesota Press, 1987, pp. 474 ff.
2. Paul Patton, *Deleuze and the Political*, Oxford: Blackwell, 2000, p. 114.
3. Ibid., p. 129.
4. Deborah Root, *Cannibal Culture: Art, Appropriation, and the Commodification of Difference*, Boulder, CO: Westview, 1996, p. 86.
5. The bulk of the on-site research for this project in Iqaluit was undertaken by Adam Bryx, who is presently a doctoral candidate in drama at the University of California.
6. Department of Communications and Department of Justice, *Privacy and Computers: A Report of a Task Force*, Ottawa: Government of Canada, 1972, p. 88.
7. Valerie Alia, *Names, Numbers, and Northern Policy: Inuit, Project Surname, and the Politics of Identity*, Halifax: Fernwood, 1994, pp. 30–1.
8. *A Thousand Plateaus*, p. 500.
9. Ibid., p. 492.

10. Ibid., p. 493.
11. Ibid., p. 494. The use of the term 'Eskimo' already signals acceptance of a deprecatory label used by outsiders, including anthropologists, and seems quite period-bound. The term's survival in *A Thousand Plateaus*, originally published in 1980, suggests that the authors were not aware that it went out of use in the mid-1970s and was replaced by 'Inuit.' Edmund Carpenter, *Eskimo Realities* (New York: Holt, Rinehart & Winston, 1973), pp. 192 ff.; cf. James Houston, *Confessions of an Igloo Dweller* (Toronto: M&S, 1995), p. 18. On the deployment of the term 'ice space,' see both Deleuze and Guattari, *A Thousand Plateaus*, p. 574, n. 28 and p. 557, n. 56, and Carpenter, *Eskimo Realities*, p. 78.
12. Christopher L. Miller, 'The Postidentitarian Predicament in the Footnotes of *A Thousand Plateaus*: Nomadology, Anthology, and Authority,' in *Deleuze and Guattari: Critical Assessments,* vol. 3, G. Genosko (ed.) (London: Routledge, 2001), p. 1117.
13. Deleuze and Guattari, *A Thousand Plateaus*, p. 574, n. 28.
14. Carpenter, *Eskimo Realities,* p. 78; Deleuze and Guattari, *A Thousand Plateaus*, pp. 475–6.
15. Ernst Roch (ed.), *Arts of the Eskimo: Prints*, Montreal: Signum Press, 1974, p. 20.
16. Department of Indian Affairs and Northern Development, *Identification and Registration of Indian and Inuit People*, Ottawa: DIAND, 1993, p. 24.
17. Richard Diubaldo, *The Government of Canada and the Inuit: 1900–1967*, Ottawa: Research Branch and Corporate Policy, Indian and Northern Affairs Canada, 1985, p. 111.
18. Deleuze and Guattari, *A Thousand Plateaus*, p. 477.
19. John MacDonald–Adam Bryx, personal communication, July 17, 2003.
20. Alan Rudolph Marcus, *Relocating Eden: The Image and Politics of Inuit Exile in the Canadian Arctic* (Hanover and London: University Press of New England, 1995), p. 33.
21. Department of Indian Affairs and Northern Development, *Identification and Registration of Indian and Inuit People*, p. 23.
22. Alia, *Names, Numbers, and Northern Policy*, pp. 14 ff.
23. Deleuze and Guattari, *A Thousand Plateaus*, pp. 456–7.
24. Ludger Müller-Wille, *Gazetter of Inuit Place Names in Nunavik (Québec, Canada)*, Inukjuak, PQ: Avataq Cultural Institute, 1987; cf. Department of Natural Resources Canada, 'Geographical Names of Canada,' <http://www.geonames.nrcan.gc.ca>.
25. See James Williams, 'Monitoring vs. Metaphysical Modeling: or, How to predict the future of the postmodern condition,' *PLI*

(October 1992): 55; and Michael Hardt, 'The Global Society of Control,' *Discourse* 20/3 (Fall 1998): 139–52.

26. R.A. Reiter, *The Fundamental Principles of Indian Law*, Edmonton: First Nations Resource Council, 1991, p. 14; and S. Imai, *The 1999 Annotated Indian Act and Aboriginal Constitutional Provisions*, Toronto: Carswell, 2000, p. 26.

27. See J. Poudrier, 'Racial Categories and Health Risks: Epidemiological Surveillance among Canadian First Nations,' in D. Lyon (ed.), *Surveillance as Social Sorting*, London: Routledge, 2003, pp. 111–34.

28. Alia, *Names, Numbers, and Northern Policy*, p. 40.

29. Marcus, *Relocating Eden*, p. 32.

30. Félix Guattari, 'Semiological Subjection, Semiotic Enslavement,' in *The Guattari Reader*, ed. G. Genosko, Oxford: Blackwell, 1996, pp. 143–5.

31. Marcus, *Relocating Eden*, p. 33.

32. Department of Indian Affairs and Northern Development, *Identification and Registration of Indian and Inuit*, p. 23.

33. Marcus, *Relocating Eden*, p. 23.

34. Deleuze and Guattari, *A Thousand Plateaus*, p. 457.

35. R. Quinn Duffy, *The Road to Nunavut: The Progress of the Eastern Arctic Inuit since the Second World War*, Montreal and Kingston: McGill-Queen's University Press, 1988, p. 10.

36. Diubaldo, *The Government of Canada and the Inuit*, pp. 4 and 51.

37. Deleuze and Guattari, *A Thousand Plateaus*, p. 491.

38. Duffy, *The Road to Nunavut*, pp. 31–2.

39. David Damas, *Arctic Migrants/Arctic Villagers: The Transformation of Inuit Settlement in the Central Arctic*, Montreal and Kingston: McGill-Queen's University Press, 2002, p. 112.

40. Deleuze and Guattari, *A Thousand Plateaus*, p. 449.

41. Ibid., p. 453.

42. Alia, *Names, Numbers, and Northern Policy*, p. 102.

43. Ibid, pp. 102–6.

44. Jim Shirley–Adam Bryx, personal communication, July 19, 2003.

45. Julie McCann, 'Reclaiming Inuit Tags,' *Canadian Geographic Magazine*, September/October 2003, p. 29.

46. Aaron Spitzer, 'Getting the names right – finally,' *Nunatsiaq News*, October 20, 2000, <http://www.nunatsiaq.com>.

47. Re Tucktoo and Kitchooalik (Re: Deborah) (1972) 27 D.L.R. (3d) 225.

48. Deleuze and Guattari, *A Thousand Plateaus*, p. 40.

49. Félix Guattari, *Cartographies schizoanalytiques*, Paris: Galilée, 1989, p. 104.

50. Zebedee Nungak, 'E9-1956,' Canadian Film Centre's Great Canadian Story Engine (n.d.), <http://www.storyengine.ca/serlet/ReadAStory?story=90>.
51. Rosalind Kidd, *The Way We Civilise*, St. Lucia, Queensland: Queensland University Press, 2000, p. 309.
52. Marilyn Wood, 'Nineteenth Century Bureaucratic Constructions of Indigenous Identities in New South Wales,' in N. Peterson and W. Sanders (eds.), *Citizenship and Indigenous Australians: Changing Conceptions and Possibilities*, Melbourne: Cambridge University Press, 1998, pp. 35–54.
53. Lauren Marsh and Steve Kinnane, 'Ghost Files: The Missing Files of the Department of Indigenous Affairs Archives,' *Studies in Western Australian History* 23 (2004): 125.
54. Tim Rowse, *White Flour, White Power: From Rations to Citizenship in Central Australia*, Melbourne: Cambridge University Press, 1998, p. 116.
55. John Murphy, *Imaging the Fifties: Private Sentiment and Political Culture in Menzies' Australia*, Sydney: University of New South Wales Press, 2000, p. 175.
56. Maggie Brady (ed.), *Giving Away the Grog*, Canberra: Commonwealth Department of Health and Ageing, 1995, pp. 54 and 63.
57. J. Milroy, 'Introduction,' *The Art of Sally Morgan*, Ringwood, Victoria: Penguin, 1996, p. 28; and Sally Morgan and Jack McPhee, *Wanamurraganya: The Story of Jack McPhee*, Fremantle: Fremantle Arts Cooperative, 1989, pp. 16–17.
58. See article 'Dog Tags,' in David Horton (ed.), *Encyclopedia of Aboriginal Australia*, vol. 1, Canberra: Aboriginal Studies Press, AIATSIS, pp. 298–9. See also the statement of Ruby Langford, *Don't Take Your Love to Town*, Ringwood, Victoria: Penguin, 1988, p. 48: 'The Dog Licence was a product of the Aborigines' Protection Board ... The main function of the APB was to discriminate against Aborigines.'
59. Murphy, *Imaging the Fifties*, p. 176.
60. Jakelin Troy, *King Plates: A History of Aboriginal Gorgets*, Canberra: Aboriginal Studies Press, 1993, p. 41.
61. See Judith Ryan, *Land Marks*, Melbourne: National Gallery of Victoria, 2006, p. 87.
62. Troy, *King Plates*, pp. 35–8.
63. Steve Butcher, 'Firm Fined over Aboriginal Relics,' *The Age*, February 10, 2005; <http://www.theage.com.au/news/national/Firm-fined-over-Aboriginal-relics/2005/02/09/1107890272567.html>.
64. Stephen Muecke, 'The Discourse of Nomadology: Phylums in Flux' in Genosko (ed.), *Deleuze and Guattari*, vol. 3, pp. 1164–81.

Elizabeth Grosz discusses two examples of western desert art at length, as cosmic and political forward-looking invocations of a future in which the earth will be returned to Aboriginal peoples; this will be accomplished by art's capacity to give autonomy to sensation as a resource for change: 'the sensations unavailable now but to be unleashed in the future on a people ready to perceive and be affected by them'. Elizabeth Grosz, *Chaos, Territory, Art: Deleuze and the Framing of the Earth*, New York: Columbia University Press, 2008, p. 103.

Chapter 6

1. Félix Guattari, 'Le Cinéma: Un Art Mineur,' in *La révolution moléculaire*, Fontenay-sous-Bois: Recherches (Encres), 1977, pp. 203–38.
2. Constantine Verevis, 'Minoritarian + Cinema,' in *The Deleuze Dictionary*, ed. A. Parr, Edinburgh: Edinburgh University Press, 2005, pp. 165–6. On the question of the character of nationalism and Third Cinema, Jim Pines and Paul Willemen clarify that it is a non-essentialist, non-transcendent nationalism that emerges through militant struggle by a people, and to which intellectuals contribute critical and lucid insights. 'Preface,' in Jim Pines and Paul Willemen (eds.) *Questions of Third Cinema*, London: BFI, 1989, pp. 19–20.
3. Félix Guattari, 'Gangs à New York,' in *La Révolution Moléculaire* (Encres), pp. 185–6. See also Guattari's comments on gangs in the South Bronx: 'on one level they reproduce the worst sorts of fascist violence, but on the other hand they are seeking their own solutions, their own desiring relations, which are often as positive as they are negative.' 'Revolution and Desire: An Interview with Félix Guattari,' Hannah Levin and Mark Seem, *State and Mind* 6/4 and 7/1 (Summer/Fall 1978): 57.
4. Félix Guattari, 'La Question des Tribunaux Populaires,' in *La révolution moléculaire*, Fontenay-sous-Bois: Recherches (10/18), 1977, pp. 89–90.
5. Fernando Solanas and Octavio Getino, 'Towards a Third Cinema: Notes and Experiences for the Development of a Cinema of Liberation in the Third World,' in *New Latin American Cinema*, vol. 1, Detroit: Wayne State University Press, 1997, p. 45.
6. Fernando Solanas, 'An Interview by James Roy MacBean,' *Film Quarterly* 24/1 (1979): 38.
7. Ibid., p. 40.
8. See Félix Guattari, 'Name-dropping,' 2 pages, typescript, signed and dated Apr. 15, 1986, Fonds Félix Guattari, L'Institut Mémoires de

l'Édition Contemporaine (IMEC), Saint-Germain-la-Blanche-Herbe, file ET02-10.

9. Dudley Andrew, 'The Roots of the Nomadic: Gilles Deleuze and the Cinema of West Africa,' in G. Flaxman (ed.), *The Brain Is the Screen: Deleuze and the Philosophy of Cinema*, Minneapolis: University of Minnesota Press, 2000, pp. 224–5.

10. Julio García Espinosa, 'For an Imperfect Cinema,' in *New Latin American Cinema*, vol. 1, p. 81.

11. Julio García Espinosa, 'Meditations on Imperfect Cinema,' in *New Latin American Cinema*, vol. 1, p. 84.

12. Félix Guattari, 'Le Divan du Pauvre,' in *La révolution moléculaire* (Encres), p. 226.

13. Espinosa, 'Meditations,' p. 84.

14. Deleuze, *Cinema 2: The Time-Image*, trans. H. Tomlinson and R. Galeta, Minneapolis: University of Minnesota Press, 1989, pp. 220–1. On the waning of the people in Third Cinema see Patricia Pisters, 'Arresting the Flux of Images and Sounds: Free Indirect Discourse and the Dialectics of Political Cinema,' in I. Buchanan and A. Parr (eds.), *Deleuze and the Contemporary World*, Edinburgh: Edinburgh University Press, 2006, pp. 177–8. Pisters refers neither to Guattari's sense of the minor nor to Espinosa's idea of a people to come, while isolating the historical failures of the 'expectation of a people to come' in many Third World countries after the hopes of the 1960s.

15. Gilles Deleuze and Félix Guattari, *A Thousand Plateaus*, trans. Brian Massumi, Minneapolis: University of Minnesota Press, 1987, p. 456.

16. Ibid., p. 473.

17. Félix Guattari, 'Le cinema doit devenir un art mineur,' in *La révolution moléculaire* (Encres), p. 206.

18. Deleuze and Guattari, *A Thousand Plateaus*, p. 470.

19. On this point see Paola Marrati, 'Against the Doxa: Politics of Immanence and Becoming-Minoritarian,' in P. Pisters (ed.), *Micropolitics of Media Culture*, Amsterdam: University of Amsterdam Press, 2001, p. 214.

20. See Gilles Deleuze and Félix Guattari, *Anti-Oedipus: Capitalism and Schizophrenia*, trans. Robert Hurley, Mark Seem, and Helen R. Lane, New York: Viking Press, 1977, pp. 3 and 124.

21. Solanas and Getino, 'Towards,' pp. 53–4.

22. Guattari, 'Tokyo, the Proud,' trans. G. Genosko, *Deleuze Studies* 1/2 (2007) (orig. 'Tokyo l'orgueilleuse,' Fonds Félix Guattari, IMEC, file ET02-12, 5 pages, typescript in French; published in Japanese in F. Guattari, Hiraï Gen, Asada Akira, Takeda Kenichi, Radio

Homerun, et al., *Tokyo Gekijou: Gatari, Tokyo wo yuku*, Tokyo: UPU, 1986).

23. On this point see Edward Fowler, *San'ya Blues: Laboring Life in Contemporary Tokyo*, Ithaca: Cornell University Press, 1996, pp. 24–5.

24. Krystian Woznicki, 'SANYA: On Marginal Space and Periphery', interview with Toshiya Ueno, 1998, <http://www.nettime.org/Lists-Archives/nettime-l-9802/msg00082.html>.

25. See Tom Gill, *Men of Uncertainty: The Social Organization of Day Laborers in Contemporary Japan*, Albany: State University of New York Press, 2001, pp. 87 and 242.

26. Mitsuo Sato, 'Appeal to the Sanya Workers,' posted on <http://www.bordersphere.com/events/yama5.htm>.

27. Félix Guattari, 'La Balade Sauvage,' in *La révolution moléculaire* (Encres), p. 206.

28. Edgar Morin, *The Stars*, trans. R. Howard, New York: Grove Press, 1961, p. 133.

29. Guattari, 'La Balade Sauvage,' p. 206.

30. Félix Guattari, 'Les Cinémachines Désirantes,' in *La révolution moléculaire* (Encres), p. 218.

31. Félix Guattari, 'La Place Du Signifiant Dans L'Institution,' in *La révolution moléculaire* (Encres), p. 282.

32. Slavoj Žižek, *For They Know Not What They Do*, London: Verso, 1991, pp. 22 ff.

33. Guattari, 'Les Cinémachines Désirantes,' p. 221.

34. Ibid., p. 221, n. 1.

35. Ibid., p. 223.

36. Ibid., pp. 222 and 233.

37. Laleen Jayamanne, '"Forty Acres and A Mule Filmworks" – *Do the Right Thing* – "A Spike Lee Joint": Blocking and Unblocking the Block,' in P. Pisters (ed.) *Micropolitics of Media Culture: Reading the Rhizomes of Deleuze and Guattari*, Amsterdam: University of Amsterdam Press, pp. 235–49.

38. Guattari, 'Les Cinémachines Désirantes,' p. 236.

39. Félix Guattari, 'La machine à images,' *Cahiers du cinéma* 437 (November 1990): 71.

40. Guattari, 'Les Cinémachines Désirantes,' p. 236.

41. Félix Guattari, 'Comme un Echo de la Mélancholie Collective,' in *La Révolution Moléculaire* (10/18), p. 200.

42. Félix Guattari, 'Urgences: la folie est dans le champ,' *Le Monde* (March 9, 1988): 22.

43. Guattari, quoted in Gilles Pial, 'Docteur Cooper et Mister Anti,' *Libération* (July 31, 1986): 20.

44. Deleuze and Guattari, *Anti-Oedipus*, p. 95.
45. Félix Guattari, 'Le cinéma doit devenir,' in *La révolution moléculaire* (Encres), p. 203.
46. Félix Guattari, *Chaosmosis*, trans. P. Bains and J. Pefanis, Bloomington: Indiana University Press, 1995, p. 92–3.
47. Félix Guattari, *Cartographies schizoanalytiques*, Paris: Galilée, 1989, pp. 27–8 and 304.
48. Félix Guattari, *L'inconscient machinique*, Fontenay-sous-Bois: Recherches, 1979, p. 191.
49. On the generative/transformational difference see ibid., pp. 192 ff.
50. Franco Basaglia, 'Institutions of Violence,' in *Psychiatry Inside Out: Selected Writings of Franco Basaglia*, ed. Nancy Scheper-Hughes and Anne M. Lovell, trans. A. M. Lovell and T. Shtob, New York: Columbia University Press, 1987, p. 63.
51. Félix Guattari, 'Franco Basaglia: Guerilla Psychiatrist,' in *The Guattari Reader*, p. 44.
52. Anne M. Lovell and Nancy Scheper-Hughes, 'Introduction – The Utopia of Reality: Franco Basagalia and the Practice of a Democratic Psychiatry,' in Basaglia, *Psychiatry Inside Out*, p. 16.
53. Félix Guattari, 'Fous à Délier (Italie, 1976),' in *La révolution moléculaire* (Encres), pp. 158–60.
54. Félix Guattari, 'La Borde: A Clinic Unlike Any Other,' in *Chaosophy*, p. 198.
55. Guattari, 'Fous à Délier,' p. 160.
56. Deleuze and Guattari, *Anti-Oedipus*, p. 342.
57. Félix Guattari, 'La Misère D'Aujourd'hui,' *La révolution moléculaire* (10/18), p. 348.
58. Ibid., p. 350.
59. Michel Foucault and René Feret, 'Sur Histoire de Paul: Entretien,' *Cahiers du cinema* 262–3 (January 1976): 63.
60. Ibid., p. 65.
61. Guattari, 'La Borde', p. 197.

Chapter 7

1. Deleuze, *Spinoza: Practical Philosophy*, trans. Robert Hurley, San Francisco: City Lights, 1988, pp. 48–51.
2. See Gilles Deleuze and Félix Guattari, *A Thousand Plateaus*, trans. Brian Massumi, Minneapolis: University of Minnesota Press, 1987, p. 260.
3. Brian Massumi, *Parables for the Virtual*, Durham, NC: Duke University Press, 2002, p. 21.

4. Félix Guattari, 'Ritornellos and Existential Affects,' trans., Juliana Schiesari and Georges van den Abbeele, *Discourse* 12/2 (1990): 66.
5. Brian Massumi, 'The Autonomy of Affect,' in Paul Patton (ed.), *Deleuze: A Critical Reader*, Oxford: Blackwell, 1996, pp. 221–2.
6. Guattari, 'Ritornellos,' pp. 66–7.
7. Herbert Spiegelberg, *Phenomenology in Psychology and Psychiatry*, Evanston, IL: Northwestern University Press, 1972, pp. 243–6.
8. Gilles Deleuze and Félix Guattari, *Anti-Oedipus: Capitalism and Schizophrenia*, trans. Robert Hurley, Mark Seem, and Helen R. Lane, New York: Viking Press, 1977, p. 361.
9. Maurice Merleau-Ponty, *Phenomenology of Perception*, trans. Colin Smith, New York: Routledge & Kegan Paul, 1962, p. 136.
10. Ibid.
11. Françoise Minkowska, quoted in Eugène Minkowski, *Lived Time: Phenomenological and Psychopathological Studies*, trans. Nancy Wetzel, Evanston, IL: Northwestern University Press, 1933, p. 203.
12. Minkowski, *Lived Time*, p. 209.
13. Ibid., p. 65; John M. Sutherland and Howard Tait, *The Epilepsies*, Edinburgh: E. & S. Livingstone, 1969, p. 113; Walter J. Friedlander, *The History of Modern Epilepsy: The Beginning, 1865–1914*, Westport, CT: Greenwood Press, 2001, pp. 220–3.
14. Massumi, 'Autonomy of Affect,' pp. 228–9.
15. Arthur Tatossian, *Phénomenologie des psychoses*, Paris: Masson, 1980, p. 42; and Guattari, 'Ritornellos,' p. 79, n. 4.
16. Tatossian, *Phénomenologie des psychoses*, p. 42.
17. Guattari, 'Ritornellos,' p. 67.
18. Daniel Stern, *The Interpersonal World of the Infant: A View from Psychoanalysis and Developmental Psychology*, New York: Basic Books, 1985, pp. 54 ff.
19. Guattari, 'Ritornellos,' p. 68.
20. Guattari, *Chaosmosis*, p. 9.
21. Guattari, 'Ritornellos,' pp. 68–9.
22. Ibid., p. 69.
23. Guattari, *Chaosmosis*, p. 17.
24. Guattari, 'Ritornellos,' p. 73.
25. Gilles Deleuze and Félix Guattari, *What is Philosophy?* trans. H. Tomlinson and G. Burchell, New York: Columbia University Press, 1994, p. 173.
26. Peter Cowie, *Revolution! The Explosion of World Cinema in the Sixties*, New York: Faber and Faber, 2004, p. 170.

27. Oswei Temkin, *The Falling Sickness: A History of Epilepsy from the Greeks to the Beginnings of Modern Neurology*, Baltimore: Johns Hopkins Press, 1971, pp. 160–1.
28. Perminder Sachdev, 'Schizophrenia-like psychosis and epilepsy,' in Daryl Fujii and Iqbal Ahmed (eds.), *The Spectrum of Psychotic Disorders: Neurobiology, Etiology and Pathogenesis*, Cambridge: Cambridge University Press, 2007, p. 270.
29. Maurizio Pompili, et al., 'Suicide Risk Among Epileptic Patients,' in K.J. Holloway (ed.), *New Research on Epilepsy and Behavior*, New York: Nova Science, 2007, pp. 147–8.
30. Deleuze and Guattari, *A Thousand Plateaus*, p. 299.
31. *Chaosmosis*, pp. 16–17.
32. Paul Virilio built his theory of disappearance as an implosive dimension of everyday life in the age of the hegemony of speed on epilepsy – to be precise, on picnolepsy, or frequent, slight epileptoid episodes. His book *The Aesthetics of Disappearance* begins on the subject of loss, lapse, and absence, and meditates on the active memory that the young picnoleptic brings to patching over, inventing what cannot be remembered from the course of existence. But Virilio's move here is not designed to ghettoize and stigmatize the picnoleptic – s/he may not be an epileptic at all, as this diagnosis is controversial. For 'childhood absences' are sometimes classed as partial and subject to criticism because 'loss' is not adequate to their epileptological description (on this point see Andrea E. Cavanna, et al., 'Epilepsy and Consciousness,' in Holloway (ed.), *New Research on Epilepsy and Behavior*, p. 300).

   Still, Virilio's main point is that this condition raises an awkward question, posed on the basis of the characteristics of a petit mal crisis, that is perceived neither by the sufferer nor by observers: 'who is picnoleptic? We could possibly respond today: who isn't, or hasn't been?' (Paul Virilio, *The Aesthetics of Disappearance*, New York: Semiotext(e), 1991, p. 14.)

   It is not that all of us have been picnoleptics; rather, all of us have been adolescents struggling to master the childhood that slips from our hands in the passage of time, and with it goes the picnoleptic experience, at least according to Virilio's sense of the epileptiform's unfolding and puberty's interferences. Picnolepsy is known 'typically' as a childhood disorder that often slowly ceases with maturation. This is the specific type of seizure that interests Virilio because of its slightness and non-convulsiveness. Indeed, it also lacks a pronounced aura or premonitory symptom – which can be a disturbance in the field of vision, or take the form of an auditory distortion or change, sensory twitchings or numbness in a limb, intensification of olfactory sense, peculiar tastes, vertigo, or malaise. This is a modest alternative to affect's epileptic void.

33. Massumi's delicate term, *Parables*, p. 30.
34. See Klaus Lehnertz, 'Epilepsy: Extreme Events in the Human Brain,' in S. Albeverio et al. (eds.), *Extreme Events in Nature and Society*, Berlin: Springer, 2006, pp. 123–43. This paper shows that 'there are currently no accepted methods for assessing performance and validating the statistical significance of seizure anticipation algorithms' (p. 138), and that the failure of randomized clinical trials is due to a variety of reasons.
35. See Isabelle Delmotte's work on the Epileptograph at <http://www.isabelledelmotte.net>.
36. See Guattari, *Chaosmosis*, pp. 83–6.

Conclusion

1. Félix Guattari, *Chaosmosis*, trans. P. Bains and J. Pefanis, Bloomington: Indiana University Press, 1995, pp. 37–8.
2. Félix Guattari, 'Machine et structure,' in *Psychanalyse et transversalité*, Paris: Maspero/La Découverte, 1972/2003, p. 243.
3. Félix Guattari, 'La causalité, la subjectivité et l'histoire,' in *Psychanalyse et transversalité*, p. 181.
4. Guattari, *Chaosmosis*, p. 40.
5. Félix Guattari, 'So What?' in *Chaosophy*, p. 21.
6. Félix Guattari, 'La revolution moleculaire,' *Le Monde* December 7, 1990; and *Chaosmosis*, p. 21.
7. Guattari, *Chaosmisis*, p. 97.
8. Félix Guattari and Suely Rolnick, *Molecular Revolution in Brazil*, trans. K. Clapshow and B. Holmes, Los Angeles: Semiotext(e), 2008, p. 381.
9. Anne Querrien, 'Le plan de consistence du felice-deleuzisme,' *Chimères* 37 (1999): 35.
10. François Dosse, *Gilles Deleuze and Félix Guattari: Biographie croisée*, Paris: La Découverte, 2007, pp. 34–5.
11. Guattari and Rolnick, *Molecular Revolution in Brazil*, p. 380.
12. Félix Guattari, 'Three Billion Perverts on the Stand,' in *The Guattari Reader*, ed. G. Genosko, Oxford: Blackwell, 1996, p. 192.
13. See Liane Mozère, 'Foucault et le CERFI: instantanés et actualité,' *Le Portique* 13–14 (2004), in which the question of Foucault's participation in the 'Three Billion Perverts' issue is discussed in terms of his reticence to get involved in the carnivalesque atmosphere around its production, keeping a 'benevolent distance,' but still

putting his name on it. Mozère directed CERFI from 1967 to 1970.

14. Dosse, *Biographie croisée*, pp. 319–24.
15. Ibid., pp. 332–5.
16. Hocquenghem, quoted by Dosse, *Biographie croisée*, p. 327.
17. Guattari, 'Three Billion Perverts,' p. 186.
18. Ibid.
19. Ibid. p. 187.
20. Ibid.
21. Gilles Deleuze and Félix Guattari, *Anti-Oedipus: Capitalism and Schizophrenia*, trans. Robert Hurley, Mark Seem, and Helen R. Lane, New York: Viking Press, 1977, p. 18.
22. Félix Guattari, 'Remaking Social Practices,' in *The Guattari Reader*, p. 263.
23. Ibid., p. 266.
24. 'It is "machinic" subjectivity that fuels great impetuses like Silicon Valley.' Félix Guattari, 'Machinic Junkies,' in *Soft Subversions*, New York: Semiotext(e), 1995, p. 103.
25. Ibid., p. 272.
26. Félix Guattari, *The Anti-Oedipus Papers*, trans. K. Gotman, New York: Semiotext(e), 2006, p. 55.

LIST OF REFERENCES

Acidus. 'NCR ATMs: Aurum Ex Machina,' *2600* 19/2 (Summer 2002): 18–19.

Alia, Valerie. *Names, Numbers, and Northern Policy: Inuit, Project Surname, and the Politics of Identity*, Halifax: Fernwood, 1994.

Alliez, Eric. 'Anti-Oedipus: Thirty Years On,' in *Deleuze and the Social*, M. Fuglsang and B. M. Sorensen (eds.), Edinburgh: Edinburgh University Press, 2006, pp. 151–68.

Andrew, Dudley. 'The Roots of the Nomadic: Gilles Deleuze and the Cinema of West Africa,' in G. Flaxman (ed.), *The Brain is the Screen: Deleuze and the Philosophy of Cinema*, Minneapolis: University of Minnesota Press, 2000, pp. 215–49.

Ashley, Richard K. 'Living on Border Lines: Mass, Poststructuralism, and War,' in James Der Derian and Michael J. Shapiro (eds.), *International/Intertextual Relations: Postmodern Readings of World Politics*, Lexington, MA: D.C. Heath, 1989, pp. 276–7.

Bains, Paul. 'Subjectless Subjectivities,' in B. Massumi (ed.), *A Shock to Thought*, London: Routledge, 2002, pp. 101–16.

Baker, S. *The Postmodern Animal*, London: Reaktion Books, 2000.

Barthes, Roland. *Elements of Semiology*, trans. A. Lavers and C. Smith, New York: Hill & Wang, 1967.

Basaglia, Franco. 'Institutions of Violence,' in *Psychiatry Inside Out: Selected Writings of Franco Basaglia*, ed. Nancy Scheper-Hughes and Anne M. Lovell, trans. A. M. Lovell and T. Shtob, New York: Columbia University Press, 1987.

Baudrillard, Jean. *Fragments: Conversations with François L'Yvonnet*, trans. Chris Turner, London: Routledge, 2004.

Beattie, Nicholas. *The Freinet Movements of France, Italy, and Germany, 1920–2000*. Mellen Studies in Education, vol. 74, Lewiston, NY: Edwin Mellen Press, 2002.

Bédarida, Catherine. 'Disparitions: Fernand Deligny – Un éducateur et un écrivain au service des enfants "anormaux",' *Le Monde*, September 21, 1996.

Berardi, Franco. *Félix Guattari: Thought, Friendship, and Visionary Cartography*, trans. G. Mecchia and C. Stivale, Basingstoke: Palgrave Macmillan, 2008.

Bleiker, Roland. *Popular Dissent, Human Agency and Global Politics*, Cambridge: Cambridge University Press, 2000.

Boiral, Pierre. 'Introduction,' in *Deligny et les tentatives de prise en charge des enfants fous: L'aventure de l'aire (1968–1973)*, Ramonville Saint-Agne: Éditions Érès, 2007, pp. 16–21.

Bosteels, Bruno. 'From Text to Diagram: Towards a Semiotics of Cultural Cartography,' in C.W. Spinks and J. Deely (eds.), *Semiotics 1994*, New York: Peter Lang, 1995, pp. 347–59.

Brady, Maggie (ed.). *Giving Away the Grog*, Canberra: Commonwealth Department of Health and Ageing, 1995.

Buchanan, Ian. 'Deleuze, Gilles and Félix Guattari,' in M. Groden et al. (eds.), *The Johns Hopkins Guide to Literary Theory and Criticism*, Baltimore: Johns Hopkins University Press, 2005, pp. 247–50.

Butcher, Steve. 'Firm Fined over Aboriginal Relics,' *The Age*, February 10, 2005, <http://www.theage.com.au/news/national/Firm-fined-over-Aboriginal-relics/2005/02/09/1107890272567.html>.

Campbell, David. 'Political Prosaics, Transversal Politics, and the Anarchical World,' in Michael J. Shapiro and Hayward R. Allier (eds.), *Challenging Boundaries*, Minneapolis: University of Minnesota Press, 1996, pp. 7–24.

Carpenter, Edmund. *Eskimo Realities*, New York: Holt, Rinehart & Winston, 1973.

Castells, Manuel. *The Rise of the Network Society*, Oxford: Blackwell, 2000.

—— *End of Millennium*, Oxford: Blackwell, 2000

Cavanna, Andrea E., Mula, Marco and Monaco, Francesco. 'Epilepsy and Consciousness,' in K. J. Holloway (ed.), *New Research on Epilepsy and Behavior*, New York: Nova Science, 2007, pp. 295–317.

CERFI, 'La grille: 1958–1973,' originally published in *Revue perspectives psychiatriques* 45 (1974). Accessed under 'Réflexions' at <http://www.cliniquedelaborde.com>.

Chesnaux, J. and Gentis, R. 'Félix, Our Friend,' trans. M. McMahon, in G. Genosko (ed.), *Deleuze and Guattari: Critical Assessments of Leading Philosophers*, vol. 2, London: Routledge, 2001, pp. 542–5.

Clastres, Pierre. *Society Against the State*, trans. R. Hurley, New York: Zone, 1987.

Club Laborde, Le. 'Le feuille de jour: traverses les cloisonnements,' listed under 'Quotidien,' (n.d.), at <http://www.cliniquedelaborde.com>.

Cooper, David. *Psychiatry and Anti-Psychiatry*, London: Tavistock, 1967.

Cowie, Peter. *Revolution! The Explosion of World Cinema in the Sixties*, New York: Faber and Faber, 2004.

Damas, David. *Arctic Migrants/Arctic Villagers: The Transformation of Inuit Settlement in the Central Arctic*, Montreal and Kingston: McGill-Queen's University Press, 2002.

De Coster, Tom, et al. 'Emancipating a Neo-Liberal Society? Initial Thoughts on the Progressive Pedagogical Heritage in Flanders Since the 1960s,' *Education Research and Perspectives* 31/2 (2004): 156–75.

DeLanda, Manuel. *War in the Age of Intelligent Machines*, New York: Zone, 1991.

Deleuze, Gilles. *Two Regimes of Madness*, trans. A. Hodges and M. Taormina, New York: Semiotext(e), 2006.

—— *Francis Bacon: The Logic of Sensation*, trans. D.W. Smith, Minneapolis: University of Minnesota Press, 2003.

—— 'Postscript on Control Societies,' in *Negotiations 1972–1990*, trans. M. Joughin, New York: Columbia, 1995, pp. 177–82.

—— *Cinema 2: The Time-Image*, trans. H. Tomlinson and R. Galeta, Minneapolis: University of Minnesota Press, 1989.

—— *Foucault*, trans. S. Hand, Minneapolis: University of Minnesota Press, 1988.

—— *Spinoza: Practical Philosophy*, trans. Robert Hurley, San Francisco: City Lights, 1988.

—— and Guattari, Félix. *What is Philosophy?* trans. H. Tomlinson and G. Burchell, New York: Columbia University Press, 1994.

—— —— *A Thousand Plateaus: Capitalism and Schizophrenia*, trans. B. Massumi, Minneapolis: University of Minnesota Press, 1987.

—— —— *Kafka: For a Minor Literature*, trans. Dana Polan, Minneapolis: University of Minnesota Press, 1986.

—— —— *Anti-Oedipus: Capitalism and Schizophrenia*, trans. Robert Hurley, Mark Seem and Helen R. Lane, New York: Viking Press, 1977.

Delmotte Isabelle. 'The Epileptograph,' at <http://www.isabelledelmotte. net>.

Department of Communications and Department of Justice. *Privacy and Computers: A Report of a Task Force*, Ottawa: Government of Canada, 1972.

Department of Indian Affairs and Northern Development. *Identification and Registration of Indian and Inuit People*, Ottawa: DIAND, 1993.

Department of Natural Resources Canada. 'Geographical Names of Canada,' (n.d.), <http://www.geonames.nrcan.gc.ca>.

Depussé, Marie. *Dieu gît dans les détails: La Borde, un asile*, Paris: P.O.L. Éditeur, 1993.

Derrida, Jacques. *Dissemination*, trans. B. Johnson, Chicago: University of Chicago Press, 1981.

Diubaldo, Richard. *The Government of Canada and the Inuit: 1900–1967*, Ottawa: Research Branch and Corporate Policy, Indian and Northern Affairs Canada, 1985.

Dosse, François. *Gilles Deleuze et Félix Guattari: Biographie croisée*, Paris: La Découverte, 2007.

Duffy, R. Quinn. *The Road to Nunavut: The Progress of the Eastern Arctic Inuit since the Second World War*, Montreal and Kingston: McGill-Queen's University Press, 1988.

Eco, Umberto. *A Theory of Semiotics*, Bloomington: Indiana University Press, 1976.

Espinosa, Julio García. 'For an Imperfect Cinema,' in M. I. Martin (ed.), *New Latin American Cinema*, vol. 1, Detroit: Wayne State University Press, 1997, pp. 71–82.

—— 'Meditations on Imperfect Cinema,' in M. I. Martin (ed.), *New Latin American Cinema*, vol. 1, Detroit: Wayne State University Press, 1997, pp. 83–5.

Foucault, Michel. 'Afterword: The Subject and Power,' in Hubert L. Dreyfus and Paul Rabinow, *Michel Foucault: Beyond Structuralism and Hermeneutics*, Chicago: University of Chicago Press, 1982, pp. 208–26.

—— *Discipline and Punish*, trans. A. Sheridan, New York: Vintage, 1977

—— and René Feret, 'Sur Histoire de Paul: Entretien,' *Cahiers du cinema* 262–3 (January 1976): 63–5.

Fowler, Edward. *San'ya Blues: Laboring Life in Contemporary Tokyo*, Ithaca, NY: Cornell University Press, 1996.

Fox, Warwick. *Toward a Transpersonal Ecology*, Albany: State University of New York Press, 1995.

Freinet, Célestin. *Oeuvres Pédagogiques*, vol. 1, Paris: Éditions du Seuil, 1994.

—— *Oeuvres pédagogiques*, vol. 2, Paris: Éditions du Seuil, 1994.

—— *Cooperative Learning and Social Change: Selected Writings of Célestin Freinet*, ed. and trans. David Clandfield and John Sivell, Toronto: OISE Publishing, 1990.

—— *La méthode naturelle. 1. L'apprentissage de la langue*, Neuchatel and Paris: Delachaux & Niestlé, 1968.

Freud, Sigmund. 'Recommendations to Physicians Practising Psycho-Analysis [1912]' *Standard Edition*, vol. 12, London: Hogarth/Vintage, 2001, pp. 111–20.

—— 'Neurosis and Psychosis' [1924], *Standard Edition*, vol. 19, London: Hogarth/Vintage, 1964, pp. 149–53.

—— 'An Outline of Psycho-Analysis' [1940], *Standard Edition*, vol. 23, London: Hogarth/Vintage, 1964, pp. 144–207.

Friedlander, Walter J. *The History of Modern Epilepsy: The Beginning, 1865–1914*, Westport, CT: Greenwood Press, 2001.

Gandy, Oscar. 'Data Mining, Surveillance, and Discrimination in the Post-9/11Environment,' in K. Haggerty and R. Ericson (eds.), *The New Politics of Surveillance and Visibility*, Toronto: University of Toronto Press, 2006, pp. 363–84.

Genosko, Gary. 'Félix Guattari: Towards a transdisciplinary metamethodology,' *Angelaki: Journal of the Theoretical Humanities* 8/1 (April 2003): 129–40.

—— *The Party without Bosses: Lessons on Anti-Capitalism from Félix Guattari and Luís Inácio 'Lula' da Silva*, Semaphore Series,Winnipeg: Arbeiter Ring, 2003.

—— *Félix Guattari: An Aberrant Introduction*, London: Continuum, 2002.

Gill, Tom. *Men of Uncertainty: The Social Organization of Day Laborers in Contemporary Japan*, Albany: State University of New York Press, 2001.

Goddard, Michael. 'Bifo's Futural Thought,' *Cultural Studies Review* 11/2 (2005): 49–56.

Goldstein, Kurt. *Aftereffects of Brain Injuries in War*, New York: Grune & Stratton, 1948.

Grassl, Anton and Heath, Graham. *The Magic Triangle: A Short History of the World Youth Hostel Movement*, Bielefeld, Germany: International Youth Hostel Federation, 1982.

Grosz, Elizabeth. *Chaos, Territory, Art: Deleuze and the Framing of the Earth*, New York: Columbia University Press, 2008.

Guattari, Félix. 'Tokyo, the Proud,' trans. and intro. G. Genosko, *Deleuze Studies* 1/2 (2007): 93–9.

—— *The Anti-Oedipus Papers*, New York: Semiotext(e), 2006.

—— 'Révolution informationnelle, écologie et recomposition subjective,' *Multitudes* 24 (2006), <http://multitudes.samizdat.net/spip.php?article2390>.

—— *La Philosophie est essentielle à l'existence humaine*, interview with Antoine Spire, Michel Field and Emmanuel Hirsch, Paris: Éditions Aube, 2002.

—— 'Towards an Ethics of the Media,' trans. J. Watson, *Polygraph* 14 (2002): 17–21.

—— 'Entretien avec John Johnston: Vertige de l'immanence,' *Chimères* 38 (2000): 13–30.

—— *The Three Ecologies*, trans. Ian Pindar and Paul Sutton, London: The Athlone Press, 2000.

—— 'La "grille",' *Chimères* 34 (1998): 7–20.

—— 'Entretien avec Félix Guattari,' interview by E. Videcoq and J.-Y. Sparel, *Chimères* 28 (Spring/Summer 1996):19–32.

—— *The Guattari Reader*, ed. G. Genosko, Oxford: Blackwell, 1996.

—— *Chaosmosis*, trans. P. Bains and J. Pefanis, Bloomington: Indiana University Press, 1995.

—— *Chaosophy*, New York: Semiotext(e), 1995.

—— *Soft Subversions*, New York: Semiotext(e), 1995.

—— 'Les machines architecturales de Shin Takamatsu,' *Chimères* 21 (1994): 127–41.

—— 'Une autre vision du futur,' *Le Monde*, February 15, 1992.

—— *Chaosmose*, Paris: Galilée, 1992.

—— 'Ecologie et politique: Un nouvel axe progressiste,' *Le Monde*, June 4, 1992.

—— 'De la pluridisciplinarité à la transdisciplinarité,' written with Sergio Vilar, Barcelona and Paris, September 1992, Fonds Felix Guattari, L'Institut Mémoires de l'Édition Contemporaine (IMEC), Saint-Germain-la-Blanche-Herbe, file ET05-13.

—— 'Pour une éthique des médias,' *Le Monde*, November 6, 1991.

—— 'Les fondements éthico-politique de l'interdisciplinarité,' handwritten text, April 1991, Fonds Félix Guattari, L'Institut Mémoires de l'Édition Contemporaine (IMEC), Saint-Germain-la-Blanche-Herbe, file ET10-24.

—— 'Les bouleversements à l'Est et `l'Ouest Réinventer la politique,' *Le Monde*, March 8, 1990.

—— 'David Wojnarowicz,' *Rethinking Marxism* 3/1 (1990): 76–7.

—— 'Introduction,' in *George Condo*, Paris: Daniel Templon, 1990, pp. 5–8.

—— 'La machine à images,' *Cahiers du cinéma* 437 (November 1990): 71–2.

—— 'La revolution moléculaire,' *Le Monde*, December 7, 1990.

—— 'Ritornellos and Existential Affects,' trans. Juliana Schiesari and Georges van den Abbeele, *Discourse* 12/2 (1990): 66–81.

—— *Cartographies schizoanalytiques*, Paris: Galilée, 1989.

—— *Les trois écologies*, Paris: Galilée, 1989.

—— 'Urgences: la folie est dans le champ,' *Le Monde*, March 9, 1988.

—— 'La grille,' typescript dated January 29, 1987, Fonds Félix Guattari, L'Institut Mémoires de l'Édition Contemporaine (IMEC), Saint-Germain-la-Blanche-Herbe, file ET04-13.

—— 'Name-dropping,' 2 pages, typescript, signed and dated April 15, 1986, Fonds Félix Guattari, L'Institut Mémoires de l'Édition Contemporaine (IMEC), Saint-Germain-la-Blanche-Herbe, file ET02-10.

—— 'Tokyo l'orgueilleuse,' 5 pages, typescript in French, Fonds Félix Guattari, L'Institut Mémoires de l'Édition Contemporaine (IMEC), Saint-Germain-la-Blanche-Herbe, file ET02-12. Published in Japanese in

F. Guattari, Hiraï Gen, Asada Akira, Takeda Kenichi, Radio Homerun, et al., *Tokyo Gekijou: Gatari, Tokyo wo yuku*, UPU, 1986.

—— 'Du Zen aux Galeries Lafayette,' interview with Jacky Beillerot, typescript dated November 23, 1986, Fonds Félix Guattari, L'Institut Mémoires de l'Édition Contemporaine (IMEC), Saint-Germain-la-Blanche-Herbe, file I02-22.

—— 'Typescript of an interview with T. Wada of the *Asahi Shimbun*, London Bureau,' October 2, 1985, Fonds Félix Guattari, L'Institut Mémoires de l'Édition Contemporaine (IMEC), Saint-Germain-la-Blanche-Herbe, file I02-21.

—— 'L'intervention institutionnelle,' typescript of an interview (1980), Fonds Félix Guattari, L'Institut Mémoires de l'Édition Contemporaine (IMEC), Saint-Germain-la-Blanche-Herbe, file ET09-26.

—— *L'inconscient machinique*, Fontenay-sous-Bois: Recherches, 1979.

—— 'Revolution and Desire: An Interview with Félix Guattari,' Hannah Levin and Mark Seem, *State and Mind* 6/4 and 7/1 (Summer/Fall 1978): 53–7.

—— *La Révolution Moléculaire*, Fontenay-sous-Bois: Recherches (Encres), 1977.

—— *La Révolution Moléculaire*, Fontenay-sous-Bois: Recherches (10/18), 1977.

—— *Psychanalyse et transversalité*, Paris: Maspero/La Découverte, 1972/2003.

—— 'La grand-peur écologique,' handwritten MS (n.d.), Fonds Félix Guattari, L'Institut Mémoires de l'Édition Contemporaine (IMEC), Saint-Germain-la-Blanche-Herbe, file ET10-03.

—— and Negri, Antonio. *Communists Like Us: New Spaces of Liberty, New Lines of Alliance*, trans. M. Ryan, New York: Semiotext(e), 1990.

—— and Rolnick, Suely. *Molecular Revolution in Brazil*, trans. K. Clapshow and B. Holmes, Los Angeles: Semiotext(e), 2008.

Hardt, Michael. 'The Global Society of Control,' *Discourse* 20/3 (Fall 1998): 139–52.

—— and Negri, Antonio. *Multitude: War and Democracy in the Age of Empire*, New York: Penguin, 2004.

—— —— *Empire*, Cambridge: Harvard University Press, 2000.

Horton, David (ed.). *Encyclopedia of Aboriginal Australia*, vol. 1, Canberra: Aboriginal Studies Press, AIATSIS, pp. 298–99.

Houston, James. *Confessions of an Igloo Dweller*, Toronto: M. & S., 1995.

Illich, Ivan. *Tools for Conviviality*, New York: Harper & Row, 1973.

Imai, Shin. *The 1999 Annotated Indian Act and Aboriginal Constitutional Provisions*, Toronto: Carswell, 2000.

Jayamanne, Laleen. '"Forty Acres and A Mule Filmworks" – *Do the Right Thing* – "A Spike Lee Joint": Blocking and Unblocking the Block,' in Patricia Pisters (ed.), *Micropolitics of Media Culture*, Amsterdam: University of Amsterdam Press, 2001, pp. 235–49.

Jonas, Hans. *The Imperative of Responsibility: In Search of an Ethics for the Technological Age*, Chicago: University of Chicago Press, 1984.

Kidd, Rosalind. *The Way We Civilise*, St. Lucia, Queensland: Queensland University Press, 2000.

Kimzeke, Piet. 'The Educational Function of the Youth Hostel,' in Graham Heath (ed.), *The International Youth Hostel Manual*, 2nd edn., Copenhagen: IYHA, 1967, pp. 97–100.

Kirksghard, Sharon. '2.8.99 – Performer turns credit card debt into art,' STTF.org (South to the Future), <http://sttf.org/wires/1999/03/22/peformer-turns-credit-card-debt-into-art/>.

Lacan, Jacques. 'The direction of the treatment and the principles of its power,' *Ecrits: A Selection*, trans. A. Sheridan, New York: W.W. Norton, 1977, pp. 226–80.

Langford, Ruby. *Don't Take Your Love to Town*, Ringwood, Victoria: Penguin, 1988.

Lash, Scott. *Critique of Information*, London: Sage, 2002.

Lazzarato, Maurizio. 'Semiotic Pluralism and the New Government of Signs: Homage to Félix Guattari,' *Semiotic Review of Books* 18/1 (2008): 9–12.

—— 'Immaterial Labor,' in Paolo Virno and Michael Hardt (eds.), *Radical Thought in Italy: A Potential Politics*, Minneapolis: University of Minnesota Press, 1996, pp. 133–46.

Lehnertz, Klaus. 'Epilepsy: Extreme Events in the Human Brain,' in S. Albeverio, V. Jentsch, and H. Kantz (eds.), *Extreme Events in Nature and Society*, Berlin: Springer, 2006, pp. 123–43.

Marcus, Alan Rudolph. *Relocating Eden: The Image and Politics of Inuit Exile in the Canadian Arctic*, Hanover and London: University Press of New England, 1995.

Margulis, Lynn and Lovelock, James. 'Gaia and Geognosy,' in M.B. Rambler et al. (eds.), *Global Ecology*, Boston: Academic Press, 1989, pp. 1–30.

Marks, John. 'Information and Resistance: Deleuze, the Virtual and Cybernetics,' in I. Buchanan and A. Parr (eds.), *Deleuze and the Contemporary World*, Edinburgh: Edinburgh University Press, 2006, pp. 195–211.

Marrati Paola. 'Against the Doxa: Politics of Immanence and Becoming-Minoritarian,' in Patricia Pisters (ed.), *Micropolitics of Media Culture*, Amsterdam: University of Amsterdam Press, 2001, pp. 205–20.

Marsh, Lauren and Kinnane, Steve. 'Ghost Files: The Missing Files of the Department of Indigenous Affairs Archives,' *Studies in Western Australian History* 23 (2004): 111–27.

Marx, Karl. *Capital*, vol. 1, trans. S. Moore and E. Aveling, Moscow: Progress Publishers, 1986.

Massumi, Brian. *Parables for the Virtual*, Durham, NC: Duke University Press, 2002.

—— 'The Autonomy of Affect,' in Paul Patton (ed.), *Deleuze: A Critical Reader*, Oxford: Blackwell, 1996, pp. 217–39.

—— *A User's Guide to Capitalism and Schizophrenia*, Cambridge, MA: MIT Press/Swerve Edition, 1992.

Mattelart, A. and M. *Rethinking Media Theory*, trans. J.A. Choen and M. Urquidi, Minneapolis: University of Minnesota Press, 1992.

McCann, Julie. 'Reclaiming Inuit Tags,' *Canadian Geographic Magazine* (September/October 2003): 29.

Merleau-Ponty, Maurice. *Phenomenology of Perception*, trans. Colin Smith, New York: Routledge & Kegan Paul, 1962.

Miller, Christopher L. 'The Postidentitarian Predicament in the Footnotes of *A Thousand Plateaus*: Nomadology, Anthology, and Authority,' in G. Genosko (ed.), *Deleuze and Guattari: Critical Assessments*, vol. 3, London: Routledge, 2001, 1113–49.

Milroy, J. *The Art of Sally Morgan*, Ringwood, Victoria: Penguin, 1996.

Minkowski, Eugène. *Lived Time: Phenomenological and Psychopathological Studies*, trans. Nancy Wetzel, Evanston, IL: Northwestern University Press, 1933.

Morgan, Sally and McPhee, Jack. *Wanamurraganya: The Story of Jack McPhee*, Fremantle: Fremantle Arts Cooperative, 1989.

Morin, Edgar. *The Stars*, trans. R. Howard, New York: Grove Press, 1961.

Mozère, Liane. 'In Early Childhood: What's Language About?' *Educational Philosophy and Theory* 39/3 (2007): 291–9.

—— 'Foucault et le CERFI: instantanés et actualité,' *Le Portique* 13–14 (2004), <http://leportique.revues.org/document642.html>.

Muecke, Stephen. 'The Discourse of Nomadology: Phylums in Flux,' in G. Genosko (ed.), *Deleuze and Guattari: Critical Assessments of Leading Philosophers*, vol. 3, London: Routledge, 2001, pp. 1164–81.

Müller-Wille, Ludger. *Gazetteer of Inuit Place Names in Nunavik*, Inukjuak, PQ: Avataq Cultural Institute, 1987.

Murphy, John. *Imaging the Fifties: Private Sentiment and Political Culture in Menzies' Australia*, Sydney: University of New South Wales Press, 2000.

Naess, Arne. *Ecology, Community and Lifestyle*, trans. D. Rothenberg, Cambridge: Cambridge University Press, 1989.

Nungak, Zebedee. 'E9-1956,' Canadian Film Center's Great Canadian Story Engine (n.d.), <http://www.storyengine.ca/serlet/ReadAStory?story=90>.

Oury, Jean. 'Une dialectique de l'amitié,' *Le Monde*, September 1, 1992.

—— *Onze heures du soir à La Borde: Essais sur la psychothérapie institutionnelle*, Paris: Galilée, 1980.

Parikka, Jussi. *Digital Contagions*, New York: Peter Lang, 2007.

Patton, Paul. *Deleuze and the Political*, Oxford: Blackwell, 2000.

Pial, Gilles. 'Docteur Cooper et Mister Anti,' *Libération*, July 31, 1986.

Pines, Jim and Willemen, Paul (eds.). *Questions of Third Cinema*, London: BFI, 1989.

Pisters, Patricia. 'Arresting the Flux of Images and Sounds: Free Indirect Discourse and the Dialectics of Political Cinema,' in I. Buchanan and A. Parr (eds.), *Deleuze and the Contemporary World*, Edinburgh: Edinburgh University Press, 2006, pp. 175–93.

Pompili, Maurizio, et al., 'Suicide Risk among Epileptic Patients,' in K.J. Holloway (ed.), *New Research on Epilepsy and Behavior*, New York: Nova Science, 2007, pp. 141–59.

Poudrier, J. 'Racial Categories and Health Risks: Epidemiological Surveillance among Canadian First Nations,' in D. Lyon (ed.), *Surveillance as Social Sorting*, London: Routledge, 2003, pp. 111–34.

'La preparation des elections régionales: Les Verts de Paris proposent une referendum sur l'aménagement de l'Ile-de-France,' *Le Monde*, February 27, 1992.

Querrien, Anne. 'CERFI 1965–87' (2002), <http://www.criticalsecret.com/n8/quer/1fr/index.html>.

—— 'Le plan de consistence du felice-deleuzisme,' *Chimères* 37 (1999): 33–43.

Reiter, R.A. *The Fundamental Principles of Indian Law*, Edmonton: First Nations Resource Council, 1991

Roch, Ernst (ed.). *Arts of the Eskimo: Prints*, Montreal: Signum Press, 1974.

Root, Deborah. *Cannibal Culture: Art, Appropriation, and the Commodification of Difference*, Boulder, CO: Westview, 1996.

Rossiter, Ned. *Organized Networks,* The Hague: NAi Publishers, 2006.

Rowse, Tim. *White Flour, White Power: From Rations to Citizenship in Central Australia*, Melbourne: Cambridge University Press, 1998.

Ruse, Michael. 'Signal,' in Paul Bouissac (ed.), *Encyclopedia of Semiotics*, New York: Oxford University Press, 1998, pp. 575–6.

Ryan, Judith. *Land Marks*, Melbourne: National Gallery of Victoria, 2006.

Sachdev, Perminder. 'Schizophrenia-like psychosis and epilepsy,' in Daryl Fujii and Iqbal Ahmed (eds.), *The Spectrum of Psychotic Disorders: Neurobiology, Etiology and Pathogenesis*, Cambridge: Cambridge University Press, 2007, pp. 262–84.

Sato, Mitsuo. 'Appeal to the Sanya Workers,' (n.d.), posted on <http://www.bordersphere.com/events/yama5.htm>.

Semetsky, Inna. 'Semiotics,' in A. Parr (ed.), *The Deleuze Dictionary*, Edinburgh: Edinburgh University Press, 2004, pp. 242–4.

Solanas, Fernando. 'An Interview by James Roy MacBean,' *Film Quarterly* 24/1 (1979): 37–43.

—— and Getino, Octavio. 'Towards a Third Cinema: Notes and Experiences for the Development of a Cinema of Liberation in the Third World,' in *New Latin American Cinema*, vol. 1, Detroit: Wayne State University Press, 1997, pp. 33–58.

Somerville, M.A. and Rapport, D. J. (eds.). *Transdisciplinarity: Recreating Integrated Knowledge*, Oxford: EOLSS, 2000.

Spelman, Nicola. 'Reversing us and them: anti-psychiatry and "The Dark Side of the Moon",' in R. Reising (ed.), *'Speak to Me': The Legacy of Pink Floyd's 'The Dark Side of the Moon'*, Aldershot: Ashgate, 2005, pp. 123–42.

Spiegelberg, Herbert. *Phenomenology in Psychology and Psychiatry*, Evanston, IL: Northwestern University Press, 1972.

Spitzer, Aaron. 'Getting the names right – finally,' *Nunatsiaq News*, October 20, 2000, <http://www.nunatsiaq.com>.

Stern, Daniel. *The Interpersonal World of the Infant: A View from Psychoanalysis and Developmental Psychology*, New York: Basic Books, 1985.

Sutherland, John M. and Tait, Howard. *The Epilepsies*, Edinburgh: E. & S. Livingstone, 1969.

Tatossian, Arthur. *Phénomenologie des psychoses*, Paris: Masson, 1980.

Temkin, Owsei. *The Falling Sickness: A History of Epilepsy from the Greeks to the Beginnings of Modern Neurology*, Baltimore: Johns Hopkins Press, 1971.

Thoburn, Nick. 'Vacuoles of Noncommunication: Minor Politics, Communist Style and the Multitude, in I. Buchanan and A. Parr (eds.), *Deleuze and the Contemporary World*, Edinburgh: Edinburgh University Press, 2006, pp. 42–56.

Troy, Jakelin. *King Plates: A History of Aboriginal Gorgets*, Canberra: Aboriginal Studies Press, 1993.

Tucktoo and Kitchooalik (Re: Deborah) (1972) 27 *D.L.R.* (3d) 225.

Vasquez, Aïda and Oury, Fernand. *Vers une pédagogie institutionnelle*, Paris: François Maspero, 1968.

Verevis, Constantine. 'Minoritarian + Cinema,' in A. Parr (ed.), *The Deleuze Dictionary*, Edinburgh: Edinburgh University Press, 2005, pp. 165–6.

Virilio, Paul. *Negative Horizon*, London: Continuum, 2005.

—— *The Aesthetics of Disappearance*, New York: Semiotext(e), 1991.

—— *Lost Dimension*, New York: Semiotext(e), 1991.

Wallace, Ian. *Clayoquot Protest (August 9, 1993)*, Windsor: Art Gallery of Windsor, 1997.

Watson, Janell. 'Guattari's Black Holes and the Post-Media Era,' *Polygraph* 14 (2002): 23–46.

Williams, James. 'Monitoring vs. Metaphysical Modeling: or, How to predict the future of the postmodern condition,' *PLI* (October 1992): 41–65.

Wood, Marilyn. 'Nineteenth Century Bureaucratic Constructions of Indigenous Identities in New South Wales,' in N. Peterson and W. Sanders (eds.), *Citizenship and Indigenous Australians: Changing Conceptions and Possibilities*, Melbourne: Cambridge University Press, 1998, pp. 35–54.

Willinsky, John. *Technologies of Knowing*, Boston: Beacon Press, 1999.

Woznicki, Krystian. 'SANYA: Marginal Space and Periphery', interview with Toshiya Ueno, 1998, <http://www.nettime.org/Lists-Archives/nettime_1_9802/msg00082.html>.

Zepke, Stephen. *Art as Abstract Machine: Ontology and Aesthetics in Deleuze and Guattari*, London: Routledge, 2005.

Žižek, Slavoj. *Organs without Bodies*, New York: Routledge, 2004.

—— *For They Know Not What They Do*, London: Verso, 1991.

LIST OF MEDIA

Agnosti, Sylvano, Bellocchio, Marco, et al. (dirs.). 1975. *Fous à délier*. 11 Marzo Cinematografica.

Bellocchio, Marco (dir.). 1965. *Fists in the Pocket*. Doria Film/The Criterion Collection.

Brustellin, Alf and Cloos, Hans Peter et al. (dirs.). 1978. *Germany in Autumn*. Filmverlag der Autoren.

Corbijn, Anton (dir.) 2007. *Control: The Tragic Tale of the Singer of Joy Division*. The Weinstein Company/The Miriam Collection.

Deligny, Fernand and Manenti, Josée. 1962–71. *Le Moindre Geste*. Éditions Montparnasse.

Depardon Raymond (dir.). 1988. *Urgences*. CNC.

Feret, René (dir.). 1974. *Histoire de Paul*. Films de l'Arquebuse.

Forman, Milos (dir.). 1975. *One Flew Over the Cuckoo's Nest*. Fantasy Films.

Goupil, Romain (dir.). 1982. *Mourir à trente ans*. MK2 Productions.

Joy Division. 1979. 'Atmosphere,' *Unknown Pleasures*. LP. Factory Records.

Karmitz, Marin (dir.). 1972. *Coup pour coup*. Cinema Services.

Lee, Spike (dir.). 1989. *Do The Right Thing*. 40 Acres and a Mule Filmworks.

Loach, Ken (dir.). 1971. *Family Life*. Kestrel/EMI Films.

Lynch, David (dir.). 1977. *Eraserhead*. American Film Institute.

Malick, Terence (dir.). 1973. *Badlands*. Badlands Co./Warner.

Mitsuo, Sato (dir.) 1985. *YAMA: An Eye for an Eye*. YAMA Production and Exhibition Committee.

Nichols, Mike (dir.) 1970. *Catch-22*. Filmways Productions.

Pop, Iggy. 1977. *The Idiot*. LP. Produced by David Bowie. RCA Records,

Robinson, Peter (dir.). 1972. *Asylum*. Peter Robinson Associates.

Schmidt, Jean (dir.). 1978. *Comme les anges déchus de la planète Saint-Michel*. Atelier 8.

Verdi, Giuseppe. 1853. *La traviata*. Opera, libretto by F.M. Piave, 1852.

Wiseman, Frederick (dir.). 1967. *Titicut Follies*. Zipporah Films.

Wright, Ben (dir.). 2004. *Slavoj Žižek: The Reality of the Virtual*. Olive Films.

INDEX